PHYTO-CHEMICALS AND ETHNOBOTANY

ENV BOOKS SERIES

PHYTO-CHEMICALS AND ETHNOBOTANY

Editor

Dr. Pawan Kumar 'Bharti'

Society for Environment, Health
Awareness of Nutrition & Toxicology (SEHAT)
B-225/5D, Top Floor, Subhash Gali, Road No. 7, Block B
Ashok Nagar, Shahdara
Delhi-110093
(India)

DPH

DISCOVERY PUBLISHING HOUSE PVT. LTD.
INDIA

Published by:
Namit Wasan
DISCOVERY PUBLISHING HOUSE PVT. LTD.
4383/4B, Ansari Road, Darya Ganj
New Delhi-110 002 (India)
Phone : +91-11-23279245; 23253475; 43596065
E-mail : discoverybooksindia@gmail.com
discoverypublishinghouse@gmail.com
namitwasan9@gmail.com
web : www.discoverypublishinggroup.com

***First Edition:* 2019**

ISBN: 978-93-86841-93-3

Phyto-chemicals and Ethnobotany

Printed at:
Infinity Imaging Systems
Delhi

PREFACE

Phytochemicals generally are regarded as research compounds rather than essential nutrients because proof of their possible health effects has not been established yet. Phytochemicals under research can be classified into major categories, such as carotenoids and polyphenols, which include phenolic acids, flavonoids, and stilbenes/lignans. Flavonoids can be further divided into groups based on their similar chemical structure, such as anthocyanins, flavones, flavanones, and isoflavones, and flavanols.

Phytochemicals, or 'plant chemicals', are bioactive non-nutrient plant compounds that provide a range of activities from inhibiting cancer cell proliferation to protecting against oxidative damage that prevent cardiovascular disease and multiple cancers. For example, lycopene, found in cooked tomatoes, has antioxidant properties linked to decreased risk of some cancers. More than 5,000 phytochemicals have been identified, and many are still unknown.

The present book updates the subject content of phyto-chemicals, medicinal plants, chemical constituents of plants, ethnobotany, useful plants, agro-chemicals, pharmacological and nutraceutical significance of plants.

Thanks are due to publisher and contributors from various institutions and universities.

The book will be helpful for the researchers, academia working in the field of phyto-chemicals, medicinal plants, chemical constituents of plants, ethnobotany, agro-chemicals, pharmacological and nutraceutical significance of plants.

Editors
(envbooks@gmail.com)

CONTENTS

Phyto-chemicals and Ethanobotany **Pages 1-5**
Edited by: **Pawan Kumar 'Bharti'**
ISBN: 978-93-86841-93-3
Edition: **2019**
Published by: **Discovery Publishing House Pvt. Ltd., New Delhi (India)**

1 Introduction

Phytochemicals are chemical compounds produced by plants, generally to help them thrive or thwart competitors, predators, or pathogens. The name comes from Greek word phyton, meaning 'plant'. Some phytochemicals have been used as poisons and others as traditional medicine.

As a term, phytochemicals is generally used to describe plant compounds that are under research with unestablished effects on health and are not scientifically defined as essential nutrients. Regulatory agencies governing food labeling in Europe and the United States have provided guidance for industry limiting or preventing health claims about phytochemicals on food product or nutrition labels.

Plants are composed entirely of chemicals of various kinds. Phytochemicals (from Greek phyto, meaning "plant") are chemicals produced by plants through primary or secondary metabolism. They generally have biological activity in the plant host and play a role in plant growth or defense against competitors, pathogens, or predators.

Phytochemicals generally are regarded as research compounds rather than essential nutrients because proof of their possible health effects has not been established yet. Phytochemicals under research can be classified into major categories, such as carotenoids and polyphenols, which include phenolic acids, flavonoids, and stilbenes/lignans. Flavonoids can be further divided into groups based on their similar chemical structure, such as anthocyanins, flavones, flavanones, and isoflavones, and flavanols. Flavanols further are classified as catechins, epicatechins, and proanthocyanidins.

Phytochemists study phytochemicals by first extracting and isolating compounds from the origin plant, followed by defining their structure or testing in laboratory model systems, such as cell cultures, in vitro experiments, or in vivo studies using laboratory animals. Challenges in that field include isolating specific compounds and determining their structures, which are often complex, and identifying what specific phytochemical is primarily responsible for any given biological activity.

Many antioxidant compounds can be found in fruits and vegetables including phenolics, carotenoids, anthocyanins, and tocopherols. Approximately 20% of known plants have been used in pharmaceutical studies, impacting the healthcare system in positive ways such as treating cancer and harmful diseases. Plants are able to produce a large number of diverse bioactive compounds. High concentrations of phytochemicals, which may protect against free radical damage, accumulate in fruits and vegetables. Plants containing beneficial phytochemicals may supplement the needs of the human body by acting as natural antioxidants. Various studies have shown that many plants are rich source of antioxidants. For instance, vitamins A, C, E, and phenolic compounds such as flavonoids, tannins, and lignins, found in plants, all act as antioxidants. The consumption of fruits and vegetables has been linked with several health benefits, a result of medicinal properties and high nutritional value. Antioxidants control and reduce the oxidative damage in foods by delaying or inhibiting oxidation caused by reactive oxygen species (ROS), ultimately increasing the shelf-life and quality of these foods. Beta carotene, ascorbic acid, and many phenolics play dynamic roles in delaying aging, reducing inflammation, and preventing certain cancers. Increasing the consumption of fruits and vegetables has been recommended by many agencies and health care systems throughout the world.

Phytochemicals, or 'plant chemicals', are bioactive non-nutrient plant compounds that provide a range of activities from inhibiting cancer cell proliferation to protecting against oxidative damage that prevent cardiovascular disease and multiple cancers. For example, lycopene, found in cooked tomatoes, has antioxidant properties linked to decreased risk of some cancers. More than 5,000 phytochemicals have been identified, and many are still unknown.

History

Without specific knowledge of their cellular actions or mechanisms, phytochemicals have been used as poison and in traditional medicine. For example, salicin, having anti-inflammatory and pain-relieving properties, was originally extracted from the bark of the white willow tree and later synthetically produced to become the common, over-the-counter drug, aspirin. The tropane alkaloids of A. belladonna were used as poisons, and early humans made poisonous arrows from the plant. In Ancient Rome, it was used as a poison by Agrippina the Younger, wife of Emperor Claudius on advice of Locusta, a lady specialized in poisons, and Livia, who is rumored to have used it to kill her husband Emperor Augustus.

The English yew tree was long known to be extremely and immediately toxic to animals that grazed on its leaves or children who ate its berries; however, in 1971, paclitaxel was isolated from it, subsequently becoming an important cancer drug.

As of 2017, the biological activities for most phytochemicals are unknown or poorly understood, in isolation or as part of foods. Phytochemicals with established roles in the body are classified as essential nutrients.

Functions

The phytochemical category includes compounds recognized as essential nutrients, which are naturally contained in plants and are required for normal physiological functions, so must be obtained from the diet in humans.

Some phytochemicals are known phytotoxins that are toxic to humans; for example aristolochic acid is carcinogenic at low doses. Some phytochemicals are antinutrients that interfere with the absorption of nutrients. Others, such as some polyphenols and flavonoids, may be pro-oxidants in high ingested amounts.

Nondigestible dietary fibers from plant foods, often considered as a phytochemical, are now generally regarded as a nutrient group having approved health claims for reducing the risk of some types of cancer and coronary heart disease.

Eating a diet high in fruits, vegetables, grains, legumes and plant-based beverages has long-term health benefits, but there is no evidence that taking dietary supplements of non-nutrient phytochemicals extracted from plants similarly benefits health. Phytochemical supplements are neither recommended by health authorities for improving health nor approved by regulatory agencies for health claims on product labels.

Significance

Phytochemicals are non-nutritive plant chemicals that have protective or disease preventive properties. They are non-essential nutrients, meaning that they are not required by the human body for sustaining life. It is well-known that plant produce these chemicals to protect themselves but recent research demonstrate that they can also protect humans against diseases. There are more than thousand known phytochemicals. Some of the well-known phytochemicals are lycopene in tomatoes, isoflavones in soy and flavanoids in fruits.

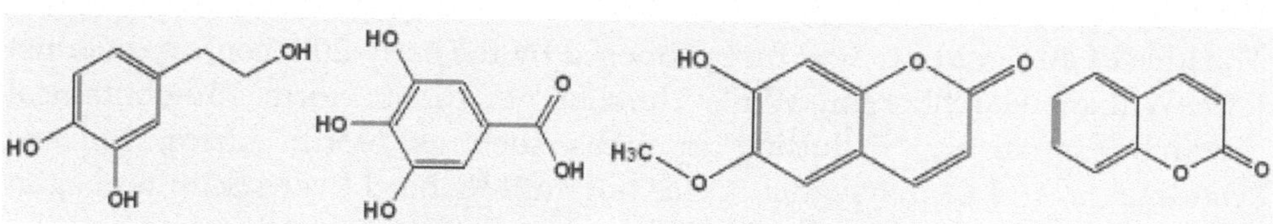

There are many phytochemicals and each works differently. These are some possible actions:

- Antioxidant - Most phytochemicals have antioxidant activity and protect our cells against oxidative damage and reduce the risk of developing certain types of cancer. Phytochemicals with antioxidant activity: allyl sulfides (onions, leeks, garlic), carotenoids (fruits, carrots), flavonoids (fruits, vegetables), polyphenols (tea, grapes).

- Hormonal action - Isoflavones, found in soy, imitate human estrogens and help to reduce menopausal symptoms and osteoporosis.
- Stimulation of enzymes - Indoles, which are found in cabbages, stimulate enzymes that make the estrogen less effective and could reduce the risk for breast cancer. Other phytochemicals, which interfere with enzymes, are protease inhibitors (soy and beans), terpenes (citrus fruits and cherries).
- Interference with DNA replication - Saponins found in beans interfere with the replication of cell DNA, thereby preventing the multiplication of cancer cells. Capsaicin, found in hot peppers, protects DNA from carcinogens.
- Anti-bacterial effect - The phytochemical allicin from garlic has anti-bacterial properties.
- Physical action - Some phytochemicals bind physically to cell walls thereby preventing the adhesion of pathogens to human cell walls. Proanthocyanidins are responsible for the anti-adhesion properties of cranberry. Consumption of cranberries will reduce the risk of urinary tract infections and will improve dental health.

Ethnobotany

Ethnobotany is the study of a region's plants and their practical uses through the traditional knowledge of a local culture and people. An ethnobotanist thus strives to document the local customs involving the practical uses of local flora for many aspects of life, such as plants as medicines, foods, and clothing.

Since the time of Schultes, the field of ethnobotany has grown from simply acquiring ethnobotanical knowledge to that of applying it to a modern society, primarily in the form of pharmaceuticals. Intellectual property rights and benefit-sharing arrangements are important issues in ethnobotany.

History

The idea of ethnobotany was first proposed by the early 20th century botanist John William Harshberger. While Harshberger did perform ethnobotanical research extensively, including in areas such as North Africa, Mexico, Scandinavia, and Pennsylvania, it was not until Richard Evans Schultes began his trips into the Amazon that ethnobotany become a more well known science. However, the practice of ethnobotany is thought to have much earlier origins in the first century AD when a Greek physician by the name of Pedanius Dioscorides wrote an extensive botanical text detailing the medical and culinary properties of "over 600 mediterranean plants" named De Materia Medica.

Historians note that Dioscorides wrote about traveling often throughout the Roman empire, including regions such as "Greece, Crete, Egypt, and Petra", and in doing so obtained substantial knowledge about the local plants and their useful properties. European botanical knowledge drastically expanded once the New World was discovered due to ethnobotany. This expansion in knowledge can be primarily attributed to the substantial influx of new plants from the Americas, including crops such as potatoes, peanuts, avocados, and tomatoes.

REFERENCES

https://en.wikipedia.org/wiki/Phytochemical

http://www.phytochemicals.info/

https://www.ncbi.nlm.nih.gov/pmc/articles/PMC5750618/

https://www.sciencedirect.com/topics/agricultural-and-biological-sciences/phytochemical

https://www.fruitsandveggiesmorematters.org/what-are-phytochemicals

https://en.wikipedia.org/wiki/Ethnobotany

Phyto-chemicals and Ethanobotany **Pages 6-40**
Edited by: Pawan Kumar 'Bharti'
ISBN: 978-93-86841-93-3
Edition: 2019
Published by: Discovery Publishing House Pvt. Ltd., New Delhi (India)

2

Prickly Pear

Phyto-Chemicals and Potential Health benefits

[1*]Zainab A. Salama, [2]Hanan F. Aly, [1]Rasha M.M. Mohasib and [3]Farouk K. El Baz[1]

ABSTRACT

Numerous epidemiological studies indicated that Prickly pear (Opuntia ficus indicia) protect humans against cancer since they are rich sources of phenolics, flavonoids, vitamins and betalains, as well as mineral nutrients. Some criteria have been proposed to evaluate the possibilities of developing new "functional foods" to reduce the risk of specific cancers; therefore, this review will be focuses on the content, composition, antioxidant capacity of both lipid- and water-soluble antioxidants in prickly pear health-promoting properties chemical and biological characterization of the pharmaceutical in prickly pear. The present review aims to summarize the updating knowledge regarding the biological activities of prickly pear with special reference to its phytochemicals, chemo preventive as anti-inflammatory, anticancer, hepatoprotective, and antidiapetic properties.

Keywords: Prickly pear, phytochemicals compounds, health benefits, food applications

Important of Prickly Pear

Prickly pear (Opuntia *ficus indica*) is family of Cactacae, it is widely distributed in the Mideternian area and south Africa (Frati et al., 1990; Fernandez et al., 1992). Prickly pear cultivars produce clear- renewable, yellow-brown, yellow-orange, red-purple chocolate (Pimienta-Barrios, 1994; Saenz and Sepulveda, 2001). The antioxidant process of the prickly pear was reported due to occurrence of vitamin C, amino acids, polyphenolics, flavonoid compounds, taurine and betalains (Butera et al., 2002; Castellar et al., 2003). Prickly pear as a source of betalain has potency as anticancer activity (Castellar et al., 2003; Chavez-Santoscoy et al., 2009; Salama et al., 2014).

1 Plant Biochemistry Department, National Research Centre, 33 El Bohouth st. (former El Tahrir st.), Dokki, Giza, Egypt, P.O. 12622.
2 Therapeutical Chemistry Department, National Research Centre (NRC), 33 EL Bohouth St. (former EL Tahrir St.), Dokki, Giza, Egypt, P.O. 12622.

Opuntia dicot genus Indica as a folk's medication for the treatment of burns, wounds, edema, and digestion. It has been reported that its alcoholic extract possesses medicine, symptom, and anti-viral activities anti-polygenic-disease. It has been tied reportable to medicinally employ in hyperlipidemia far more than lipids within the blood) (Saenz, 2000). Much attention has been focused on prickly pear as a source of bioactive compounds which possess antioxidant and anticancer effects (Chavez-Santoscoy et al., 2009). Apart from other nutritional antioxidants, prickly pear is also a significant source of calcium, folic acid, carotenoids, ascorbic acid and known to reduce risk of colon, prostate and kidney cancer (Castellar et al., 2003).

Fig. 2.1: Prickly pear

Antioxidants

Antioxidants are substances which when present at low concentration are able to prevent or delay oxidative damage of lipids, proteins and nucleic acids by reactive oxygen species. These reactive oxygen species mainly are reactive free radicals such as superoxide, hydroxyl, peroxyl, alkoxyl and non- radicals such as hydrogen peroxide. They scavenge radicals by inhibiting initiation and breaking chain propagation or suppressing formation of free radicals by binding to the metal ions, reducing hydrogen peroxide, and quenching superoxide and singlet oxygen (Shi et al., 2001). The most abundant antioxidants in fruits and vegetables are polyphenols, vitamins C , A, B and E whereas; carotenoids are present to a lesser extent in some fruits. These polyphenols, most of which are flavonoids, are present mainly in ester and glycoside forms (Fleuriet and Macheix, 2003) .The three major groups: vitamins, especially vitamin C; phenolics; and betalain, is responsible for the defensive effect of antioxidants in prickly pear. Vitamin C and phenolics are known as hydrophilic antioxidants, and carotenoids are known as lipophilic antioxidants. A number of researches have been made in the antioxidant capacity of prickly pear fruits.

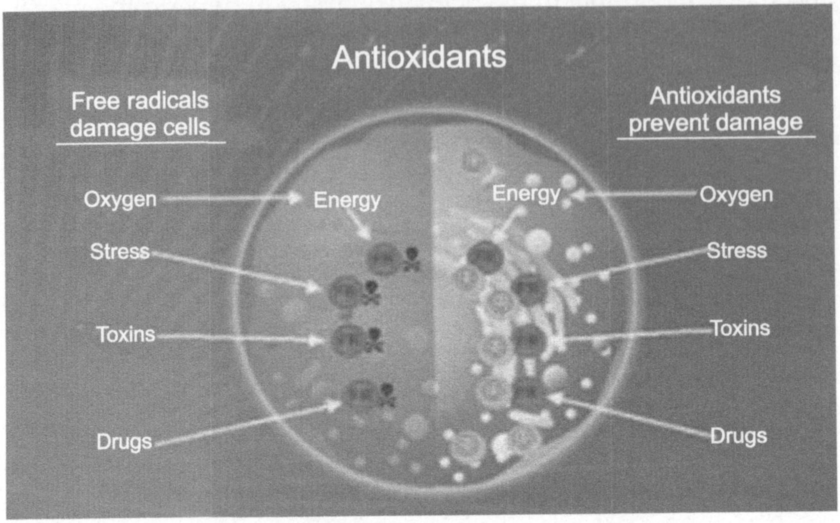

Fig. 2.2: Role of antioxidant in living cell

Factors Affecting Antioxidant Compounds of Prickly Pear

Recently, an increased interest in antioxidant activity and health-improving capacity of cactus pear has been registered. Cardador Anaberta et al. (2011) examined the total phenolics, flavonoids and tannins of peel and seeds of four cactus pear cultivars as well as their antioxidant capacity (Tables 2.1 & 2.2). Tannins were the major phenolics in cactus pear seeds accounting for almost fifty percent for all cultivars. Analysis of variance revealed that ripeness, cultivar, and its interaction had highly significant effect on the total phenolics, tannin, and flavonoid contents of cactus pear peel. With regard to the seeds, only the stage of ripeness and interaction (ripeness stage × cultivar) are significant on total phenolics and tannins contents. The flavonoid content in seeds is not affected by any of the factors or their interactions (Tables 2.3 & 2.4). The antioxidant capacity is higher in the peel than in the seeds.

Table 2.1: Phenolic Content in Cactus Pear Peels

Sample	Concentration[1]				%Content[2]	
	Ripeness stage	Total phenolics	Tannins	Flavonoids	Tannin	Flavonoid
Esmeralda	Ripe	362[a]	53[c]	66[a]	15[c]	18[b,c]
	Unripe	376[a]	95[b]	57[b]	25[d]	15[c,d]
Pelon-Liso	Ripe	193[c]	144[a]	21[d]	74[a]	11[c]
	Unripe	44[c]	23[c]	8[c]	52[c]	17[c]

Cristalina	Ripe	141^{d}	30^{d,c}	36^{c}	21^{d,c}	26^{a}
	Unripe	172^{c}	32^{d}	36^{c}	19^{d,c}	21^{b}
Montesa	Ripe	229^{b}	144^{a}	35^{c}	63^{b}	15^{d}
	Unripe	223^{b}	52^{c}	32^{c}	23^{d}	14^{d}

[1]Concentration expressed as mg equivalent of gallic acid, catechin or rutin for total phenolics, tannins and flavonoids, respectively, per 100 g of peel in dry basis.

[2]Percentage of tannins and flavonoids in relation to total phenolics. Means in a column followed by the same letter are not significantly different (Tukey, α=0.05).

Source: Cardador Anaberta et al. (2011)

Table 2.2: Phenolic Content in Cactus Pear Seeds

Sample	Concentration[1]				%Content[2]	
	Ripeness stage	Total phenolics	Tannins	Flavonoids	Tannin	Flavonoid
Pelon-Liso	Ripe	354^{a}	171^{b}	46^{a}	50^{a}	13^{a}
	Unripe	414^{b}	205^{a}	47^{a}	49^{a}	11^{b}
Cristalina	Ripe	337^{d}	174^{a,b}	46^{a}	52^{a}	14^{a}
	Unripe	373^{c}	169^{b}	49^{a}	45^{a}	13^{a}
Montesa	Ripe	373^{c}	172^{b}	49^{a}	46^{a}	13^{a}
	Unripe	460^{a}	137^{c}	50^{a}	30^{b}	11^{b}

[1]Concentration expressed as mg equivalent of gallic acid, catechin or rutin for total phenolics, tannins and flavonoids, respectively, per 100 g of seed in dry basis.

[2]Percentage of tannins and flavonoids in relation to total phenolics. Means in a column followed by the same letter are not significantly different (Tukey, α = 0.05)

Source: Cardador Anaberta et al. (2011)

Table 2.3: Antioxidant Capacity of Cactus Pear Extracts

Sample 1	Ripe ness stage	ARA2	TEAC3
BHT	—	59^{c}	299^{d}
Catechin	—	67^{b}	577^{b}
Gallic acid	—	91^{a}	646^{a}
Esmeralda	Ripe	21^{c}	322^{d}
	Unripe	49^{c}	534^{b,c}
Pelon-Liso	Ripe	14^{f}	291^{d}
	Unripe	13^{f}	380^{d}
Cristalina	Ripe	33^{d}	430^{c,d}
	Unripe	15^{f}	313^{d}
Montesa	Ripe	14^{f}	484^{c}
	Unripe	33^{d}	529^{b,c}

[1]Concentration for standards were 250 μm, and for extracts it was 500 μm equivalent gallic acid.

[2]ARA = Antiradical activity expressed as percent DPPH discoloration at 500 μm, or standards at 250 μm, Means in a column followed by the same letter are not significantly different (Tukey, α=0.05)

Source: Cardador Anaberta et al. (2011)

Table 2.4: Antioxidant Activity in Cactus Pear Seed Extracts

Sample1	Ripe ness stage	ARA2	TEAC3
BHT	—	59[c]	299[c]
Catechin	—	67[b]	577[b]
Gallic acid	—	91[a]	647[a]
Pelon-Liso	Ripe	38[d]	47[d]
	Unripe	32[c]	45[d]
Cristalina	Ripe	32[c]	24[c]
	Unripe	36[d]	40[d]
Montesa	Ripe	38[d]	19[c]
	Unripe	32[c]	12[c]

[1]Concentration for standards were 250 μm, and for samples it was 500 μm equivalent gallic acid.

[2]ARA = Antiradical activity expressed as percent DPPH discoloration, TEAC = Trolox antixiodant equivalent capacity in μm of Trolox equivalent to seeds extracts at 500 μm, or standards at 250 μm, Means in a column followed by the same letter are not significantly different (Tukey, $\alpha = 0.05$).

Cardador Anaberta et al. (2011) observed a significant relationship between total phenolics and flavonoids in both peels and seeds and only significant correlation between flavonoids and ARA activity (Table 1.5). Cactus pear by-products can indeed be exploited as a good and cheap source of natural antioxidants.

Table 2.5: Correlation Coefficients for Total Phenolics, Flavonoids, Tannins, and Antioxidant Activities in Cactus Pear Fruit Peel

	Tannin content	Flavonoid content	Antioxidant activities	
			ARA	TEAC
Total phenolics	0.3551[c]	0.8820[a]	0.5210[a]	0.2323
Tannin content	—	0.0296	–0.0934	0.1058
Flavonoids	—	—	0.5036[b]	0.1305
ARA	—	—	—	0.6377[a]

Source: Cardador Anaberta et al. (2011).

Nutrients Composition

Griffith (2004) reported that prickly pear pulp is an important source of calcium, potassium, and magnesium. However, in the peel the concentration of these minerals is 13, 6, and 4 times higher than in the pulp, respectively. The amount of calcium, potassium, and magnesium in the prickly pear pulp, is higher than that in the mango, papaya, pineapple, granadilla, and guava while the levels of potassium are similar than in the banana and sour-sop (Roman-Ramos et al., 1995). Recommended Daily Allowance (RDA) of calcium and potassium are 1,000 mg and 2,000 mg respectively in adult women and men, while for magnesium are 400-420 mg and 310-320 for men and women, respectively (Becerra-Jiménez; Andrade-Cetto, 2012) 250 g of prickly pear pulp could contribute with 40, 140, and 19 mg of calcium, potassium and magnesium, amounts that are not even close to the 10% of the daily requirements.

Sawaya et al. (1983) reported that about the dietary nature of prickly pear seeds, *Opuntia ficus indica*. The seeds contained 16.6% protein, 17.2% fat, 49.6% fiber and 3.0% fiery debris (Table 2.6). The feast demonstrated a high measure of iron (9.45 %). The substance of Mg, P, K, Zn and Cu were nutritiously noteworthy contributing roughly 10-20% of the Recommended Dietary Allowances (RDA) of these components per 100g of dry weight.

Table 2.6: Approximate Analysis of Prickly Pear Seeds (dry weight basis)

Components	Mean standard deviation
Moisture	5.3 ± 0.51
Protein (N x 6.25)	16.6 ± 0.40
Fat %	17.2 ± 0.22
Fiber %	49.6 ± 1.46
Ash %	3.0 ± 0.16
Na(mg/100 g)	67.6 ± 3.5
K(mg/100 g)	163.0 ± 5.1
Ca(mg/100 g)	16.2 ± 1.3
Mg(mg/100 g)	74.0 ± 1.1
P(mg/100 g)	152.0 ± 4.8
Fe(mg/100 g)	9.45 ± 1.2
Zn(mg/100 g)	1.45 ± 0.3
Cn(mg/100 g)	0.32 ± 0.1
Mn(mg/100 g)	Traces

Source: Sawaya et al. (1983)

Amino Acids

Sawaya *et al.* (1983) reported that aspartic, glutamic arginine and glycine were the richest amino acids influencing almost 50% of the sum amino acids content. Lysine was the principal restriction amino acids bringing about a concoction score of 62 for the protein (Table 2.7).

Table 2.7: Amino Acid Composition of Prickly Pear Seed Meal (g amino acid/100 g protein)

Amino acid	Prickly pear meal[a]	FAO/WAOReference patter (1973)
Aspartic acid	8.60	-
Threonine	3.96	4.0
Serine	4.14	-
Glatarnic acid	20.27	-
Protine	5.66	-
Glycine	7.67	-
Alanine	4.58	-
Valine	5.69	5.0
Methionine	2.61	-
Cystine (C)	3.10	-
M+C	5.71	3.5
Isoleucine	3.66	4.0
Leucine	6.90	7.0
Tyrosine (T)	3.56	-
Phenylalanine (P)	4.46	-
T + P	8.02	6.0
Lysine	3.39	5.5
Histidine	3.36[b]	-
Arginine	2.46	-
Tryptophan	14.62	1.0
Total amino acids/100 g protein	106.23	-
Chemical score	62	100

Source: Sawaya et al. (1983).

Sarbojeet Jana (2012) determined the content of amino acids in prickly pear pulp found that it contains a wide variety of free amino-acids, predominating glutamine, proline, and taurine (Table 2.8), although in the yellow pulp predominate the reduced glutathione and in the white pulp the cysteine. Taurine is a preventive agent of the hepatic or fatty diseases in the liver, it is effect in detoxification, and is considered an antioxidant and a stabilizer of the membrane cell, providing osmoregulation, neuromodulator, and hypercholesterolemia (Van Proeyen et al., 2012). It has been found that four hundred mg of taurine lower the platelet aggregation in healthy individuals and the consumption of 300 ml of prickly pear pulp can contribute with 40% of the previously mentioned taurine (Deldicque et al., 2013; Kaastra et al., 2006).

Table 2.8: Amino Acids Contents in Cladodes and Fruit Pulps from *Opuntia ficus indica*

Amino acids	Fresh weight basis	
	Cladodes(g/100g)	Fruit juice(mg/L)
Alanine	0.6	87.2
Arginine	2.4	30.5
Asparagine	1.5	41.6
Asparaginic acid	2.1	Not valid
Glutamine acid	2.6	66.1
Glutamine	17.3	346.2
Glycine	0.5	11.33
Histidine	2.0	45.2
Isoleucine	1.9	31.2
Leucine	1.3	20.6
Lysine	2.5	17.4
Methionine	1.4	55.2
Phenylalanine	1.7	23.3
Serine	3.2	174.5
Threonine	2.0	13.3
Tyrosine	0.7	12.3
Tryptophan	0.5	12.6
Valine	3.7	39.4
Alpha-Aminobutyric acid	Not Available	1.1
Carriosine	Not Available	5.9
Carrulline	Not Available	16.3
Oraithine	Not Available	Not detectable
Proline	Not Available	1265.2
Faurine	Not Available	434.3

Source: Sarbojeet Jana (2012)

Fatty acids

Esther Ramírez-Moreno et al. (2017) investigated the oil fatty acids profiles of both varieties green and red cactus pear were similar and exhibited a high content of linoleic acid, while two fatty acids (linolenic and behenic) found in red cactus pear were not observed in the green variety (Table 2.9).

Table 2.9: Percentages of FAMEs in Crude Pear Seed Oil Extracts

FAMEs	Green cactus pear seed oil extract	Red cactus pear seed oil extract
C14:0	0.078 ± 0.00	0.066 ± 0.01
C16:0	12.327 ± 0.09	12.887 ± 0.02
C16:1	0.429 ± 0.02	0.570 ± 0.01
C16:2	0.073 ± 0.00	0.540 ± 0.00
C17:0	0.060 ± 0.01	0.075 ± 0.00
C18:0	3.436 ± 0.01	3.389 ± 0.07
C18:1	16.215 ± 0.03	17.061 ± 0.01
C18:2	67.448 ± 0.08	65.407 ± 0.01
C18:3	Ni	0.372 ± 0.01
C22:0	Ni	0.160 ± 0.01

Source: Esther Ramírez-Moreno et al. (2017).

Patricia Morales (2012) found that the pulp of the studied xoconostle cultivars had an appreciable amount of soluble fiber and antioxidant compounds such as ascorbic acid, while the seeds are a source of fiber, phenolics, flavonoids, PUFAs and tocopherols (especially γ-tocopherol), which provide a good antioxidant capacity (Tables 2.9 & 2.10). In the light of these results, xoconostle fruits should be considered of great interest for either promoting the conventional consumption, and also as sources of bioactive compounds for the addition to other food products, so that all the nutrients present are fully used, instead of being discarded.

Table 2.10: Antioxidant Compounds and Antioxidant Properties (EC50 values) of Cultivated Xoconostle

Fatty acids	*Opuntia joconostle*, cv. Cuaresmeno		*Opuntia matudae*, cv. Rosa	
	Pulp	Seeds	Pulp	Seeds
Ascorbic acid^A	20.63 ± 0.32^a	nd	31.67 ± 6.67^b	nd
Total tocopherols^A	0.22 ± 0.01^b	3.23 ± 0.18^c	0.14 ± 0.00^a	6.71 ± 0.38^s
α-tocopherol^A	0.16 ± 0.01^b	0.09 ± 0.02^a	0.10 ± 0.00^a	0.19 ± 0.01^c
β-tocopherol^A	0.01 ± 0.00^a	0.01 ± 0.00^a	Traces	0.02 ± 0.00^b
γ-tocopherol^A	0.05 ± 0.00^a	3.07 ± 0.15^b	0.03 ± 0.00^a	6.43 ± 0.73^c
δ-tocopherol^A	Traces	0.06 ± 0.01^b	0.01 ± 0.00^a	0.08 ± 0.00^c
Total Phenolica^B	38.57 ± 6.87^b	50.43 ± 4.86^c	33.71 ± 2.09^b	59.48 ± 0.69^d
Total Flavonoidsc	3.93 ± 0.19^b	24.18 ± 1.69^c	0.86 ± 0.09^a	54.40 ± 0.78^d
Antioxidant activity EC_{50} values				
DPPH Scacenging activity^D	5.14 ± 0.20^c	1.53 ± 0.05^a	$> 16^d$	1.88 ± 0.11^b

Reducing power[D]	3.16 ± 0.12[c]	0.27 ± 0.04[a]	5.35 ± 0.63[d]	1.58 ± 0.01[b]
β-carotene bleaching inhibition[D]	0.32 ± 0.02[b]	2.11 ± 0.30[c]	0.02 ± 0.00[a]	4.75 ± 0.03[d]

[A]Results were expressed as mg/100 g of fresh weight (fw).

[B]Results were expressed as mg of gallic acid equivalents (GAE)/g of extract.

[C]Results were expressed as mg of catechin equivalents (CE)/g of extract.

[D]Results were expressed as mg/mL of extract

Mean+ SD, n=3. In each row, different letters mean statistically significant difference (P<0.05).

nd (not detected).

Traces (<0.005 mg/100 g fw).

Source: Patricia Morales (2012)

Table 2.11: Fatty Acids Composition of Cultivated Xoconostle Fruits[A]

Fatty acids	*Opuntia joconostle*, cv. Cuaresmeno		*Opuntia matudae*, cv. Rosa	
	Pulp	Seeds	Pulp	Seeds
C6:0	nd	0.75 ± 0.03	0.24 ± 0.00	0.09 ± 0.02
C8:0	31.35 ± 3.55	0.01 ± 0.00	8.04 ± 0.67	traces
C10:0	0.16 ± 0.10	0.01 ± 0.00	0.05 ± 0.00	traces
C12:0	0.82 ± 0.41	0.09 ± 0.00	0.19 ± 0.01	traces
C13:0	nd	0.01 ± 0.00	nd	traces
C14:0	0.84 ± 0.19	0.04 ± 0.00	0.28 ± 0.00	0.4 ± 0.00
C14:1	nd	nd	nd	traces
C15:0	0.32 ± 0.02	0.01 ± 0.00	0.48 ± 0.04	0.01 ± 0.00
C15:1	nd	0.01 ± 0.00	nd	0.01 ± 0.00
C16:0	15.03 ± 1.59	12.35 ± 0.40	12.74 ± 0.18	9.42 ± 0.78
C16:1	0.48 ± 0.06	0.40 ± 0.01	0.50 ± 0.00	0.31 ± 0.03
C17:0	2.08 ± 0.12	0.04 ± 0.00	nd	0.02 ± 0.00
C18:0	2.81 ± 1.04	3.28 ± 0.18	2.05 ± 0.02	2.04 ± 0.34
C18:1n9c	3.68 ± 1.29	9.72 ± 0.03	2.45 ± 0.06	7.82 ± 0.84
C18:2n6c	32.70 ± 2.30	72.49 ± 0.13	64.29 ± 0.46	79.15 ± 1.96
C18:3n3c	8.64 ± 1.97	0.36 ± 0.01	7.67 ± 0.21	0.41 ± 0.04
C20:0	0.25 ± 0.15	0.26 ± 0.01	0.15 ± 0.06	0.19 ± 0.01
C20:1	nd	0.07 ± 0.02	nd	0.05 ± 0.00
C22:0	0.30 ± 0.12	0.19 ± 0.02	0.23 ± 0.06	0.04 ± 0.01
C23:0	0.10 ± 0.08	nd	nd	0.10 ± 0.02
C23:1n9c	nd	0.05 ± 0.01	nd	0.04 ± 0.01
C23:0	nd	nd	nd	0.03 ± 0.00
C24:0	0.38 ± 0.26	0.09 ± 0.03	0.53 ± 0.23	0.06 ± 0.00

C24:1	nd	0.02 ± 0.00	0.09 ± 0.03	0.01 ± 0.00
SFA (% of total FA)	54.43 ± 0.92	16.86 ± 0.17a	25.00 ± 0.22b	12.10
MUFA (% of total FA)	4.16 ± 1.23a	10.28 ± 0.03c	3.05 ± 0.03a	7.64 ± 0.86b
PUFA (% of total FA)	41.11 ± 0.74a	4.32 ± 0.05b	2.88 ± 0.03a	6.67 ± 0.73c
PUFA/SFA (% of total FA)	1.28 ± 0.74a	4.32 ± 0.05b	2.88 ± 0.03a	6.67 ± 0.73c
n-3/n-6	0.20 ± 0.01b	0.01 ± 0.00a	0.12 ± 0.00b	0.01 ± 0.00a

[A]Results were expressed as relative percentage of each fatty acid, Mean + SD, n=3. In each row, different letters mean statistically significant difference (P <0.05).Traces (<0.005%); nd (not detected).

Source: Patricia Morales et al. (2012).

Phytochemicals

Phytochemicals are promoted for the prevention and treatment of many health conditions, including cancer, heart disease, diabetes, and high blood pressure. There is some evidence that certain phytochemicals may help prevent the formation of potential carcinogens (substances that cause cancer), block the action of carcinogens on their target organs or tissue, or act on cells to suppress cancer development. Many experts suggest that people can reduce their risk of cancer significantly by eating more fruits, vegetables, and other foods from plants that contain phytochemicals. Secondary compounds in plants are known as secondary metabolites or phytonutrients. General categories of these compounds in prickly pear are phenolics including flavonoids, vitamins, minerals and pigments (betaline). These compounds are employing in the treatment of human diseases through quenching free radicals which act as anti-proliferative agents, promoting detoxifying enzymes, inducing differentiation of cancer cells, stimulating immune system thereby inhibiting tumor blood vessel formation (*12000070"Heaton*, 2001).

Groups of phytochemicals

(a) Vitamin C

Vitamin C (ascorbic acid) is found in several varieties of prickly pear with concentrations up to 95 mg/l of juice (Stintzing et al., 2005; Wit et al., 2010). This vitamin can be found in fruits and vegetables such as: melon (68.3 mg/g), yellow water-melon (55.2 mg/g), magenta granadilla (49.3 mg/g), water-melon (39.1 mg/g), and nectarine (32.2 mg/g) (Griffith, 2004) (Table 2.9). In the human body, nutritional C performs as a metabolic element, and as an enzyme cofactor, antioxidant, and in the preventation of the scurvy (Stintzing and Carle, 2005). Natural capacity of L-vitamin c can be clarified as a catalyst cofactor, a radical scrounger, at that point when a donor/acceptor in electron transport on the plasma layer. Vit. C will be able to scavenge the superoxide and hydroxyl radicals, in addition to regenerate α-tocopherol (Davey et al., 2000).Results clearly point towards a positive correlation between cancer prevention of many target organs and consumption of prickly pear.

(b) Vitamin E

Vitamin E can be observed that in the oil of the seeds and pulp of prickly pear *O. ficus-indica* has high levels of tocopherols (vitamin E);-tocopherol and tocopherol are the key chemical substances of seeds and pulp oils, respectively .Vitamin E is the main liposoluble antioxidant, and helps to protect biological systems from de-gradable oxidation (Ramadan et al., 2003) .

Vitamin E (tocopherols) including the α-, β-, γ, δ-tocopherols, which have a long iso-prenic saturated side chain at C2 and a variable group of methyl groups bound to the chromanol ring; and 2). When vitamin E functions as an antioxidant and donates its electron, it cannot function again until it has been 'recharged' by vitamin C. The tocotrienols, divided into the α-, β-, γ-, δ-tocotrienols, which have the same structure as the related tocopherols, except for the side chain, which is unsaturated with three double bonds (Pennock et al., 1964). The tocopherols have been found in cereal sprouts, green leafy vegetables, oleic fruits, seeds, and their respective oils. Vitamin E is a powerful lipid-soluble antioxidant, which acts synergistically with selenium to prevent the oxidation of fatty acids, membrane phospholipids, and proteins α- and β-tocopherols have a neuroprotective role by preventing apoptosis and prolonging newborn neuron life (Brigelius et al., 1999). RDA values are of main and 10 mg vitamin E equivalents for adult men and women, the fat extracted from pulp has 13 times more tocopherols content than the olive oil obtained from the seed products. Tocopherol concentration in prickly pear seeds oil (4030 mg/kg) is higher than other oils such as soy (1342. 84 mg/L), squash (1235 mg/L), sunflower (531 mg/L), sesame (253 mg/L), canola (200 mg/L), olive (130 mg/L) and avocado (65 mg/L) (Becerra-Jiménez et al., 2012).

(c) Vitamin K

Vitamin K is a cofactor for the synthesis of blood stream coagulation factors (II, VII, IX and X), of the coagulation inhibitor, and of the proteins of the bone matrix. The deficiency of this nutritional can cause thrombotic or hemorrhagic syndrome, and change of bone mass (Kuti, 2004). RDA values for this vita-min are sixty-five and 80/ g for adult women and men (Ramadan et al., 2003; Becerra and Andrade, 2012). Oils from the seeds and pulp contain high concentrations of vitamin K (Table 2.12).

Table 2.12: Vitamins Levels as (mg/100 g tissue) in the Fruit and Cladode from Prickly Pear of *O. ficus-indica*

	Pulp	Seeds	Skin	Cladode
Vitamin K1	53.2	52.5	109	——
Vitamin C.	34-40	——	——	7-22
Vitamin B1	——	——	——	0.144
Vitamin B2	——	——	——	0.60
Vitamin B3	——	——	——	0.46
α-Tocopherol	84.9	56	1760	——
β-Tocopherol	12.6	12	222	——
c-Tocopherol	7.9	33	174	——
σ-Tocopherol	422	5	26	——
Total vitamin E	517.4	106	2182	——

Source: Kuti 2004 ; Ramadan et al. (2003)

(d) Phenolic Compounds

Phenolic compounds are a large group of the secondary metabolites widespread in plant kingdom. The phenolic composition and their specific effects on human metabolism have been reviewed (Stintzing et al., 2005 & 2005a). The phenolic compounds can defer prooxidative impacts on proteins, DNA and lipids by the generation of stable radicals (Shahidi et al. 1992). Furthermore, *O. ficus* indica polyphenolic compounds have been uncovered to induce a hyperpolarization of the plasma membrane and to raise the intracellular pool of calcium in human T-cell lines (Aires et al., 2004).

Guzman-Maldonado et al. (2010) found that Prickly pear is a source of gallic, vanillic, 4-hydroxybenzoic acids, catechin, epicatechin, and vanillin were also identified by high-performance liquid chromotography in peel and skin of fruit.The main polyphenols in *O. dicot* genus indica peel were flavonols, additional exactly isorahamnetin derivatives (Figure 2.2). The quercetin 3-O-rutinoside was solely found within the bristled *O. dicot* genus-indica. (Figure 2.3). Cactus (Opuntia species) was found an expensive supply of Conjugated flavonoids (quercetin, kaempfeol and isorhamnetin) in four (Opuntia species) were isolated. Kaempferol was found in green injured Isorhamnetin in inexperienced injured and purple injured varieties (Kuti, 2004).

(A)

(B)

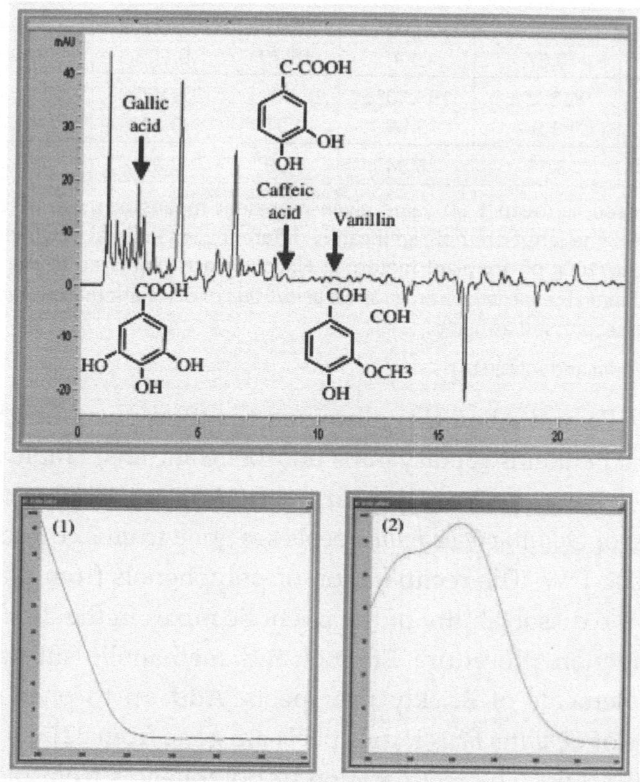

Fig. 2.2: (A) HPLC profile at 280 nm of Myrtillocactus Geometrizans Fruit Harvested in Queretaro (Mg-Qro). (B) UV Spectra of (1) Gallic Acid and (2) Caffeic Acid Standards

Source: Guzman-Maldonado et al. (2010).

Table 2.13: Total Phenolics, Flavonoids, Tannins, Total Betalains (Betacyanins and Betaxanthins) Contents and Yield of Different Extracts of Prickly Pear Peels

Extract	Total polyphenols	Flavonoids	Tannins	Total betatains		Yield %
				Betacynins mg/L	Betaxanthio^{b} mg/L	
Ethanol/water (80:20vly)	1501^{e} ± 2.0	472.33^{e} ± 4.87	72.14^{e} ± 2.52	0.73^{e} ± 0.09	1.045^{e} ± 0.02	84.74^{e} ± 0.42
Chloroform	352.3^{e} ± 11	127.43^{e} ± 2.21	28.11^{e} ± 7.81	0.4121^{e} ±0.001	0.431^{e} ± 0.00	4.8^{e} ± 0.48
Ethyl- acetate	221.3^{e} ± 11	90.58^{e} ± 0.4	13.42^{e} ± 1.24	0.080^{e} ± 0.001	0.072^{e} ± 0.004	8.18^{e} ± 0.10
Acetone	241.2^{e} ± 0.05	74.12^{e} ± 0.12	18.75^{e} ± 1.75	0.173^{e} ± 0.001	0.147^{e} ± 0.00	2.5^{e} ± 0.5
Ethanol	848.9^{e} ± 4.44	328.30^{e} ± 5.0	47.31^{e} ± 2.91	0.395^{e} ± 0.001	0.429^{e} ± 0.007	34.13^{e} ± 1.00

Methanol	$1078^{b} \pm 0.67$	$358.00^{e} \pm 3.4$	$48.91^{e} \pm 0.29$	$0.2471^{e} \pm 0.009$	$0.594^{e} \pm 0.001$	$50.7^{e} \pm 0.4$
Distilled water	$812.1^{e} \pm 1.9$	$194.50^{e} \pm 3.39$	$28.90^{e} \pm 0.07$	$2.946^{e} \pm 0.12$	$2.062^{e} \pm 0.21$	$38.12^{e} \pm 0.70$
LSD	3.55	5.34	6.09	0.09	0.1	0.09

Data ate expressed as mean ± SD value given represent means of three determinations values followed by the same letter are not significantly different (p<05). Total polyphenois are expressed as mg garlic acid /100g of dry plant maternal. Flavonids are expressed as mg catechin/100g dry plant material Tannin is expressed as mg tannic acid/100g of dry plant material and Setacyanins and Setaxanthins are expressed as mg/L

Source: Abou-Elella and Ali (2014)

Abou-Elella and Ali (2014) examined the total phenolics, bio-flavonoids, tannins, total betalains (Betacyanins and Betaxanthins) (Table 2.12).The yield of various elements of Prickly pear peels. Add up to phenolics of various concentrates of *Opuntia ficus indica* peels are gone from 221. 3 to 1501.7/g gallic corrosive/100g DW. The recuperation of polyphenols from plant materials is spurred by the dissolvability of the phenolic mixes in the dissolvable utilized for the extraction procedure Ethanol and methanolic substance and yield of various elements of Prickly pear peels. Add up to phenolics of various concentrates of *Opuntia ficus* indica peels are gone from 221.3 to 1501.7/g gallic corrosive/100g DW. The recuperation of polyphenols from plant materials is spurred by the dissolvability of the phenolic mixes in the dissolvable utilized for the extraction procedure Ethanol and methanolic extracts had significantly (p < 0. 05) the highest amounts of total phenolics (1501.7and 1078 /g gallic equivalents (GAE) / g DW. The phenolic compounds values of water extracts was 612.10 /g GAE/ g DW. These results showed that higher amount of phenol compounds was obtained with solvent which has high polarity.

Fatima et al. (2013) established the antioxidant activity, total phenolic, flavonoid, flavonol and betalain content of seven selected promising cactus pear (*Opuntia ficus indica*. The antioxidant capacity was evaluated by methods for two unique assays: the 2, 2-azinobis (3-ethylbenzothiazoline-6-sulfonic corrosive) (Trolox equivalent prevention agent) (ABTS) technique and the 2, 2-diphenyl-1-picrylhydrazyl (DPPH) scavenging activity. The results revealed qualitative and quantitative dissimilarities in the physico-chemical characteristics of cactus pear accessions. Total phenolics and bio-flavonoids content were found between 354. 37 and 643.66/g gallic eq/g and 24.67 and 49.03/ g catechin eq. /g dry weight basis. (Table 2.13).

Table 2.14: Total Phenols, Flavonoids, Flavonols, Betaxanthins and Betacyanins Pigments Antioxidant Capacity of Juices Extracted from Nine Moroccan Prickly Pears

Cultivars	Total phenols µg GA eq.lg of juice	Betaxanthins mg indicaxantin/l of juice	Betacyanins mg betanin/ l of juice	ABTS mM TE/g of Dry Weight of juice	DPPH EC50 µg/ml of juice
Skhour Rhamna	476.37 ± 5.13	37.66 ± 4.77	-	0.17 ± 0.02	91.2 ± 3.63
Alkalaa	632.11 ± 5.50	42.83 ± 3.00	-	0.24 ± 0.02	65.85 ± 5.20
Yellow Khoribga	354.37 ± 5.37	26.68 ± 2.12	-	0.16 ± 0.03	135.96 ± 12.50
Red Khouribga	358.99 ± 6.10	15.84 ± 0.08	52.04 ± 0.93	0.16 ± 0.03	131.82 ± 11.55
Tamellalet	467.22 ± 3.79	36.96 ± 0.34	-	0.16 ± 0.02	104.71± 6.24
Doukkala	394.9 ± 7.40	18.28 ± 1.48	-	0.16 ± 0.02	112.51± 9.83
Ras Elain	587.11 ± 4.42	41.61 ± 2.15	-	0.24 ± 0.02	75.86 ± 8.16
Ben Guerir	524.63 ± 7.27	22.96 ± 0.24	-	0.18 ± 0.02	82.86 ± 5.64
Ait Baamrame	643.66 ± 3.25	51.33 ± 4.10	-	0.24 ± 0.02	52.48 ± 6.17

Source*:* Fatima et al. (2013)

Salama et al. (2014) determined the total phenolic compounds content (TPC), total flavonoid content (TFC), their antioxidant and antitumor properties. The TPC was 6.34 mg and 4.86 mg as Gallic/g DW, respectively. The total flavonoid content was 3.35 mg and 2.0 mg as qurectein/g DW, respectively (Table 2.14). The scavenging activity of the methanolic extract (100 µg/ml) of prickly pear peel (58.65%) was significantly lower than that of the synthetic antioxidant BHT (79.36%) (Table 2.15).

Table 2.15: Total Phenolic (TP) and Total Flavonoid (TF) in 80% Methanolic Extract of Red Prickly Pear Peel

Plant extract	Total phenolic (TPC)mg as gallic acid /gDW	Total flavonoid (TFC)mg as qurestin /gDW
Red Prickly pear peel	6.34 ± 0.02	3.35 ± 0.10

All values are the mean of three replicate + Standard deviation

Table 2.16: Percent of DPPH Inhibition of Prickly Pear Methanolic Extracts

ConcentrationsPlant extract	Antioxidant inhibition %		
	25µg/ml	50µg/ml	100 µg/ml
Prickly pear peel	15.65 ± 0.32	27.85 ± 0.69	58.65 ± 0.72
BHT	29.47 ± 0.76	57.21 ± 0.34	79.36 ± 0.34

Source: Salama et al. (2014)

Esther Ramírez Moreno et al. (2017), evaluated different solvent system Hexane, ethanol, and ethyl acetate to extract the oil from cactus pear seeds. The extraction yields are compared in (Fig. 2.3), which shows that the higher amount of oil was obtained from the green cultivar and that yield depended on the solvent used. Oil extraction with hexane was higher for both fruit varieties (11.83% for GCPS and 6.89% for RCPS), followed by ethanol, which reached the same yield as ethyl acetate.

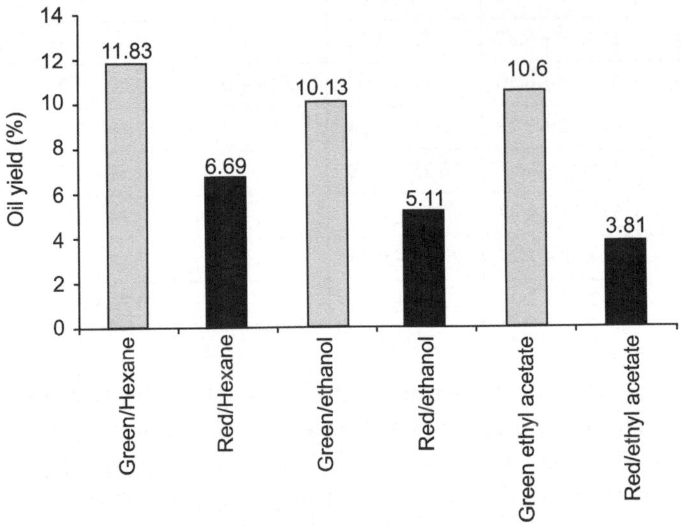

Fig. 2.3: Oil yields (%) extracted from GCPS and RCPS with hexane, ethanol, and ethyl acetate

Source: Esther Ramírez-Moreno et. al. (2017)

(e) Betalains and betacyanins

They are the main pigments in prickly pear. The two isolated betalain pigments were subjected to UV and Densitometer spectral analysis for identification by Abou-Elella and Ali (2014).

Abou-Elella and Ali (2014) studied spectroscopic results of opuntia ficus indica. This research relates to the isolation and identification of bioactive compounds through the ethanol (80%) extract of *Opuntia ficus indica* peel which have anticancer and antioxidant activities. The ethanolic extract of opuntia ficus indica was first fractionated using TLC technique and nine fractions (E1-E9) were separated. The chromatographic and spectroscopic analysis suggested two active compounds are highlighted below: first compound is 17-hydroxy betanin with molecular weight 507 Dalton chemical formula $C_{23}H_{26}N_2O_{11}$ and the second compound is betanin with molecular weight 551 Dalton and chemical formula $C_{24}H_{26}N_2O_{13}$ and the both are alkaloids (Figure 1.4).

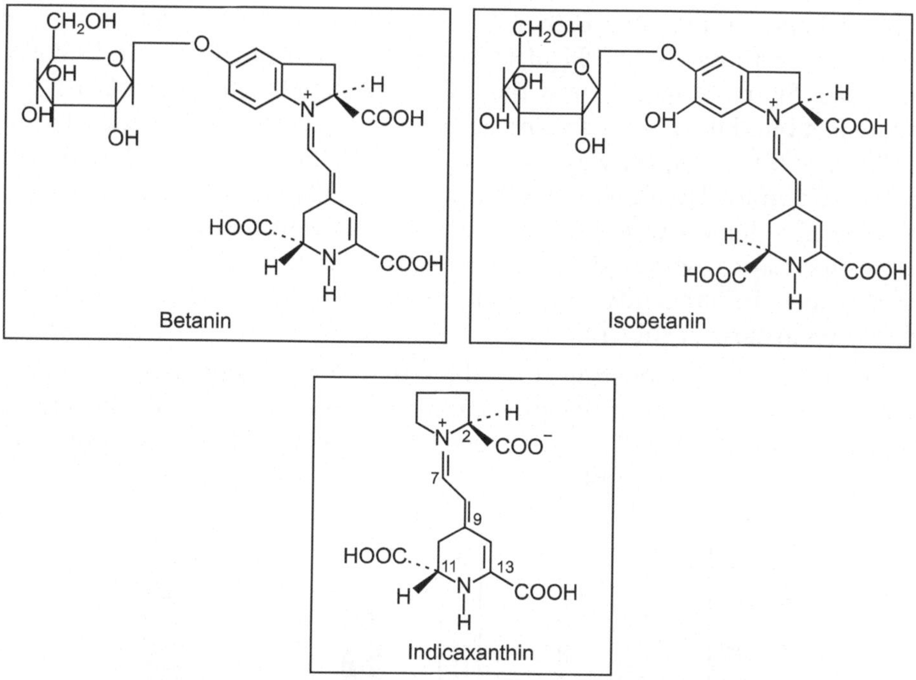

Fig. 2.4: Chemical structure of betanin (A), chemical structure of 17 decarboxy betanin (B)

Source: Abou-Elella and Ali (2014).

Pharmacological Activities

The oil from cactus pear seed has been found to have an appreciable amount of oil with high levels of unsaturated fatty acids (Chougui et al., 2013) with antioxidant (Liu et al., 2013) antimicrobial activity (Zito et al., 2013) as well as cardioprotective, antithrombotic, anti-inflammatory, antiarrhythmic, hypolipidemic, and antihyperglycemic effect (Mobraten et al 2013; Berraaouan et al., 2014).These properties are of interest for the pharmaceutical and food industry. However, the concentration and effectiveness of these oils may vary among cultivars or varieties, crop environmental factors (e.g., light, temperature, and type of soil nutrients), or methods and solvents used for their extraction.

Role of Secondary Metabolites in Prickly Pear as Antioxidant and Antimicrobial Effect

(a) Antioxidant Activity

Esther Ramírez-Moreno et al. (2017) determined the antioxidant and antimicrobial activities of seed oils from two Mexican varieties of cactus pear (green: Opuntia albicarpa and red: Opuntia ficus indica) were extracted with different solvents (hexane, ethanol, and ethyl acetate) to evaluate their antioxidant activity. Esther Ramírez-Moreno (2017) determined the antioxidant activity by DPPH of the oil extracted from RCPS and GCPS is shown in (Figure 2.5). Oil from the GCPS extracted with ethanol and ethyl acetate exhibited the higher antioxidant activity ($p < 0.05$) of 323 and 316 μmol TE/20mg extract, respectively, followed by RCPS oil extracted with ethyl acetate (274 μmol TE/20mg extract) and ethanol (247 μmol TE/20mg extract). These results demonstrate that the extraction solvent had a significant effect on the free radical scavenging capacity of the oil, where the hexane had the lower values. In our study, the green variety exhibited a higher antioxidant activity regardless of solvent.

These results demonstrate that the extraction solvent had a significant effect on the free radical scavenging capacity of the oil, where the hexane had the lower values. In our study, the green variety exhibited a higher antioxidant activity regardless of solvent.

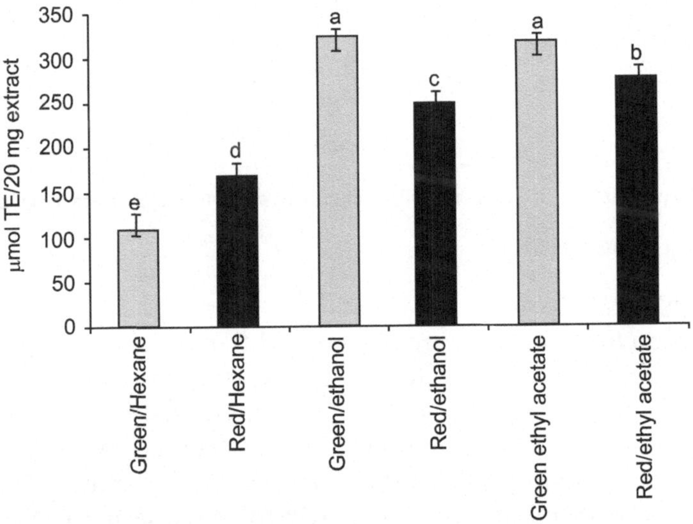

Fig. 2.5: Antioxidant activity of GCPS and RCPS oils extracted with different solvents. A–different letters above bars indicate that samples are significantly different (*p* < 0.05)

The seed oil with higher antioxidant activity was selected to evaluate antimicrobial activity. Oil from green cactus pear seeds obtained with ethanol and ethyl acetate exhibited higher antioxidant activity of 323 and 316μmol TE/20mg ($p < 0.05$), respectively, compared to red cactus pear seed oil (≈274 and 247μmol TE/20mg with ethyl acetate and ethanol, resp.).

(b) Antimicrobial activity

Esther Ramírez- Moreno et al. (2017) found that the oil obtained with ethanol and higher antioxidant activity was used to determine the antimicrobial activity (Figure 2.6). Both cactus pear oils produced a microbial inhibition zone in most of the microorganisms evaluated, particularly Saccharomyces cerevisiae which had similar diameter (38–40 mm).

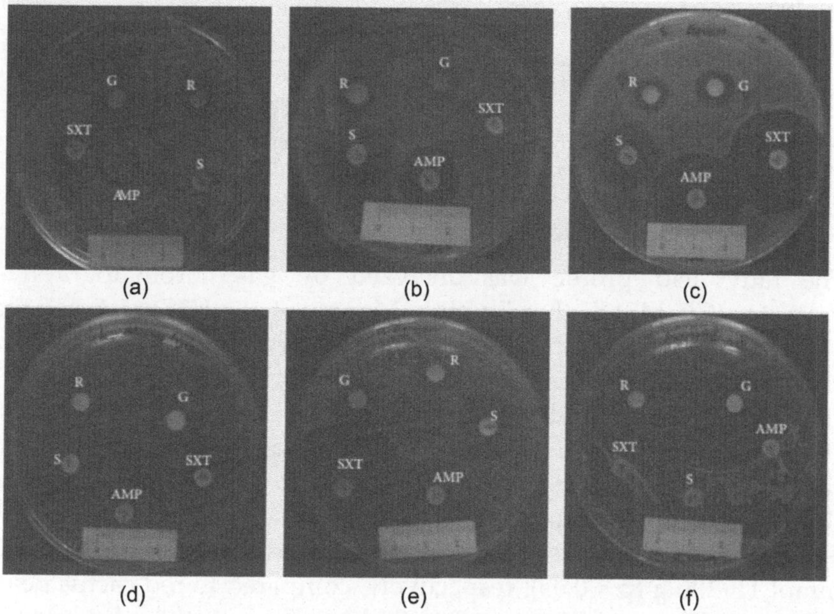

Fig. 2.6: Antimicrobial activity of oil extracted from green cactus pear (G); oil extracted from red cactus pear seeds (R); streptomycin(S); ampicillin (AMP); and sulfamethoxazole/trimethoprim (SXT). Candida. albicans (ATCC 10231) (a); *Escherichia. Coli* O58:H21 (ATCC10536) (b); *Staphylococcus aureus* (ATCC 13565) (c); *Listeria monocytogenes* (CCUG15526) (d); *Pseudomonas aeruginosa* (ATCC15442) (e); *Saccharomyces cerevisiae* (CECT1942) (f).

Table 2.17: Diameters of Growth Inhabitation Zones (mm) in the Presence of Oil Extracted from Cactus Pear Seeds and Conventional Antimicrobials[A].

Microbial cultures	Extract			Antimicrobial agent	
	GCPS	RCPS	S	AMP	SXT
Saccharomyces cerevisiae (CECT1942)	38.3 ± 4.22	40.3 ± 4.5[a]	ND	ND	ND
Escherichia coli O58:H21 (ATCC 10536)	11.9 ± 0.7[d]	11.4 ± 0.9[d]	19.5 ± 1.4[b]	17.8 ± 1.5[c]	29.9 ± 0.9[a]
Escherichia coli O157:H7 (CCUG 44857)	NDB	ND	ND	ND	25.3 ± 1.0
Staphylococcus aureus (ATCC 13565)	12.1 ± 1.0[c]	11.1 ± 1.1[c]	18.3 ± 0.9[b]	28.3 ± 15[a]	33.3 ± 1.9[a]
Listeria monocytogenes (CCUG15526)	13.3 ± 1.5[c]	11.4 ± 0.9[d]	21.3 ± 1.2a	17.3 ± 0.8[c]	37.6 ± 1.8[a]
Pseudomonas aeruginosa (ATCC15442)	16.4 ± 2.1[c]	15.1 ± 2.0[c]	20.1 ± 1.5[b]	24.1 ± 2.54	36.6 ± 2.9[a]

Salmonella typhi (CCUG29478)	ND	ND	14.6 ± 0.4[b]	11.3 ± 1.8[c]	27.3 ± 0.8[a]
Candida albicans (ATCC 10231)	11.1 ± 1.0[a]	11.0 ± 1.8[a]	ND	ND	ND

Source: Esther- Ramírez Moreno et al. (2017)

[A]Inhibition zone diameters for oil and reference antibiotics are means + SE of three replicas. **GCPS**: green cactus pear seed oil extract, **RCPS**: red cactus pear seed oil extract, **S** : streptomycin (10μg/disc), **AMP** : ampicillin (10 μg/disc), and **SXT** : sulfamethoxazole/trimethoprim (10 μg/disc). [B]**ND**: not detected activity. [A-D]Different letters in the same row indicate significant differences.

Source: Esther-Ramírez Moreno et al. (2017).

The fatty acid profile was analyzed by gas chromatography-mass spectrometry (GC-MS). Esther Ramírez-Moreno et al. (2017) reported that the seed oils from two Mexican varieties of cactus pear (green: *Opuntia albicarpa* and red: *Opuntia ficus indica*) were extracted with different solvents (hexane, ethanol, and ethyl acetate) to evaluate their antioxidant activity. The seed oil with higher antioxidant activity was selected to evaluate antimicrobial activity. The fatty acid profile was analyzed by gas chromatography-mass spectrometry (GC-MS) (Table 1.9). Oil from green cactus pear seeds obtained with ethanol and ethyl acetate exhibited higher antioxidant activity ($p < 0.05$) of 323 and 316 mmol TE/20mg ($p < 0.05$), respectively, compared to red cactus pear seed oil (≈274 and 247mmol TE/20mg with ethyl acetate and ethanol, resp.). The oil obtained with ethanol and higher antioxidant activity was used to determine the antimicrobial activity. Both cactus pear oils produced a microbial inhibition zone in most of the microorganisms evaluated, particularly Saccharomyces cerevisiae which had similar diameter (38–40mm).

Role of Secondary Metabolites in Prickly Pear in the Prevention of Neuroprotective Disease

Anti-ulcer

Anti-ulcer activity in Sicily folk's medication, *Caryophylloid dicot* genus genus *Ficus indica* (L.) Mill cladodes area unit being employed for treating peptic ulcer.

Galati et al. (2003) studied the pre-treatment in rats and discovered a protecting action against ethanol-induced-lesion. It was apparent that acute administration of *Ficus indica* lyophilised cladodes typically maintains the structure of the internal organ, digestive. The mucilage might forest all penetration of the necrotizing agent within the stomatal tissue layer. It forms a protecting layer and inhibits the deep death lesions iatrogenic by grain alcohol (Trachtenberg and Mayer, 1981). The most important elements of genus *Ficus indica* cladodes contains a combination of mucilage and cellulose. The cellulose polysaccharides from *O.ficus indica* cladodes most likely might have an effect on the canal tissue layer regeneration. O. genus *Ficus arata* cladodes bring about to cyto- protection phenomena by ignoring up the animal tissue cellular cells and stimulating a rise in mucous secretion production in grain alcohol induce lesion that tends to dissolve the elements of the tissue layer of the abdomen and lowers the amount of tissue macromolecule, however preventive treatment with O. genus *Ficus indica* cladodes will stop the ulcer genic agent to stop injury (Galati et al., 2003).

Role of Secondary Metabolites in Prickly Pear in the Prevention of Anti-inflammatory Disease

Pain and inflammation are part of the body's immune response. They are a common symptom and affect a large number of patients with many types of disease. Because of the significant side effect profiles of steroidal and nonsteroidal anti-inflammatory drugs (NSAIDs), there is a greater interest in natural compounds, such as dietary supplement and herbal remedies, which have been used to reduce pain and inflammation. The presence of potentially active nutrients and their multifunctional properties make fruits and cladodes of *Opuntia* spp. ideal candidates for the production of phytopharmaceutical products. *Opuntia* species have been used as analgesic and anti-inflammatory, anticancer, antidiabetic, anti-hyperlipidemic and anti hypercholesterolemic, antioxidant, antiulcer, antiviral, diuretic, immunomodulatory, neuroprotective, and monoamino-oxidase inhibitors; in addition, the species are nutritionally important, promote wound healing, and improve platelet function. Chauhan et al.(2015) suggested that fruits of *O. elatior* Mill. Has potential analgesic and anti-inflammatory properties. The fruit juice was reddish purple due to the presence of betanin in high concentration. Therefore, betanin might be responsible for this action due to its antioxidant and/or other properties.

Park et al. (1998) found that unending irritation will regularly get activated by overexposure to hypersensitivity related substances. The family Opuntia by utilizing either natural product extricates, the lyophilized cladodes, or the phytosterols from leafy foods separates β-sitosterol from the stem remove in spite of the fact that its movement is by all accounts relatively weaker looked at immediately of cortisol. The fluid concentrate (100– 400 mg/kg.) of the products of *Opuntia dillenii* (Ker-Gawl) was assessed *in vivo* for pain relieving action. The outcomes displayed measurements subordinate activity (Loro et al., 1999). It's also supply of kaempferol has the ability to limit the effect of sensitivity related substances (by bringing down the insusceptible framework's generation of IgE-antibodies). The *Opuntia ficus indica* (OFI) or nopal has been utilized as a part of customary society drug in light of its part in treating various ailments including diabetes, hypertension, and gastric mucosa torment, cardiovascular and mitigating infections in numerous nations over the world.

Farah et al. (2017) assess the hydroethanolic and watery concentrates of (OFI) seeds (500 mg/kg) for *in vivo* mitigating movement. The mitigating movement of OFI was tried in rats weighting 200-300 g by following strategy physiological saline (0.09%) for control gathering, the two concentrates (500 mg/kg) and brexin (12 mg/kg) was controlled for 30 min before an edema was prompted in the rodent paw by subcutaneous infusion of carrageenan. The rat volume was measured 1 h 30 min and 3 h and 6 h after infusion. The OFI demonstrated huge diminishment of edema in carrageenan actuated rodent paw edema display for 44%, half at 1 h 30 min and 3 h for hydro-ethanolic separately, contrasted with the watery concentrate which decreases the expansion in paw volume with a similar level of 25%, for the reference brexin (12 mg/kg) showed % lessening in paw volume 72.71%, 71.32% and 28.72% after 1 h 30 min, 3 h, 6 h individually contrasted with control gathering. Besides the phytochemical tests distinguish the nearness of flavonoids, tannins, sterols, and alkaloids in the seeds of thorny pear desert flora (OFI). The got consequences of the present examination uncovered that the concentrate of OFI seeds (fluid, hydro-ethanolic) has noteworthy calming action (Table 2.18).

Table 2.18: Effect of Opuntia Ficus-indicaseeds Extracts and Brexin on the Edema Induced by the Carrageenan and the Percentage of Inhibition

Treat-ment	Doses (Mg/Kg)	30 min	% inhi-bition	1h, 30 min	3 h	% inhi-bition	% inhi-bition	6 h	% inhi-bition
Controls	0	0.975± 0.091	-	1.025± 0.247	-	1.730± 0.764	-	0.935± 0.177	-
Brexin	12	0.835± 0.63	10.47	0.675± 0.008	72.71	0.375	71.32	0.590± 0.084	28.72
Ext Ag	500	1.007± 0.092	6.20	1.530± 1.211	25	1.477± 0.912	25.18	0.820± 0.322	14.19
Ex (50%)	500	0.885± 0.008	1.16	1.075± 0.785	44.09	0.720± 0.070	50.31	0.635± 0.0495	24.46

Source: Farah et al., (2017)

Gavilán et al. (2015) assess the potential defensive impact of phenolic extracts from various parts of prickly pear on the generation of expert incendiary arbiters by lipopolysaccharide (LPS)-fortified N13 microglia. Initiation of microglia, the sign of neuro inflammation, is critical to have protection and tissue repair in cerebrum. Notwithstanding, enacted microglia secretes cytokines and different elements that are known to add to neurodegeneration. To safe guard mind trustworthiness, accordingly, it is vital to hold microglia initiation under strict control.

The outcomes demonstrate that the concentrates examined fundamentally restrained the arrival of professional incendiary cytokines, for example, tumor putrefaction factor-alpha (TNF-α), interleukin 1-beta (IL-1β), and inducible nitric oxide synthase (iNOS). The present examination, notwithstanding, does not demonstrate an unmistakable direct relationship between cell reinforcement mixes content (add up to phenolic and flavonoid substance) and calming movement shows that there must be some extra segments inside the concentrates that assume a significant part in the mitigating impact and consequently promote portrayal is required. The present examination does, in any case, show that the phenolic separates from various parts of thorny pears are strong inhibitors of microglial initiation and along these lines a potential preventive restorative specialist for neurodegenerative illnesses including neuroinflammation (Figure 2.7).

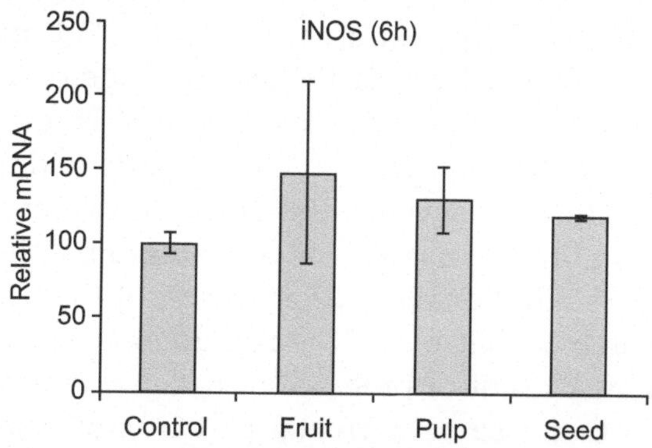

Fig. 2.7: Effect of different extracts of prickly pear on the expression of TNF- (A), IL-1β (B) and iNOS (C) mRNA in control (non- stimulated with LPS) N13 microglia. No significant difference were found in the expression of mRNA of any of the pro inflammatory factors studied between control microglia and control microglia treated with prickly pear extracts. All data are presented as the means SD of three independent experiments.

Source: Gavilán et al. (2015).

Role of Secondary Metabolites in Prickly Pear in the Prevention of Neuroprotective Disease

Dok- Go et al. (2003) reported that Opuntia *ficus-indica* have neuroprotective action in primary cultured rat cortical cells (*Opuntia ficus indica* contains three flavonoid, quercetin, (+)-dihydroquercetin, and quercetin 3-methyl ether, are reported as active antioxidative neuroprotectants that exhibiting protective actions. *Opuntia ficus indica* shows protective action against the oxidative injury induced by H_2O_2, Xanthine/Xanthine Oxidase (X/XO), or Buthione sulfoximine (BSO) in primary cultured rat cortical cells, inhibiting lipid peroxidation, and scavenging DPPH radicals .Moreover, Dok-Go et al. (2003) reported that quercetin, a component of *Opuntia ficus-indica,* had a neuroprotective action against Nmethyl-D-aspartate (NMDA), kainate (KA), and oxygen–glucose deprivation (OGD)-induced neurotoxicity in cultured rat cortical cell Methanol extract of *Opuntia ficus-indica* (MEOF) has a neuroprotective action against (NMDA), (KA), and (OGD)-induced neuronal injury in cultured mouse cortical cells and also reported the neuroprotective effect of MEOF in the hippocampal against neuronal damage evoked by global ischemia in gerbils (Kim et al., 2006).

Role of Secondary Metabolites in Prickly Pear in the Prevention of Anticancer Disease

Abou-Elella and Ali (2014) utilized typan blue test for investigation of the harmful tumor movement of the different concentrates furthermore to 9 portions got from grain liquor eightieth concentrate of sort *Opuntia magnoliopsid* class indica peel. The most astounding percent of anticancer movement was seen by chloroform and ethanol extracates (96% and 83%, individually. Table (10) demonstrated that 9 portions (E1-E9) were secluded exploitation tending were tried for their antitumor action. 2 divisions (E8-E9) gave high antitumor movement as fifty one.70%, severally so these 2 parts with chemicals known range examination. The other seven parts (Zheng and Wang, 2003; Stintzing et al., 2005) gave low antitumor movement. The absolute best antitumor action of the concentrates is additionally a direct result of the nearness of betanin colors that known in ethanolic parts. The antitumor consequence of ethanolic effect is additionally a result of presence of Betanin, and nearness of upper % of poly phenols that assume a pivotal part in inhibitor action and have clearly indicated anti-proliferative action or poisonous quality to human oral malignancy cells (Seeram et al., 2005; María et al., 2007).

Table 1.19: Anticancer Activity of Various Solvent Extracts of Prickly Pear Peels and Ethanol/Water (80:20 v/v) Fractions

Control	Dead cells/ 20 µg/ml	Dead cells/ 50 µg/ml	Dead cells/ 100 µg/ml	Fraction	Dead cells/ 100 µg/ml
Ethanol/water (80:20v/v)	0.0 ± 0.0	0.0 ± 0.0	0.0 ± 2.0	E1	4.0 ± 0.58
Chloroform	22 ± 0.1	30^{e} ± 1.0	28.11^{e} ± 7.81	E2	24.5^{e} ± 0.57
Ethyl acetate	18^{e} ± 0.2	27^{e} ± 0.5	83^{b} ± 1.24	E3	9.0^{e} ± 0.02
Acetone	8^{e} ± 0.5	10^{e} ± 1.0	0.0 ± 0.0	E4	12.0^{e} ± 0.4
Ethanol	20^{e} ± 41.0	33^{e} ± 1.0	24^{e} ± 0.31	E5	4.0^{e} ± 0.05
Methanol	20^{b} ± 1.0	0.0^{e} ± 0.0	0.0^{e} ± 0.0	E6	4.0^{e} ± 0.03
Distilled water	24^{e} ± 1.0	0.0 ± 3.39	80. ± 0.5	E7	8.0^{e} ± 0.2
				E8	78.0^{e} ± 0.5
				E9	51.6^{e} ± 0.35
LSD at 0.05	1.13				0.74

Source: Abou-Elella and Ali (2014).

Fatima et al. (2013) measured the in vitro cytotoxicity toward P-815 cell line by the improvement restriction look at directed by the MTT appropriateness test. They found that juice of different cultivars apply an estimation subordinate advancement hindrance against P-815 cell line (Figure 2.8).

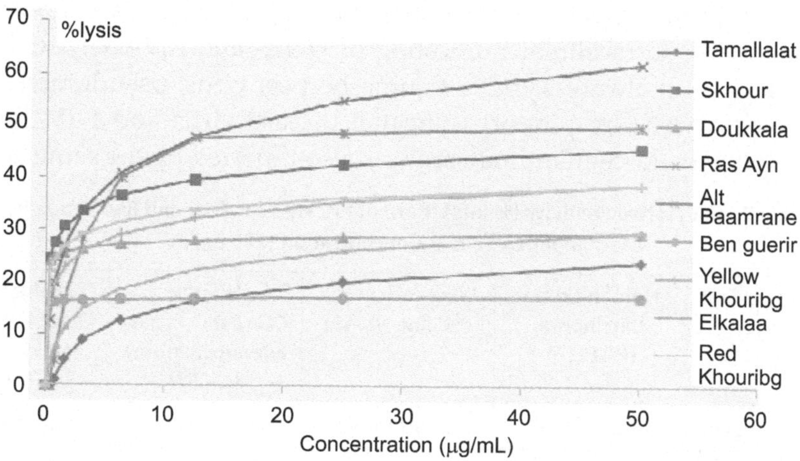

Fig. 2.8: Effect of thorny pear squeezes on cell feasibility of four tumor cell line

Source: Fatima et al. (2013)

García et al. (2009) assessed the anti-proliferative impact of fluid concentrates of four unique cultivars of prickly pear organic product on the malignancy cell line MCF-7 measured by the ferric decreasing/cell reinforcement control and the 2, 2-diphenyl-1, 1-picrylhydrazyl radical searching tests. B-Carotene, phenolics and gallic corrosive substance and the cancer prevention agent limit, were broke down in each concentrate. They didn't find a connection between the aggregate phenolic content and the cancer prevention agent limit with anti-proliferative impact.

Salama et al. (2014) analyzed the cytotoxic impacts of prickly pear peels extract on tumor human cells (Table 2.11). Prickly pear peels methanolic remove displayed cytotoxic consequences for tumor human cells in a measurement subordinate way evaluated by MTT examine. Treatment with methanolic concentrate of thorny pear peels for 24 h brought about a critical contrasts at $p>0.05$ in cell feasibility for a wide range of Human disease cell lines. A critical increment was seen in hepatocellular carcinoma cell line (HePG 2) 33.5% treated with thorny pear peel extricate Low cytotoxic movement in lung carcinoma cell line (A549) 9.86% in red thorny pear peel separate 33.5%. HCT116 20.6% and 20.5 % for MCF7 . The outcomes recommend that red thorny pear peels organic products are rich in dynamic constituents, for example, phenols and flavonoids, which have been proposed to be in charge of their cell reinforcement and anticancer impacts.

Role of Secondary Metabolites in Prickly Pear as Antiviral Effects

An interesting study by Ahmad et al. (1996) suggested that administration of a cactus stem extract (*Opuntia streptacantha*) to mice, race horses, and humans inhibits intracellular replication of DNA- and RNA-viruses such as Herpes simplex malware Type 2, Equine herpes, virus, pseudorabies virus, autorevolezza virus, respiratory syncytial disease virus and HIV-1.A great inactivation of extra-cellular malware was also reported by the same authors.

Table 2.20: Cytotoxic Activity (% Inhibition) of Prickly Pear Peel and Red Grape Peel Methanolic Extract at Concentration (100 μg/ml)

Cancer typePlant extract	Human Colon Carcinoma (HCT116)	Lung carcinoma cell line (A549)	Human Caucasian breast adenocarcinoma (MCF7)	Human hepatocellular carcinoma cell line (HePG 2)
Prickly pear peel	20.6 b + 0.25	9.86b + 0.50	20.5 a + 0.25	33.5 a + 0.30

Source: Salama et al. (2014)

Role of Secondary Metabolites in Prickly Pear as Alcohol Hangover

The main logical proof for the utilization of *Opuntia ficus-indica* against hepatotoxic substances was depicted by Wiese et al. (2004), who detailed that this cactaceous species was valuable for lessening the manifestations of after effects in the wake of expending liquor in over abundance. Weise et al. (2004) demonstrated that the seriousness of the after effect created by liquor utilization may be caused by aggravation prompted by the pollutions in drinks or their data indicated that the severity of the hangover produced by alcohol consumption might be caused by inflammation induced by the impurities in beverages or by alcoholic metabolism sub products and that an extract of *Opuntia ficus-indica* could diminish nausea, dry mouth, and anorexia, which are characteristic signs of alcoholic hangovers in humans. Saida et al. (2017) showed that a concentrate of *Opuntia ficus-indica-cladodes* (CCE) could decrease the hepatic toxicity of the organo phosphorous insecticide spray chlorpyrifos (CPF), which could altogether standardize biochemical parameters, for example, ALAT, ASAT, ALP, LDH, cholesterol, and albuimin, conversely with animals treated with the pesticide alone, in which the biochemical parameters were quite influenced (Wiese et al., 2004). Hostile to diabetic The present study was done to take a gander at the effect of thorny plant pear (*Opuntia ficus-indica*) natural concentrate on biochemical parameters, substance activities and lipid peroxidation in alloxan-actuated diabetic mice.

Role of Secondary Metabolites in Prickly Pear in the Prevention of Diabetic Disease

The present survey was done to look at the impact of prickly plant pear (*Opuntia ficus-indica*) organic extract on biochemical parameters, substance exercises and lipid peroxidation in alloxan-instigated diabetic mice. Prickly pear was utilized as a part of conventional medication for its hypoglycemic and hypolipidemic activities (Frati et al., 1990; Hegwood, 1990 ; Fernandez et al., 1992). Blossoms, stems, leafy foods juices show intriguing wellbeing properties, for example, calming action (Ahmed et al., 2005) and liver security (Galati et al., 2005). Further, Sreekantha et al. (2007) found that betalains repressed the cell development, and incited radical auxiliary changes and discontinuity of K562 cells on human incessant myeloid. Chang et al. (2007) educated that the phenolic acids and flavonoids, however not vitamin C, betanin and isobetanin in Opuntia millennia Haw natural product (ODHF), assume an urgent part in inhibitor action and hostile to LDL peroxidation. They found that vitamin C and betalain pigment is likewise important inhibitor parts inside the peel. The outcomes got by Pimienta-Barrios et al. (2008) who found that ODHF results could assume potential part as a supply of well-being elevating phenolics identified with inhibitor action along these lines, there's a guarantee for the work of ODHF peels for making new accommodating wellbeing item for nutraceutical advertises inside the future Pimienta-Barrios et al. (2008) agreeing that the utilization of *Opuntia joconostle* characteristic covering caused a rebate in steroid levels, a progressive diminishing on aldohexose-levels .Natural betalains are non-harmful cancer prevention agents outstanding to organic layers and move with human lipoproteins, apparently in view of their conjugated amphiphilic concoction structures (Tesoriere-et-al.,2013).

Role of Secondary Metabolites in Prickly Pear in the Prevention of Hepatoprotective Disease

Opuntia ficus arata cladodes extract have safety effect against liver body damage induced in rats by Antioxidant property. The hepatoprotective effect of *Opuntia robusta* and *Opuntia strepta cantha* extracts against APAP-induced ALF was evaluated by Herson et al. (2016). The results recorded in Table 11 showed a significant elevation of ALT ($p<0.05$) and AST ($p<0.001$) enzymes in CCl_4 application compared with normal animals with no alliteration of other measured parameters. The organization of *Opuntia ficus-indica* at a dosage 2 mL/kg has brought about a huge decrease of AST ($p<0.001$) in OFI1 assemble when contrasted with CCl_4 gather with no huge effect on the other tried parameters. In any case, the utilization of the watery concentrate at a measurement of 5 mL/kg has highlighted the height of AST and ALT yet none altogether in the OFI2 amass contrasted with CCl_4-gathering (Table 1.12).

Table 2.21: Biochemical Parameters of the Different Rat Group

	AST(IUL)		ALT(IUL)		Urea(mg/dL)		Creatinin (mg/dL)		Uric acid (mg/dL)	
	Mn	Var.	Mn	Var.	Mn	Var.	Mn	Var.	Mn	Var.
CR1	74.0	28.00	45.66	12.33	0.25	0.0008	6.25	10.91	16.66	25.33
CC14	250.33	960.33	59.33	32.33	0.19	0.0015	6.40	3.80	10.20	8.20
OF11	116.00	15.33	60.5	387.00	0.20	0.0004	5.50	3.60	14.25	231.58
OF12	187.25	1294.25	144.00	12474.60	0.20	0.0026	5.50	3.00	22.00	247.30
Statistical data										
CC14 Vs CRL	P<0.001		P<0.05		NS		NS		NS	
OF11 Vs CC14	P<0.001		NS		NS		NS		NS	
OF12 Vs CC14	NS		NS		NS		NS		NS	
OF11 Vs OF12	NS		NS		NS		NS		NS	

Source: Herson et al. (2016).

For histological investigations, rats were anesthetized with sodium pentobarbital and perfused through entrance vein with saline arrangement (sodium chloride .9%), containing 0.5% heparin and 0.1% procaine and settled in formalin (10%). In this manner, there's certainly worth inside the prophylactic utilization of Opuntia removes as antioxidant, and that we are directly trying Opuntia separates in elective models of oxidative liver-damage. Liver of those rats not only showed solely slight hydropic degeneration of hepatocytes, whereas alternative sections showed apparent traditional-hepatocytes. This study ended that prickly pear have a protecting impact against hepatocarcinoma in rats. Lib et al. (2015) concluded that the mechanism of reduced activities of the tested enzymes and hepatoprotective impact of prickly pear extract is also associated with their inhibitor impact of the phenolic and flavonoids compounds.

Role of Secondry Metabolites in Prickly Pear in Loss of Body Weight (Obesity)

Cactus (*Opuntia ficus-indica*) fiber was shown to promote weight loss in a 3-month clinical investigation. As demonstrated by *in vitro* studies, cactus fiber binds to dietary fat and its use results in reduced absorption, which in turn leads to reduced energy absorption and ultimately the reduction of body weight.

Uebehlhack et al. (2014) elucidated the dietary fat binding capacity of cactus fiber through determination of fecal fat excretion in healthy volunteers. This clinical investigation was performed as a double-blind, randomized, placebo-controlled, crossover study in healthy subjects for a period of approximately 45 days. Twenty healthy volunteer subjects were randomized to receive cactus fiber or placebo, 2 tablets thrice daily with main meals. All subjects were provided with meals during the study period (except washout) according to a standardized meal plan, with 35% of daily energy need coming from fat. Two 24-hour feces samples were collected during both the baseline and treatment periods for analysis of the fat content.Cactus fiber showed an increased fecal fat excretion compared with placebo (mean [SD] = 15.79% [5.79%] *vs* 4.56% [3.09%]; $P < 0.001$). No adverse events were reported throughout the study period. Cactus fiber has been shown to significantly promote fecal fat excretion in healthy adults. The results of the study support the hypothesis that cactus fiber helps in reducing body weight by binding to dietary fat and increasing its excretion, thus reducing dietary fat available for absorption.

Other Diseases and Pharmacological Effects

Distinctive reports suggested that *Opuntia ficus-indica* has a remedial effect in a combination of pains. The difference in bone mineral occasion and calciuria to sidestep osteoporosis was represented by (Aguilera et al. 2013). For this, a randomized 2-years non-never-ending examination was occupied with 181 women. The usage of dried *Opuntia ficus-indica* following a month and a half declared upgraded calciuria levels and turned them again to run of the mill, remaining progressive for whatever is left of the treatment. Bone supplement thickness extended in the general hip and lumbar area in those get-togethers who ate up 600 g of dried *Opuntia ficus-indica*. The makers have suggested that the high measure of calcium in got dried out *Opuntia ficus-indica* could fill in as a supplementary resource.

Food Applications

Desert plant organic products are generally devoured crisp, but at the same time are put to various conventional and modern uses (Saenz, 2000). It is viewed as an important sustenance that is expended as new natural product, as a vegetable in servings of mixed greens and sauces, as a fundamental fixing in treats, a hors d'oeuvre, (Barbera et al., 1992). It is additionally handled on a little scale in the nourishment businesses as a jam and stick, as entire organic product in syrup to be utilized to refresh prepared to serve sauces and mixers, limited by other sustenance items (Sawaya et al., 1983). Additionally, prickly plant pear organic product contains betalain pigment which have supportive potential for assess as regular natural colorants (Clara et al., 2015). Prickly pear fruit have high counts in vitamin C and calcium. They are also high in dietary fiber, which explains why they helped with indigestion. They also contain a high amount of kaempferol, which is an additional aid against cancer and heart disease, and many antioxidants and proteins that aid the body against infection and other maladies. Beyond that, they are also low in cholesterol, sugars and fats, making the fruit an overwhelmingly healthy treat (Fernando et al., 2006).

Conclusion

Prickly pear (Opuntia *ficus indica*) is family of Cactacae is reported to have antioxidant process due to the occurrence of vitamin C, amino acids, polyphenolics, flavonoid compounds, taurine and betalain, so it has anticancer activity. Additionally prickly pear is used in a folk's medication for the treatment of burns, wounds, edema, and digestion. It has been reported that its alcoholic extract possesses medicine, symptom, anti-viral activities, anti-polygenic-disease and anti-hyperlipidemia. Prickly pear pulp is considered as an important source of calcium, potassium, and magnesium. The seeds of Prickly pear contained 16.6% protein, 17.2% fat, 49.6% fiber and 3.0% fiery debris. While, aspartic, glutamic arginine and glycine were the richest amino acids influencing almost 50% of the sum amino acids content. Also, it exhibited a high content of linoleic and behenic fatty acids. The oil from cactus pear seed has been found to have an appreciable amount of oil with high levels of unsaturated fatty acids with antioxidant, antimicrobial activities as well as cardioprotective, antithrombotic, anti-inflammatory, antiarrhythmic, hypolipidemic, and antihyperglycemic effects. The hepatoprotective impact of prickly pear extract is also associated with their inhibitor impact of the phenolic and flavonoids compounds. The cactus fiber helps in reducing body weight by binding to dietary fat and increasing its excretion, thus reducing dietary fat available for absorption. It has a protecting action against ethanol-induced-lesion (anti-ulcer effect), potential analgesic, anti-inflammatory properties and it is vital to hold microglia initiation under strict control, so it is a potential preventive restorative specialist for neurodegenerative illnesses including neuroinflammation. Bone supplement thickness extended in the general hip and lumbar area in those get-togethers who ate up 600 g of dried *Opuntia ficus-indica*. The makers have suggested that the high measure of calcium in got dried out *Opuntia ficus-indica* could fill in as a supplementary resource. Finally, it is used in many food applications due to its high content of kaempferol, which is an additional aid against cancer and heart disease, and many antioxidants and proteins, that aid the body against infection and other maladies.

REFERENCES

Abou-Elella FM, Ali RFM ((2014): Antioxidant and Anticancer Activities of Different Constituents Extracted from Egyptian Prickly Pear Cactus (Opuntia Ficus-Indica) Peel. Biochem Anal Biochem. 3: 158.

Aguilera-Barreiro ML, Rivera-Márquez JA, Trujillo-Arriaga HM, and Tamayo Y. (2013) : Intake of Dehydrated Nopal (Opuntia Ficus Indica) Improves Bone Mineral Density and Calciuria in Adult Mexican Women. Food Nutri Res. 57. 71.

Ahmad A, Davies J, Randall S, Skinner GR. Antiviral Properties of Extract of Opuntia Streptacantha. Antiviral Res.; 30: 75-85.

Aires V., S. Adote, A. Hichami, K. Moutairou, E. S. E. Boustani & N. A. Khan (2004): Modulation of Intracellular Calcium Concentrations and T cell Activation by Prickly Pear Polyphenols. Mol Cell Biochem. 260, 103-110.

Barbera, G., F. Carimi, P. Inglese and M. Panno (1992): Physical, Morphological and Chemicalchanges during Fruit Development and Ripening in three Cultivars of Prickly-pear (Opuntia ficus-indica (L.) Miller). Journal of Horticultural Science 67:307-312.

Becerra-Jiménez J, Andrade-Cetto A (2012): Effect of Opuntia Streptacantha Lem. On Alpha-glucosidase Activity. J Ethnopharmacol 139: 493-496.

Berraaouan, A. Ziyyat, A. Mekhfi H.,(2014): "Evaluation of Antidiabetic Properties of Cactus Pear Seed Oil in Rats," Pharmaceutical Biology, vol. 52, no. 10, pp. 1286–1290, 2014.

Brigelius-Flohoe, R. and Traber, M.G. (1999): Vitamin E: Function and Metabolism. *FASE Journal*, 13, 1145-1156.

Butera , D.; Tesoriere, L.; Di Gaudio, F.; Bongiorno, A.; Allegra, M.; Pintaudi, A.M.; Kohen, R.and Livrea ,M.A. (2002): Antioxidant Activities of Sicilian Prickly Pears (Opuntia Ficus Indica) Fruit Extracts and Reducing Properties of its Betalains: Betanin and Indicaxanthin. J.Agric.Food Chem. 50:6895–6901.

Cardador Anaberta - Cristian Martínez, Martínez Jiménez,Sandoval, Georgina (2011: Evalorization of Cactus Pear (Opuntia spp.) Wastes as a Source of Antioxidants. Original Ciênc. Tecnol. Aliment. Campinas, 31(3): 782-788.

Castellar, R.; Obón, J.M.; Alacid, M.and Fernández-López, J.A. (2003): Color Properties and Stability of Betacyanins from Opuntia Fruits. J. Agric. Food Chem. 51: 2772–2776.

Chougui, N., Tamendjari A., Hamidj W. et al., (2013): "Oil Composition and Characterisation of Phenolic Compounds of Opuntia ficusindica seeds," Food Chemistry, vol. 139, no. 1–4, pp. 796–803,

Chavez-Santoscoy, R .A. Gutierrez-Uribe, J.A.and Serna-Saldívar, S.O. (2009): Phenolic Composition, Antioxidant Capacity and in Vitro Cancer Cell Cytotoxicity of Nine Prickly Pear (*Opuntia spp.*) juices Plant Foods Hum. Nutr. 64:146–152.

Clara Albano, Carmine Negre,Noemi Tommasi, Carmela Geradi, Giovanni Mita, Antonio Miceli,Luigi De bellis and Federica Blando (2015): Betalains, Phenols and Antioxidant Capacity in Cactus Pear [Opuntia ficus-indica (L.) Mill.] Fruits from Apulia (South Italy) Genotypes , Antioxidants 2015, 4, 269-280.

Chang SF, Hsieh CL, Yen GC (2008). The Protective Effect of Opuntia Dillenii Haw Fruit Against Low-density Lipoprotein Peroxidation and its Active Compounds. Food Chem 106:569–575.

Fatima Dehbi, Aziz Hasib, Mounir Tilaoui Abdelmajid Zyad (2013) Bioactive Constituents, Antioxidant Activity and in Vitro Cancer Cell Cytotoxicity of Moroccan Prickly Pear (Opuntia Ficus Indica L.) Juices. Journal of Natural Sciences Research. Vol.3, No.14,1-20.

Davey, M. W., van Montagu, M., Inze, D., Sanmartin, M., Kanellis, A., Smirnoff, N., et al. (2000): Plant L-ascorbic acid: Chemistry, Function, Metabolism, Bioavailability and Effects of Processing. Journal of the Science of Food and Agriculture 80, 825–860.

Deldicque L, Van Proeyen K, Ramaekers M, Pischel I, Sievers H, et al. (2013): Additive Insulinogenic Action of Opuntia Ficus-indica Cladode and Fruit Skin Extract and Leucine after Exercise in Healthy Males. J Int Soc Sports Nutri 10: 45.

Dok-Go H, Lee KH, Kim HJ, Lee EH, Song JLY, Lee YH, Jin C et al., (2003): Neuroprotective Effects of Antioxidative Flavonoid, Quercetin, (1) dihydroquercetin and Quercetin 3-methyl ether, Isolated from Opuntia ficus-indica var. saboten. Brain Research; 965: 130–136.

Esther Ramírez-Moreno, Raquel Cariño-Cortés, Nelly Del Socorro Cruz-Cansino, Luis Delgado-Olivares, José Alberto Ariza-Ortega, Vanessa Yelina Montañez- Izquierdo,(2017): Antioxidant and Antimicrobial Properties of CactusPear (Opuntia) Seed Oils. Hindawi Journal of Food Quality 1-8.

Farah Kenza Benattia1, Zoheir Arrar1, Youssef Khabbal (2017): Evaluation of the Anti-inflammatory Activity of the Seeds Extracts of Prickly Pear (Opuntia ficus-indica L.) Der Pharma Chemica, 2017, 9 (11): 14-17.

Fernandez, M. L.; Lin, E. C.; Trejo, A.and McNamara, D. J. (1992): Prickly Pear (Opuntia sp.) Pectin Reverses low-density Lipoprotein Receptor Suppression induced by a Hyper Cholesterolemic diet in Guinea Pigs, J. Nutr.122: 2330-2340.

Fernando Díaz Sánchez, Eva Maria Santos López, Santiago Filardo Kerstupp, Roberto Villagómez Ibarra, Leia Scheinvar, (2006): Colorant Extraction From Red Prickly Pear (Opuntia Lasiacantha) For Food Application. Electronic Journal of Environmental, Agricultural and Food Chemistry 5(2):1330-1337.

Fleuriet, A., & Macheix, J. J. (2003): Phenolic Acids in Fruits and Vegetables. In C. A. Rice-Evans & L. Packer (Eds.), Flavonoids in Health and Disease. Marcel Dekker Inc.

Forni, E. Polesello, A. Montefiori, D. Maestrelli. A. (1992): J. Chromatography, 593, 177-183.

Frati, A. C.; Jimenez, E.and Ariza, C. R. (1990): Hypoglycemic Effect of Opuntia Ficus Indica in Non-insulin-dependent Diabetes mellitus Patients. Phytother, Res. 4:195 -197.

Galati EM, Mondello MR, Lauriano ER, Traviano MF, Galluzzo M, Miceli N (2005): Opuntia ficus-indica (L.) Miller fruit juice protects liver from Carbon Tetrachloride Induced Injury. Phytother Res, 19:796-800.

Gavilán MP, Castaño A, Torres M, Revilla E, Caballero C, Jiménez S, García-Martínez A, Parrado J, Vitorica J, Ruano D. (2013): Age-related increase in the Immunoproteasome Content in Rat Hippocampus: Molecular and Functional Aspects. J Neurochem 2013; 108: 260-270.

Griffith. MP. (2004): The Origins of an Important Cactus Crop, Opuntia Ficus-Indica (Cactaceae): New Molecular Evidence. Am J Bot 91: 1915-1921.

Guzman-Maldonado, S. H. Morales-Montelongo, A. L C. Mondragon-Jacobo, Herrera Hernandez, G. Guevara-Lara, Reynoso-Camacho, F. R. (2010): J. Food Sci. 75 (6) 485-492.

Heaton S (2001): Organic Farming, Food Quality and Human Health. Soil Association report, Bristol UK, 87.

Hegwood, D.A. (1990): Human Healthy Discoveries with Opuntia sp. (prickly pear). Journal of Horticulture Science, 25: 1515–1516.

Herson Antonio González-Ponce, María Consolación Martínez-Saldaña, Ana Rosa Rincón-Sánchez, María Teresa Sumaya-Martínez, Manon Buist-Homan, Klaas Nico Faber, Han Moshage, and Fernando Jaramillo-Juárez (2016): Hepatoprotective Effect of Opuntia robusta and Opuntia streptacantha Fruits against Acetaminophen-Induced Acute Liver Damage, Nutrients. Oct. 8(10): 607.

Kaastra B, Manders RJ, Van Breda E, Kies A, Jeukendrup AE, et al. (2006): Effects of Increasing Insulin Secretion on Acute Postexercise Blood Glucose Disposal. Med Sci Sports Exerc 38: 268-275.

Kim JH, Park SM, Ha HJ, Moon CJ, and Shin TK, et al. (2006): Opuntia Ficus-Indica Attenuates Neuronal Injury in in Vitro and in Vivo Models of Cerebral Ischemia. J Ethnopharmacol 104: 257-262.

Kuti, J.O. (2004): Antioxidant compounds from four Opuntia cactus pear fruit varieties. Food Chem, 85:527-33.

Li b.B Smith B. and Hossain Md. M (2006): Extraction of Phenolics from Citrus Peels: I. Solvent Extraction Method. Separation and Purification Technology 48: 182–1883.

Liu, W. Fu, Y.-J. Zu Y.-G. (2009): "Supercritical Carbon Dioxide Extraction of Seed Oil from Opuntia dillenii Haw. And its Antioxidant Activity," Food Chemistry, vol. 114, no. 1, pp. 334–339.

Loro, J.F.; Del Rio, I.and Pérez-Santana, L. (1999): Preliminary Studies of Analgesic and Anti-inflammatory Properties of Opuntia Dillenii Aqueous Extract. J. Ethnopharmacol, 67: 213-218.

María Manuela Hernández-Herrero, and Tomás Filardo-Kerstupp4Fatima Dehbi1, Aziz Hasib1, Mounir Tilaoui2, Hicham El Batal1, Naïma Zaki1, Aaziz Ouatmane1, Abderrahim Jaouad1, Abdelmajid Zyad (2013): Bioactive Constituents, Antioxidant Activity and in Vitro Cancer Cell Cytotoxicity of Moroccan Prickly Pear (Opuntia ficus indica L.) Juices .Journal of Natural Sciences Research Vol.3, No.14, 12-20.

Park, E.J. And Pezzuto, J. (2002): Botanicals in Cancer Chemo Prevention. Can. Metas Res.21: 231-237.

Patricia Morales, Esther Ramírez-Moreno1, María de Cortes Sanchez-Mata, Ana Maria Carvalho, Isabel C.F.R. Ferreira, (2012): Nutritional and Antioxidant Properties of Pulp and Seeds of two Xoconostle Cultivars (Opuntia joconostle F.A.C. Weber ex Diguet and Opuntia matudae Scheinvar) of high consumption in Mexico. Food Research International 46(1): 279-285.

Pennock, J.F. Hemming, F.W. and Kerr, J.D. (1964): A Reassessment of Tocopherol in Chemistry. Biochemical and Biophysical Research Communications, 17: 542-548.

Pimienta- Barrios, E. (1994): Prickly pear (Opuntia spp.): A valuable fruit crop for the semi-arid lands of Mexico. Journal of Arid Environments. 28: 1-11.

Pimienta-Barrios, E., Méndez-Morán, L., Ramírez-Hernández, B., García A.and Domínguez-Arias, R. (2008): Efecto de la ingestión Del fruto de xoconostl (Opuntia joconostle Web.) sobre la glucosa y lípidos séricos. Agrociencia. 42:645-653.

Ramadan MF, Mörsel JT. Oil cactus pear (Opuntia ficus-indica L.) (2003): Food Chem . 82: 339-45.

Roman-Ramos R, Flores-Saenz JL, Alarcon-Aguilar FJ (1995): Antihyperglycemic effect of some edible plants. J Ethnopharmacol 48: 25-32.

Saenz C. (2000): Processing technologies: an alternative for cactus pear (Opuntia spp.) Fruits and Cladodes. Journal of Arid Environments 46: 209–225.

Saenz, C. and Sepulveda, E. (2001): Cactus-Pear Juices. Journal of the Proffesional Association of Cactus, 4: 3-10.

Saida Ncibi Mahmoud Ben Othman Amira Akacha, Mohamed Naceur Krifi, Lazhar Zourgui (2017): Opuntia ficusindica extract protects against Chlorpyrifos-induced damage on mice liver. Food and Chemical Toxicology Volumes 101 – 109.

Salama Z., Abd El Moneem NAGIB, Abd El Kader Moursy Abd El Samad, Hanan Anwar Aly TAIE, Rasha Mohamed Mohamed Mohasib (2014): Radical Scavenging Activity, and in vitro cancer cell Cytotoxicity of cactus (Opuntia Ficus Indica) and Grape Peel (vitis species)Extracts. Analele Universitγώii din Oradea, V: XXI, Issue: 2, 2014, pp. 84-91.

Sarbojeet Jana (2012): Nutraceutical and Functional Properties of Cactus Pear (Opuntia Spp.) And it's Utilization for Food Applications Journal of Engineering Research and Studies. JERS 3: 60-66.

Sawaya, W.N., H.A. Khatchadourian, W.M. Safi and H.M. Al-Hammad (1983): Chemical Characterization of Prickly Pear Pulp, Opuntia ficus-indica, and the Manufacturing of Prickly Pear jam. Journal of Food Technology 18:183-193.

Seeram, N.P.; Adams, L.S.; Henning, S.M, Niu, Y.; Zhang, Y.; Nair, M.G. and Heber, D. (2005): In Vitro Antiproliferative, Apoptotic and Antioxidant Activities of Punicalagin, Ellagic Acid and a total Pomegranate Tannin Extract are Enhanced in Combination with other Polyphenols as found in Pomegranate juice. J. Nutr. Biochem., 16(6): 360-367.

Shahidi F, Wanasundara PK (1992): Phenolic Antioxidants. Crit Rev Food Sci Nutr 32: 67-103.

Shi, H. L., Noguchi, N., & Niki, E.(2001): Introducing Natural Antioxidants. In J. Pokorny et al. (Eds.), Antioxidants in Food: Practical Applications. Woodhead Publishing Ltd. and CRC.

Sreekanth, D.; Arunasree, M.K.; Roy, K.R.; Chandramohan, R.T.; Reddy, G.V. and Reddanna, P. (2007): Betanin a Betacyanin Pigment purified from Fruits of Opuntia ficus-indica induces Apoptosis in Human Chronic Myeloid Leukemia Cell line-K562. Phytomedicine, 14: 739-746.

Stintzing F.C. & R. Carle R. (2005): Cactus Stems (Opuntia spp.) A Review on their Chemistry, Technology, and Uses. Mol Nutr Food Res 49, 175-194.

Stintzing FC, Herbach KM, Mosshammer MR, et al.(2005a): Color, betalain Pattern, and Antioxidant Properties of Cactus Pear (Opuntia spp.) Clones. J Agric Food Chem. 2005; 53: 442-51.

Tesoriere, L.; Gentile, C.; Angileri, F.; Attanzio, A.; Tutone, M.; Allegra, M.; Livrea, M. A. (2013): Transepithelial Transport of the Betalain Pigments Indicaxanthin and Betanin Across Caco-2 cell Monolayers and Influence of Food Matrix. Eur. J. Nutr, 52(3):1077-87.

Trachtenberg S, Mayer, A.M. (1981): Composition and Properties of Opuntia Ficus Indica Mucilage. Photochemistry, 20: 2665–2668 Uchoa AF, Souza PAS., Zarate RML, Gomes-Filho E. and Campos FAP. Isolation and Characterization of a Reserve Protein from the Seeds of Opuntia ficus-indica (Cactaceae). Bsi-oinlodgicicaal Research. 31: 757-761.

Uebelhack R, Busch R, Alt F, Beah ZM, Chong PW.(2014): Effects of Cactus Fiber on the Excretion of Dietary Fat in Healthy Subjects: A Double Blind, Randomized, Placebo-Controlled, Crossover Clinical Investigation, Curr Ther Res Clin Exp. 76:39-74.

Van Proeyen K, Ramaekers M, Pischel I, Hespel P (2012): Opuntia Ficusindica Ingestion Stimulates Peripheral disposal of oral glucose before and after exercise in healthy men. Int J Sport Nutr Exerc Metab 22: 284-291.

Wiese J, McPherson S, Odden MC, Shlipak MG (2004): Effect of Opuntia Ficus Indica on Symptoms of the Alcohol Hangover. Arch Intern Med 164: 1334-1340.

Wit M, Nel P, Osthoff G, Labuschagne MT. (2010): The Effect of Variety and Location on Cactus pear (Opuntia ficus-indica) Fruit Quality. Plant Foods Hum Nutr 2010; 65:136-45.

Zheng W, Wang SY. (2003): Oxygen Radical Absorbing Capacity of Phenolics in Blueberries, Cranberries, Chokeberries, and Lingonberries. J. Agric Food Chem; 51: 502-9.

Zito, P. Sajeva. M. Bruno, M.S. Rosselli, A. Maggio, and F. Senatore, (2013): "Essential Oils Composition of two Sicilian Cultivars of Opuntia Ficus-indica (L.) Mill. (Cactaceae) fruits (prickly pear)," Natural Product Research, Vol. 27, no. 14, pp. 1305–1314, 2013.

Phyto-chemicals and Ethanobotany
Edited by: Pawan Kumar 'Bharti'
ISBN: 978-93-86841-93-3
Edition: 2019
Published by: Discovery Publishing House Pvt. Ltd., New Delhi (India)

Pages 41-77

3

Plant Secondary Metabolites

A Key Review

[1]Prasann Kumar, [2]Shweta Pathak

ABSTRACT

The use of natural products as medicines has been described throughout history in the form of traditional medicines, remedies, potions and oils with many of these bioactive natural products still being unidentified. The biosynthesis and breakdown of proteins, fats, nucleic acids and carbohydrates, which are essential to all living organisms, are known as primary metabolism with the compounds involved in the pathways known as "primary metabolites".

Keywords: Agriculture, Biotic, Crop, Density, Energy, Forage

Introduction

Natural Products in History

Natural products (secondary metabolites) have been the most successful source of potential drug leads. However, their recent implementation in drug discovery and development efforts have somewhat demonstrated a decline in interest. Nevertheless, natural products continue to provide unique structural diversity in comparison to standard combinatorial chemistry, which presents opportunities for discovering mainly novel low molecular weight lead compounds. Since less than 10% of the world's biodiversity has been evaluated for potential biological activity, many more useful natural lead compounds await discovery with the challenge being how to access this natural chemical diversity. The earliest records of natural products were depicted on clay tablets in cuneiform from Mesopotamia (2600 B.C.) which documented oils from Cupressus sempervirens (Cypress) and Commiphora species (myrrh) which are still used today to treat coughs, colds and inflammation. The Ebers Papyrus (2900 B.C.) is an Egyptian pharmaceutical record, which documents over 700 plant-based drugs ranging from gargles, pills, infusions, to ointments. The Chinese Materia Medica (1100 B.C.) (Wu Shi Er Bing Fang, contains 52

[1] Department of Agronomy, School of Agriculture, Lovely Professional University, Jalandhar, Punjab, 144411, India.

[2] Department of Plant Physiology, I.Ag. Sci., BHU., Varanasi, 221005, U.P., India.

prescriptions), Shennong Herbal (~100 B.C., 365 drugs) and the Tang Herbal (659 A.D., 850 drugs) are documented records of the uses of natural products. The Greek physician, Dioscorides, (100 A.D.), recorded the collection, storage and the uses of medicinal herbs, whilst the Greek philosopher and natural scientist, Theophrastus (~300 B.C.) dealt with medicinal herbs. During the Dark and Middle Ages the monasteries in England, Ireland, France and Germany preserved this Western knowledge whilst the Arabs preserved the Greco-Roman knowledge and expanded the uses of their own resources, together with Chinese and Indian herbs unfamiliar to the Greco-Roman world. It was the Arabs who were the first to privately own pharmacies (8th century) with Avicenna, a Persian pharmacist, physician, philosopher and poet, contributing much to the sciences of pharmacy and medicine through works such as the Canon Medicinae.

Medicinal Plants in Folklore

The use of natural products as medicines has been described throughout history in the form of traditional medicines, remedies, potions and oils with many of these bioactive natural products still being unidentified. The dominant source of knowledge of natural product uses from medicinal plants is a result of man experimenting by trial and error for hundreds of centuries through palatability trials or untimely deaths, searching for available foods for the treatment of diseases. One example involves the plant genus Salvia which grows throughout the southwestern region of the United States as well as northwestern Mexico and which was used by Indian tribes of southern California as an aid in childbirth. Male newborn babies were "cooked" in the hot Salvia ashes as it was believed that these babies consistently grew to be the strongest and healthiest members of their respective tribes and are claimed to have been immune from all respiratory ailments for life. The plant, Alhagi maurorum Medik (Camels thorn) secretes a sweet, gummy material from the stems and leaves during hot days. This gummy sap is called "manna" and consists mostly of melezitose, sucrose and invert sugar and it has been documented and claimed by the Ayurvedic people that the plant aids in the treatment of anorexia, constipation, dermatosis, epistaxis, fever, leprosy, and obesity. It was also used by the Israelis who boiled the roots and drank the extract as it stopped bloody diarrhea. The Konkani people smoked the plant for the treatment of asthma, whilst the Romans used the plant for nasal polyps. The plant Ligusticum scoticum Linnaeus found in Northern Europe and Eastern North America was eaten raw first thing in the morning and was believed to protect a person from daily infection; the root was a cure for flatulence, an aphrodisiac and was used as a sedative in the Faeroe Islands. Atropa belladonna Linnaeus (deadly nightshade) is found in central and Southern Europe, Western Asia, North Africa, North America and New

Zealand. Its notoriously poisonous nature (three berries are sufficient to kill a child) firmly excluded it from the folk medicine compilation and seemed to have been accepted as dangerous to handle or to experiment with.

Medicinal Natural Products from Other Sources Used in Folklore

The fungus Piptoporus betulinus, which grows on birches was steamed to produce charcoal, valued as an antiseptic and disinfectant. Strips of P. betulinus were cut and used for staunching bleeding and were also found to make very comfortable corn pads. Another example is the fungus Agaricus campestris Linnaeux ex Fries (field mushroom) found in the northern and southern temperate zones and the Caribbean. A. campestris, had reportedly been stewed in milk to soothe cancer of the throat. As early as the 17th–18th century, lichens had been used as dyes and were far more valued than oriental spices. To date there are no lichen derived drugs approved on the market but their applications in folklore has been well documented. Lichens have been used as the raw materials for perfumes and cosmetics, medicine from the time of the early Chinese and Egyptian civilizations. Well known examples include Usnea dillenius ex Adanson which was traditionally used for curing diseases of the scalp and is still sold in pharmacies as an ingredient in anti-dandruff shampoos and in Ireland to treat sore eyes. The lichen U. subfloridana Stirton was mixed with tobacco and butter, boiled and then cooled and applied as a lotion. Parmelia omphalodes (Linnaeus) Acharius, which is abundant in the British Isles, was used in brown dyes. In the highlands it was traditionally sprinkled on stockings at the start of a journey to prevent inflammation of the feet and in Ireland it was used as a cure for bad sores under the chin as well as for burns and cuts. By comparison, the marine environment has very few reported applications in traditional medicine. The red algae Chondrus crispus and Mastocarpus stellatus were sources of a beverage, which was popular as a folk cure for colds, sore throats, chest infections including tuberculosis. The alga was also boiled in milk or water and used for kidney trouble and burns. Furthermore, three spoonfuls of the juice of the red alga Porphyra umbilicalis (Linnaeus) Kützing, taken every morning followed by fasting for three weeks was found to be effective against cancers, in particular breast cancer. P. umbilicalis has also been described in the Aran Islands for easing indigestion. and was also boiled and given to cows to relieve their springtime constipation.

Primary and Secondary Metabolites (Natural Products)

The biosynthesis and breakdown of proteins, fats, nucleic acids and carbohydrates, which are essential to all living organisms, is known as primary metabolism with the compounds involved in the pathways known as "primary metabolites". The mechanism by which an organism biosynthesizes compounds called 'secondary metabolites' (natural products) is often found to be unique to an organism or is an expression of the individuality of a species and is referred to as "secondary metabolism". Secondary metabolites are generally not essential for the growth, development or reproduction of an organism and are produced either as a result of the organism adapting to its surrounding environment or are produced to act as a possible defense mechanism against predators to assist in the survival of the organism. The biosynthesis of secondary metabolites is derived from the fundamental processes of photosynthesis, glycolysis and the Krebs cycle to afford biosynthetic intermediates which, ultimately, results in the formation of secondary metabolites also known as natural products. It can be seen that although the number of building blocks are limited, the formation of novel secondary metabolites is infinite. The most important building blocks employed in the biosynthesis of secondary metabolites are those derived from the intermediates: Acetyl coenzyme A (acetyl-CoA), shikimic acid, mevalonic acid and 1-deoxyxylulose-5-phosphate. They are involved in countless biosynthetic pathways, involving numerous different mechanisms and reactions (e.g., alkylation, decarboxylation, aldol, Claisen and Schiff base formation. It is hypothesized that secondary metabolism utilizes amino acids and the acetate and shikimate pathways to produce "shunt metabolites" (intermediates) that have adopted an alternate biosynthetic route, leading to the biosynthesis of secondary metabolites. Modifications in the biosynthetic pathways may be due to natural causes (e.g., viruses or environmental changes) or unnatural causes (e.g., chemical or radiation) in an effort to adapt or provide longevity for the organism. It is the unique biosynthesis of these natural products, produced by the countless number of terrestrial and marine organisms, which provides the characteristic chemical structures that possess an array of biological activities.

Historically Important Natural Products

Traditional medicinal practices have formed the basis of most of the early medicines followed by subsequent clinical, pharmacological and chemical studies. Probably the most famous and well known example to date would be the synthesis of the anti-inflammatory agent, acetylsalicyclic acid (1) (aspirin) derived from the natural product, salicin (2) isolated from the bark of the willow tree

Salix alba L. Investigation of Papaver somniferum L. (opium poppy) resulted in the isolation of several alkaloids including morphine (3), a commercially important drug, first reported in 1803 (Figure 3.1). It was in the 1870s that crude morphine derived from the plant P. somniferum, was boiled in acetic anhydride to yield diacetylmorphine (heroin) and found to be readily converted to codeine (painkiller). Historically, it is documented that the Sumerians and Ancient Greeks used poppy extracts medicinally, whilst the Arabs described opium to be addictive. Digitalis purpurea L. (foxglove) had been traced back to Europe in the 10th century but it was not until the 1700s that the active constituent digitoxin (4), a cardiotonic glycoside was found to enhance cardiac conduction, thereby improving thestrength of cardiac contractibility. Digitoxin (4) and its analogues have long been used in the management of congestive heart failure and have possible long term detrimental effects and are being replaced by other medicines in the treatment of "heart deficiency". The anti-malarial drug quinine (5) approved by the United States FDA in 2004, isolated from the bark of Cinchona succirubra Pav. ex Klotsch, had been used for centuries for the treatment of malaria, fever, indigestion, mouth and throat diseases and cancer. Formal use of the bark to treat malaria was established in the mid 1800s when the British began the worldwide cultivation of the plant. Pilocarpine (6) found in Pilocarpus jaborandi (Rutaceae) is an L-histidine-derived alkaloid, which has been used as a clinical drug in the treatment of chronic open-angle glaucoma and acute angle-closure glaucoma for over 100 years. In 1994, an oral formulation of pilocarpine (6) was approved by the FDA to treat dry mouth (xerostomia)

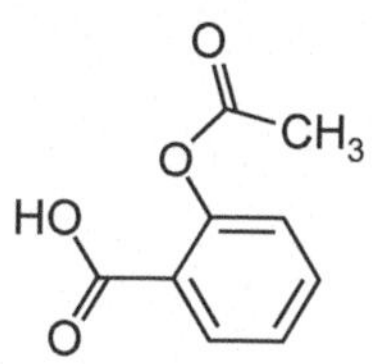

1

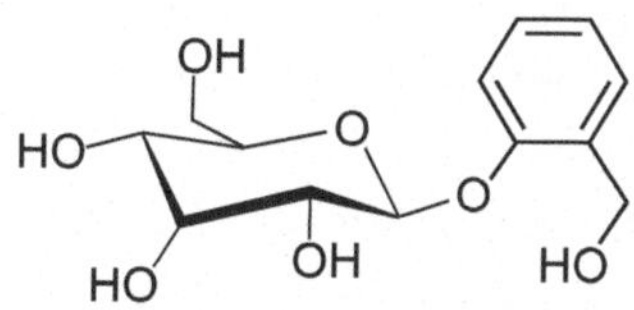

2

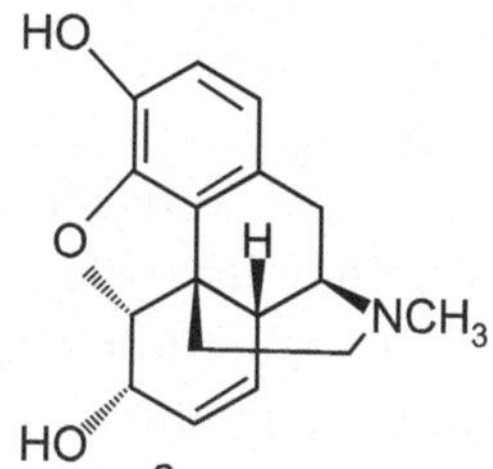

3

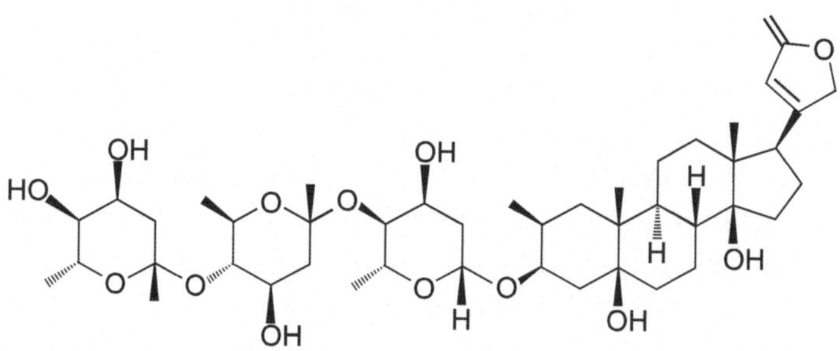

4

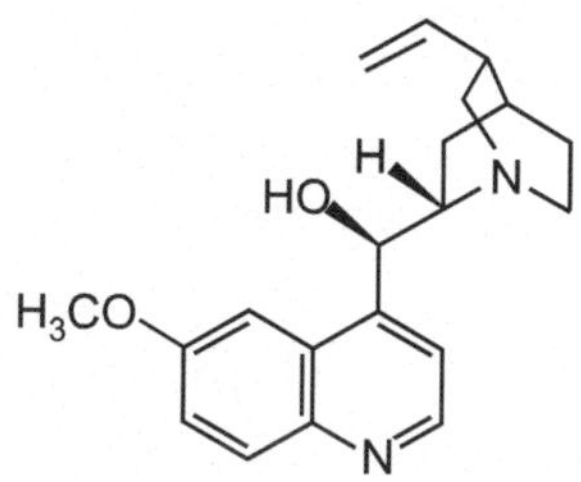

5

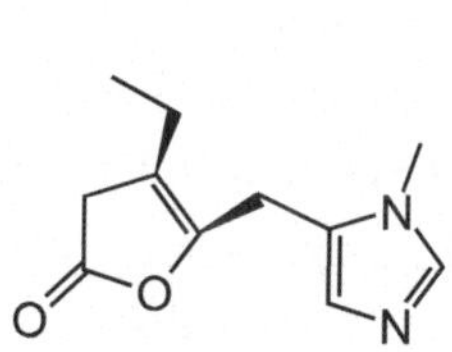

6

Fig. 3.1: Acetylsalicylic acid (1), Salicin (2), Morphine (3), Digitoxin (4), Quinine (5)

(Source: Based on Review of Literature)

which is a side effect of radiation therapy for head and neck cancers and also used to stimulate sweat glands to measure the concentrations of sodium and chloride (Figure 3.1). In 1998, the oral preparation was approved for the management of Sjogren's syndrome, an autoimmune disease that damages the salivary and lacrimal glands.

Natural Products from Fungi

Macro and micro fungi have been part of human life for thousands of years. They were used as food (mushrooms), in preparation of alcoholic beverages (yeasts), medication in traditional medicine and for cultural purposes. Currently with the advances in microbiology, their uses have extended to enzymes, biological control, antibiotics and other pharmacologically active products. Undoubtedly one of the most famous natural product discoveries derived from a fungus (microorganism) is that of penicillin (7) from the fungus, Penicillium notatum discovered by Fleming in 1929. A countercurrent extractive separation technique which produced 7 in high yields was required for the in vivo experimentation that ultimately saved countless lives and won Chain and Florey (together with Fleming) the 1945 Nobel prize in Physiology and Medicine (Figure 3.2). This discovery led to the re-isolation and clinical studies by Chain, Florey and co-workers in the early 1940s and commercialization of synthetic penicillins, which ultimately revolutionized drug discovery research. After publication of the first clinical data on penicillin G (7) between 1942–1944 there was a worldwide endeavor to discover new antibiotics from microorganisms and bioactive natural products. Up until 1968, old methods for detecting β-lactams were still being utilized and it was concluded that all natural β-lactams had been discovered. Nevertheless, this was not the case as with the introduction, in the 1970s, of new screening methods, the production of bacterial strains supersensitive to β-lactams, tests for the inhibition of β-lactamases and specificity for sulphurcontaining metabolites resulted in the discovery of novel antibiotic structural classes (norcardicins, carbapenems and monobactams) including the isolation of the antibiotics, norcardicin (8), imipenem (9) and aztreonam (10), respectively (Figure 3.2). There are presently nine β-lactams (two cephalosporins, six carbapenems and one penem) in clinical trials or undergoing drug registration, along with the novel class of broad spectrum antibiotics called the glycylcyclines.

Macro fungi such as polypores are a large group of wood-rotting fungi of the phylum Basidiomycota (basidiomycetes) and Ascomycota, which are a major source of pharmacologically active substances. There are about 25,000 species of basidiomycetes, of which about 500 are members of the Aphyllophorales [42]. Approximately 75% of tested polypore fungi have shown strong antimicrobial activities and may constitute a viable source for the development

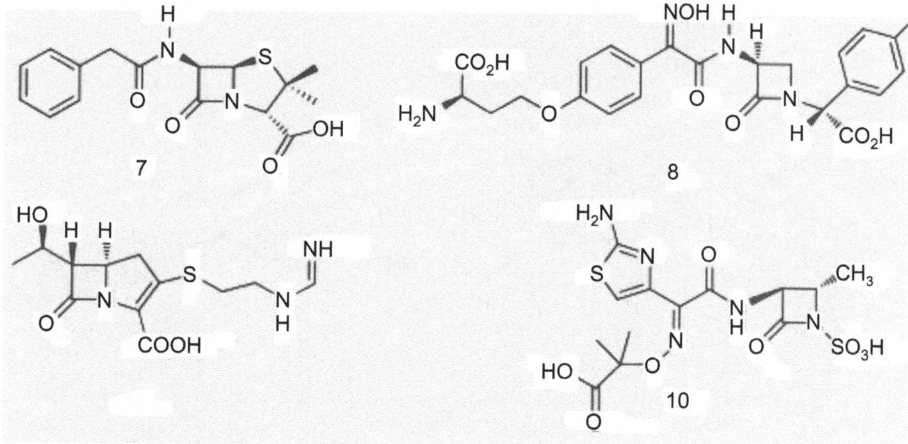

Fig. 2.2: Penicillin (7), Narcardicin (8), Imipenem (9) and Aztreonam (10)

(Source: Based on Review of Literature)

of novel antibiotics. Many compounds have displayed antiviral, cytotoxic, antineoplastic, cardiovascular, anti-inflammatory, immune-stimulating and anticancer activities. Fungi are more commonly microorganisms, some of which can spend at least part of their life cycle inside plant tissues without causing any visiblesign of infection or disease. They have been found to inhabit trees, grasses, algae and herbaceous plants and live in the intercellular spaces of plant stems, petioles, roots and leaves without affecting the host organism. Collectively these fungi are known as endophytes. Novel bioactive secondary metabolites derived from fungal sources have yielded some of the most important natural products for the pharmaceutical industry. In 1953, Edmund Kornfeld first isolated vancomycin (11) a glycopeptide antibiotic produced in cultures of Amycolatopsis orientalis which is active against a wide range of gram-positive organisms such as Staphylococci and Streptococci and against gram-negative bacteria, mycobacteria and fungi and was approved by the FDA in 1958 (Figure 3.3). It is used for the treatment of severe infection and against susceptible organisms in patients hypersensitive to penicillin (7). The macrolide erythromycin (12) from Saccharopolyspora erythraea is an antibacterial drug, which contains a 14-membered macrocycle composed entirely of propionate units (Figure 3.3). Erythromycin (12) has broad spectrum activities against gram-positive cocci and bacilli and is used for mild to moderate, upper and lower respiratory tract infections [5,26]. Currently there are three semisynthetic ketolide derivatives of erythromycin (12), cethromycin (ABT-773, Restanza™), EP-420 (by Enanta Pharmaceuticals) and BAL-19403 (by Basilea) which are in clinical development.

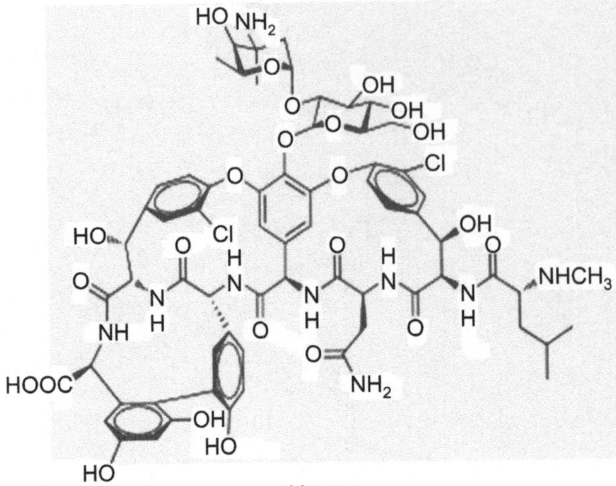

11

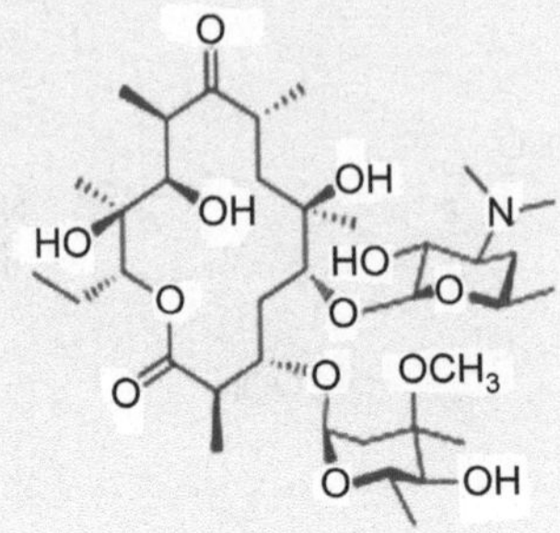

12

Fig. 3.3: Vancomycin (11) and Erythromycin (12)

(**Source:** Based on Review of Literature).

Single cell viruses represent the smallest existing life forms causing cold, influenza, ebola and SARS. Presently, there seems to be a limited number of antiviral natural products or synthetically derived analogues from fungi. Betulinic acid (13), a triterpenoid obtained from the bark of Betula pubescens was originally identified as a weak inhibitor of HIV replication. Betulinic acid can inhibit topoisomerase I and is being evaluated in Phase I trials as a cancer chemo-preventive agent (Figure 3.4). Bevirimat (PA-457) (14),

13

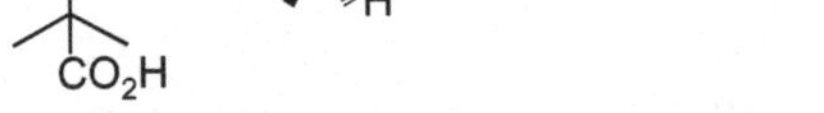

14

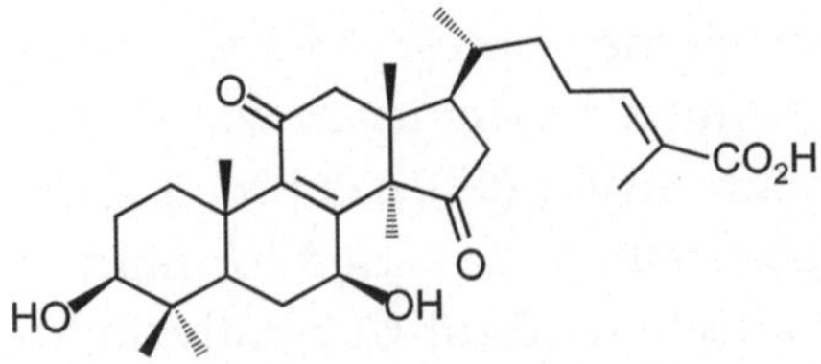

15

Fig. 3.4: Betulinic acid (13), Bevirimat (PA-457) (14) and Ganoderic acid β (15)

(**Source:** Based on Review of Literature).

extracted from a Chinese herb Syzygium claviflorum is in Phase IIb clinical trials and is believed to inhibit the final step of the HIV Gag protein processing. Ganoderic acid β (15), isolated from the fruiting bodies and spores of Ganoderma lucidum, displayed significant anti-HIV-1 protease activity with an IC50 value of 20 μM (Figure 3.4).

In 2002, amrubicin hydrochloride (16), related to the anthracycline, doxorubicin (17) (Adriamycin®), was isolated from the fungus Streptomyces peucetius. Doxorubicin (17) is used to treat acute leukaemia, soft tissue and bone sarcomas, lung cancer, thyroid cancer and both Hodgkins and non-Hodgkins lymphomas (Figure 3.5). Torreyanic acid (18) was isolated from an endophyte from the endangered tree, Torreya taxifolia and was tested in several cancer cell lines and found to display 5–10 times greater potentency/cytotoxicity in cell lines that are sensitive to protein kinase C causing cell death by apoptosis (Figure 3.5).

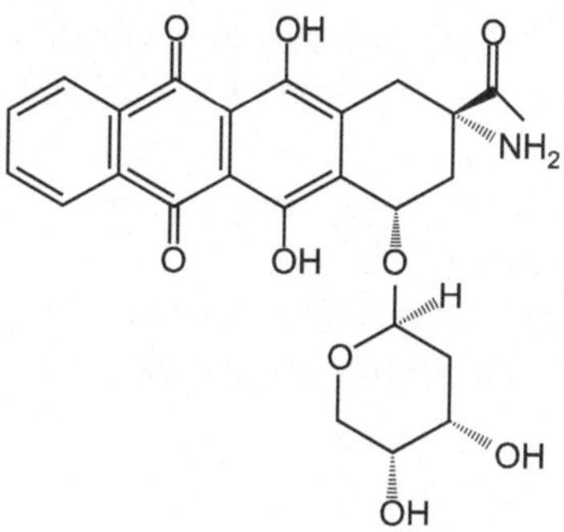

16

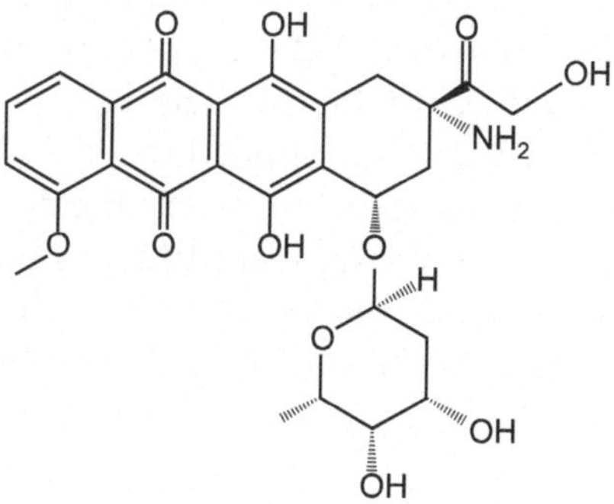

17

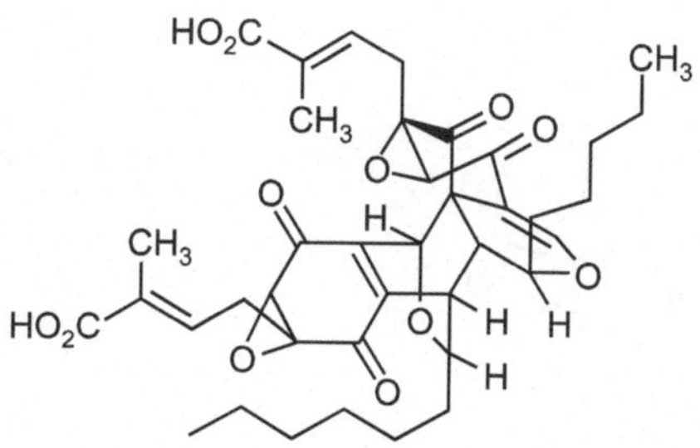

18

Fig. 3.5: Amrubicin hydrochloride (16), Doxorubicin (17) and Torreyanic acid (18)
(**Source:** Based on Review of Literature).

Natural Products from Plants

Plants have been well documented for their medicinal uses for thousands of years. They have evolved and adapted over millions of years to withstand bacteria, insects, fungi and weather to produce unique, structurally diverse secondary metabolites. Their ethnopharmacological properties have been used as a primary source of medicines for early drug discovery. According to the World Health Organization (WHO), 80% of people still rely on plant-based traditional medicines for primary health care and 80% of 122 plant derived drugs were related to their original ethnopharmacological purpose. The knowledge associated with traditional medicine (complementary or alternative herbal products) has promoted further investigations of medicinal plants as potential medicines and has led to the isolation of many natural products that have become well known pharmaceuticals. The most widely used breast cancer drug is paclitaxel (Taxol®) (19), isolated from the bark of Taxus brevifolia (Pacific Yew). In 1962 the United States Department of Agriculture (USDA) first collected the bark as part of their exploratory plant screening program at the National Cancer Institute(NCI) (Figure 2.6). The bark from about three mature 100 year old trees is required to provide 1 gram of 19 given that a course of treatment may need 2 grams of the drug. Current demand for 19 is in the region of 100–200 kg per annum (i.e., 50,000 treatments/year) and is now produced synthetically. The first of several FDA approvals for various uses for Taxol® was announced in 1992. Taxol® (19) is present in limited quantities from natural sources, its synthesis (though challenging and expensive) has been achieved. Baccatin III (20) present in much higher quantities and readily available from the needles of T. brevifolia and associated derivatives is an example of a structural analogue that can be efficiently transformed into 19 (Figure 2.6).

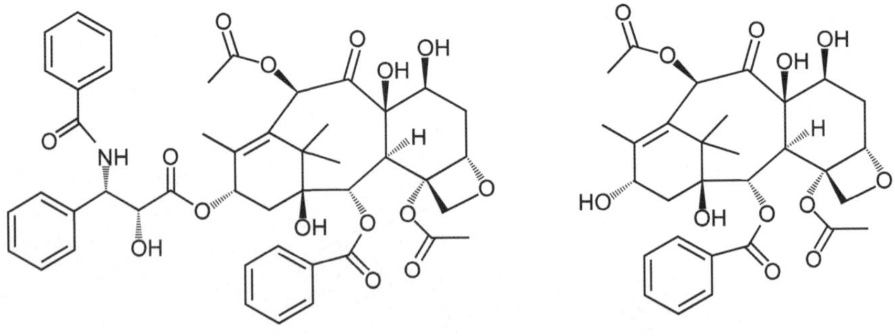

19 20

Fig. 3.6: Paclitaxel (Taxol@) (19) and baccatin III (20)

(**Source:** Based on Review of Literature)

Other examples of antitumor compounds currently in clinical trials include ingenol 3-O-angelate (21) a derivative of the polyhydroxy diterpenoid ingenol isolated from the sap of Euphorbia peplus (known as "petty spurge" in England or "radium weed" in Australia) which is a potential chemotherapeutic agent for skin cancer is currently under clinical development by Peplin Biotech for the topical treatment of certain skin cancers (Figure 3.7). PG490-88 (22) (14-succinyl triptolide sodium salt), a semisynthetic analogue of triptolide is a diterpene-diepoxide isolated from Tripterygium wilfordii which is used for autoimmune and inflammatory diseases in the People's Republic of China [64,65]. Combretastatin A-4 phosphate (23) a stilbene derivative from the South African Bush Willow, Combretum caffrum acts as an anti-angiogenic agent causing vascular shutdowns in tumors (necrosis) and is currently in Phase II clinical trials (Figure 3.7).

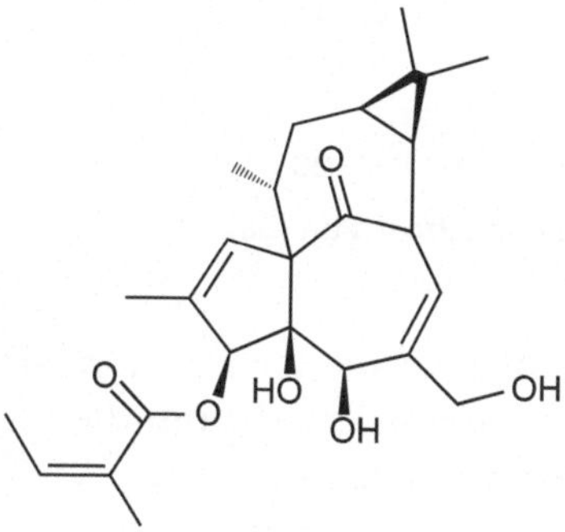

21

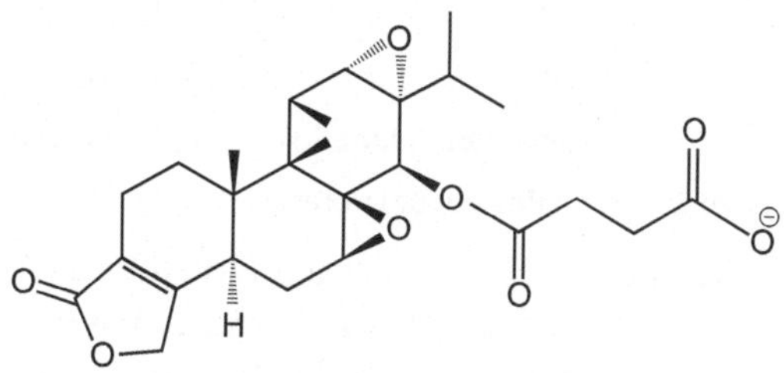

22

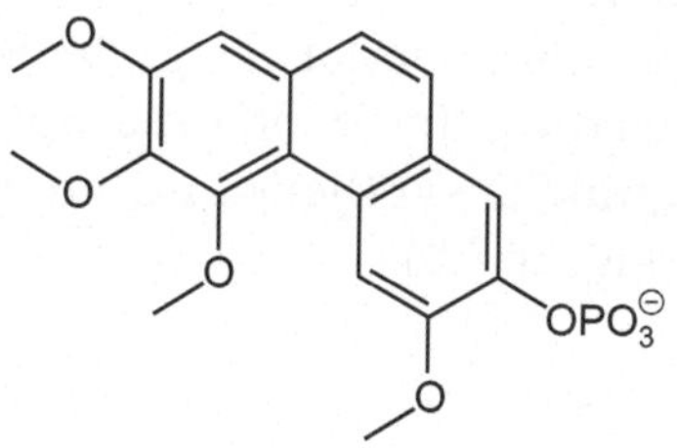

23

Fig. 3.7: Ingeonol 3-O-angelate (21), P?G490-88 (22) and Combretastatin A-4 phosphate (23)
(**Source:** Based on Review of Literature)

The Acquired Immune Deficiency Syndrome (AIDS) pandemic in the 1980s forced the National Cancer Institute (NCI) and other organizations to explore natural products as sources of potential drug candidates for the treatment of AIDS. Over 60,000 extracts of plants and marine organisms were tested against lymphoblastic cells infected with HIV-1. The most important result of these tests is the class of compounds known as the calanolides. In particular the isolation of calanolide A (24) and calanolide B (25) from the Calonphyllum species, along with prostratin (26) from Homalanthus nutans, have now progressed into clinical and preclinical development (Figure 3.8). Calanolide A (24) was licensed and evaluated to Phase II clinical trials by Sarawak Medichem Pharmaceuticals, however there has been no subsequent announcement for further drug development. In 2010, Phase I human clinical trials of prostratin (26) were carried out by the AIDS Research Alliance in Los Angeles, California (Figure 3.8).

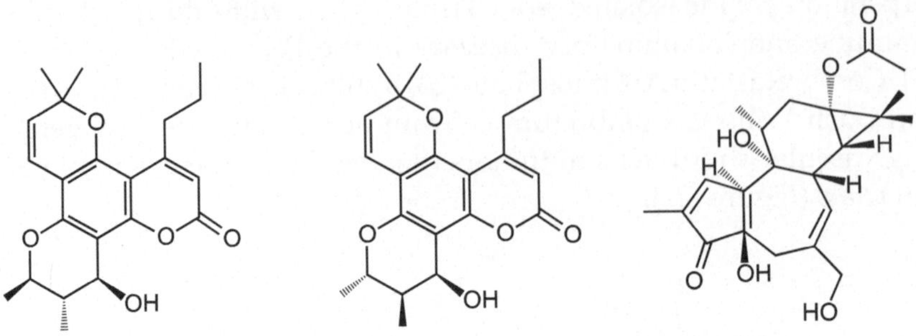

24 25 26

Fig. 3.8: Calanolide A (24), Calanolide B (25) and Prostratin (26)

(**Source:** Based on Review of Literature).

Arteether (27), introduced in 2000, as Artemotil is derived from artemisinin (28) (introduced in 1987 as Artemisin) which was first isolated from the plant Artemisia annua and are both approved antimalarial drugs (Figure 3.9). The plant was originally used in traditional Chinese medicine as a remedy for chills and fevers. Other derivatives of artemisinin (28) are in various stages of clinical development as antimalarial drugs in Europe [3,26]. To date, a synthetic trioxolane modeled on the 28 pharmacophore, is being assessed in combination with piperaquine (a synthetic bisquinoline antimalarial drug) in an effort to treat malaria (Figure 3.9).

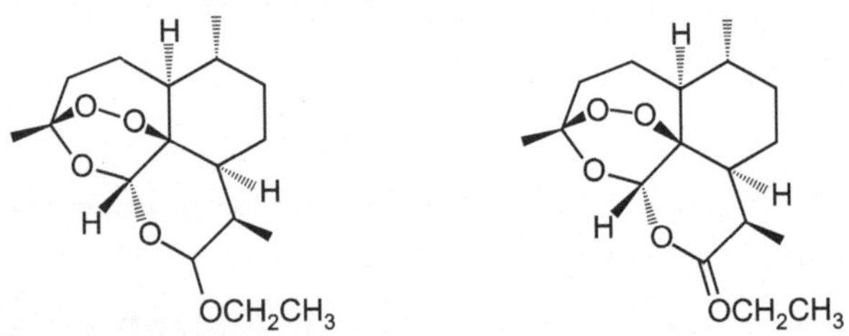

27 28

Fig. 3.9: Arteether (27) and artemisnin (28)

(**Source:** Based on Review of Literature)

Grandisines A (29) and B (30) are two indole alkaloids which were isolated from the leaves of the Australian rainforest tree, Elaeocarpus grandis (Figure 2.10). Grandisine A (29) contains a unique tetracyclic skeleton, while Grandisine B (30) possesses an unusual combination of isoquinuclidinone and indolizidine ring systems. Both 29 and 30 exhibit binding affinity for the human δ-opioid receptor and are potential leads for analgesic agents [72]. Galantamine hydrobromide (31) is an Amaryllidaceae alkaloid obtained from the plant Galanthus nivalis and has been used traditionally in Turkey and Bulgaria for neurological conditions and is used for the treatment of Alzheimer's disease. Apomorphine (32) is a derivative of morphine (31) isolated from the poppy (P. somniferum) and is a short-acting dopamine D1 and D2 receptor agonist, as well as a potent dopamine agonist, used to treat Parkinson's disease (Figure 10). "Curare" is the arrow poison of the South American Indians and is prepared in the rain forests of the Amazon and Orinoco. Tubocaurarine (33) isolated from the climbing plant, Chondrodendron tomentosum (Menispermaceae) is one of the active constituents used as a muscle relaxant in surgical operations, reducing the need for deep anesthesia. The limited availability of tubocurarine (33) has led to the development of a series of synthetic analogues which are now preferred over the natural product (Figure 3.10).

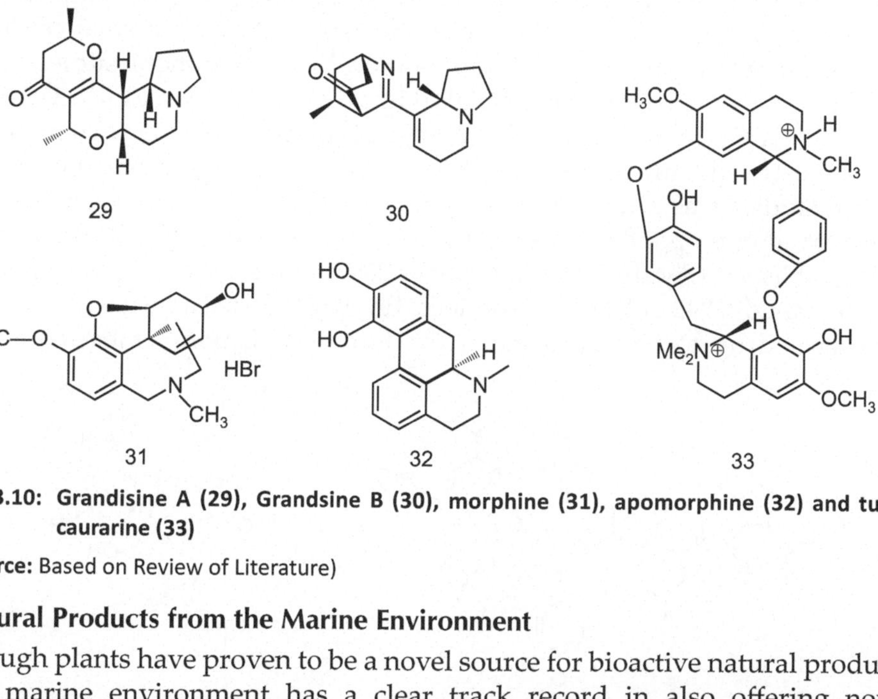

Fig. 3.10: Grandisine A (29), Grandsine B (30), morphine (31), apomorphine (32) and tubocaurarine (33)

(**Source:** Based on Review of Literature)

Natural Products from the Marine Environment

Though plants have proven to be a novel source for bioactive natural products the marine environment has a clear track record in also offering novel structural entities. "We are not marine organisms", says Fenical, "so until about 1970, no one even thought of the ocean. It was left as a deep secret. It seemed ridiculous to me that the ocean – with such a vast habitat – had escaped anyone's notice. But there are good reasons. People fear the ocean; it has been considered a very hostile, inhospitable place". Given that 70% of planet earth's surface is covered by ocean, pharmaceutical companies began to realize that the ocean would possess unique biodiversity and may be a possible source for potential drug candidates. Exploration of the marine environment and organisms (algae, sponges, ascidians, tunicates and bryozoans) became possible due to modern snorkeling, the introduction of SCUBA (1970s), to the use of manned submersibles (1980s) and more recently the use of remotely operated vehicles (ROVs) (1990s). These progressive advancements in the past 40 years of exploration of the marine environment have resulted in the isolation of thousands of structurally unique bioactive marine natural products. To date, the global marine pharmaceutical pipeline consists of three Food and Drug Administration (FDA) approved drugs, one EU registered drug, 13 natural products (or derivatives thereof) in different phases of the clinical pipeline and a large number of marine chemicals in the pre-clinical pipeline. Some examples include, Ziconotide (Prialt®, Elan Corporation) a peptide first discovered in a tropical cone snail, which was approved in December 2004 for the treatment of pain. Plitidepsin (34) (Aplidin®, PharmaMa), a depsipeptide was isolated from the Mediterranean tunicate Aplidium albicans. Plitidepsin (34) is effective in treating various cancers, including melanoma, small cell and non-small cell lung, bladder as well as non-Hodgkin lymphoma and acute lymphoblastic leukemia and is currently in Phase II clinical trials (Figure 2.11). Ecteinascidin 743 (ET743; Yondelis™) (35) was isolated in very low yields from the ascidian Ecteinascidia turbinata. The quantities of ET743 (35) required for advanced pre-clinical and clinical studies was achieved by adopting very large-scale aquaculture of E. turbinata in open ponds, however the semisynthesis of ET743 (35) has been well established (Figure 2.11). In October 2007, Trabectedin (35) (also known as Ecteinascidin 743 or ET-743) (Yondelis, PharmaMar) became the first marine anticancer drug to be approved in the European Union. Trabectedin (35)

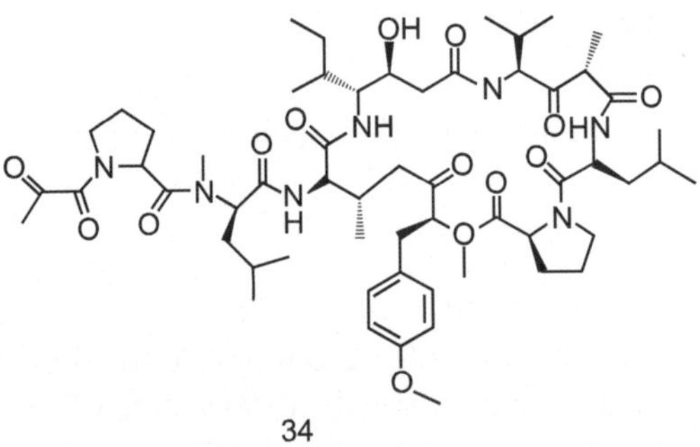

34

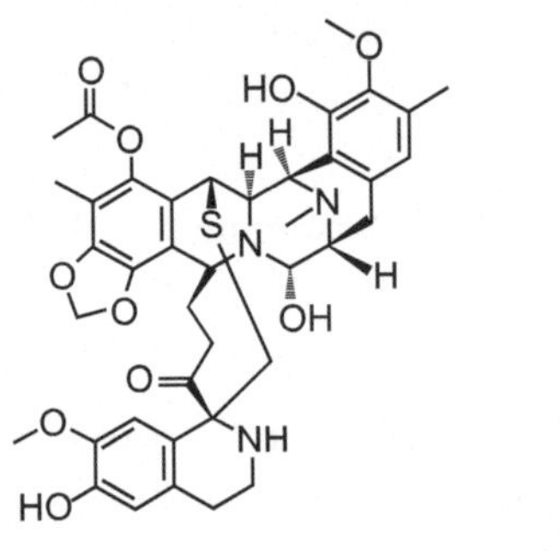

35

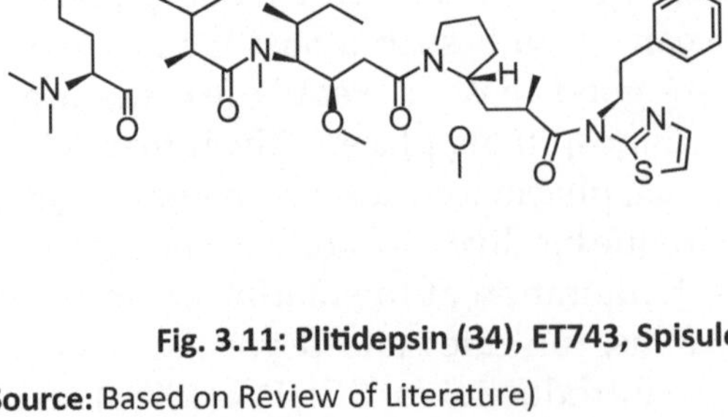

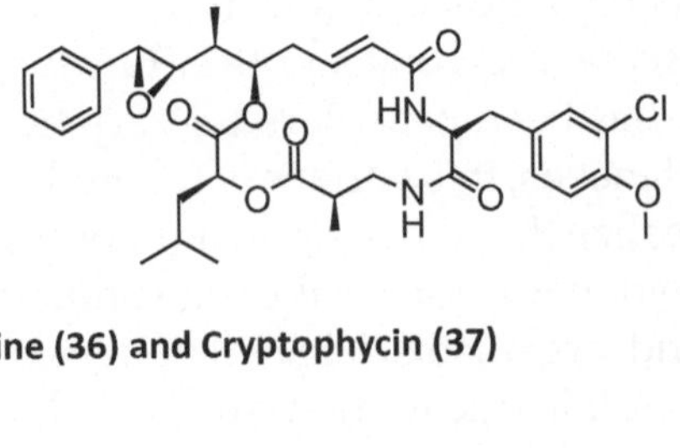

Fig. 3.11: Plitidepsin (34), ET743, Spisulosine (36) and Cryptophycin (37)

(**Source:** Based on Review of Literature)

has been approved by the European Agency for the Evaluation of Medicinal Products (EMEA) and is completing key Phase III studies in the US for approval. Spisulosine (36), isolated from the marine clam Spisula polynyma, exhibited substantial selective activity against tumor cells compared to normal cells [86]. It advanced to Phase I clinical trials against solid tumors but was withdrawn in late 2006. Cryptophycin (37) was selected for clinical trials in the mid 1990s then advanced to phase II trials but was terminated in 2002 due to toxicity and lack of efficacy (Figure 3.11).

Natural Products from Marine Algae

Algae (macroalgae, seaweed) are represented by at least 30,000 species worldwide supplying oxygen to the biosphere, food for fish and man, medicine and fertilizers as well as being a prolific source of structurally unique natural products. The terpenoids are a class of compounds predominantly isolated from marine algae in the 1970–1980s. Chemical investigations into

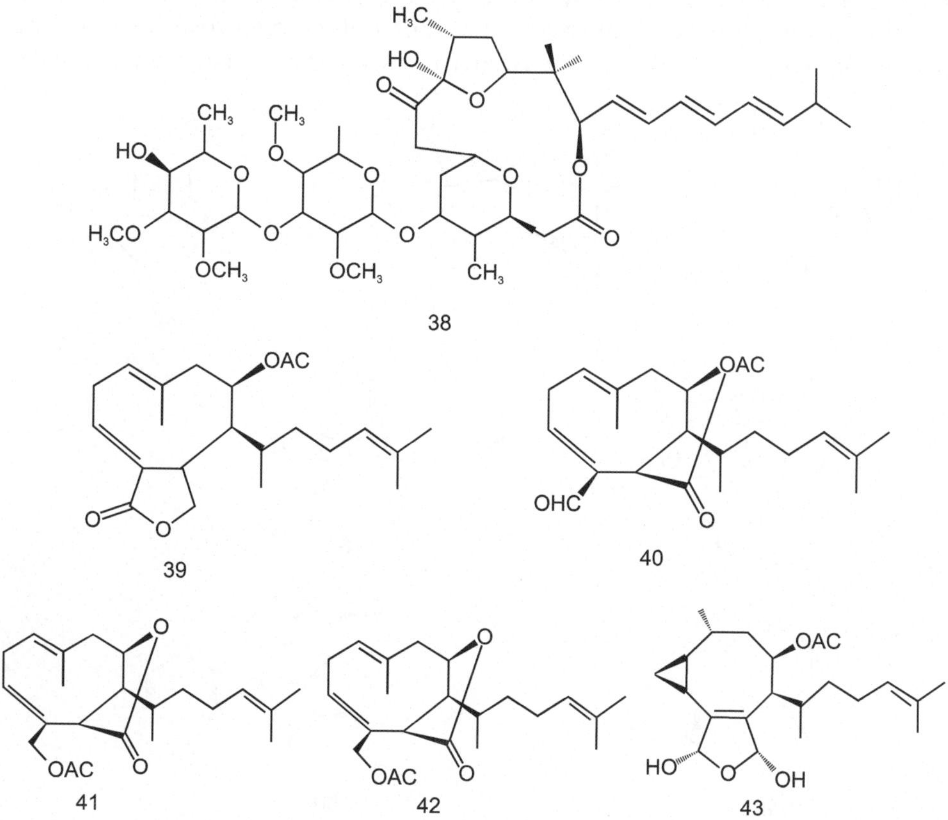

Fig. 3.12: Polycavernoside A (38), 4-acetoxydictylolactone (39), Dictyolide A (40), Dictyolide B (41), Nordictyolide (42) and Crenuladial (43)

(**Source:** Based on Review of Literature)

terpenoidtype structures have led to the isolation of many classes including brominated, nitrogen and oxygen heterocycles, phenazine derivatives, sterols, amino acids, amines and guanidine derivatives. With respect to biological activity, green, brown and red algae have been intensively assessed for their antibacterial and antifungal activities. Polycavernoside-A (38) isolated from the red alga Polycaverosa tsudai was suspected to be the toxic glycoside responsible for seafood poisoning, when, in 1991 thirteen people became ill and three died in Japan (Figure 2.12). The brown alga, Dictyota dichotoma afforded diterpenes, 4-acetoxydictylolactone (39), dictyolides A (40), B (41) and nordictyolide (42) which display antitumor activities. Another example is crenuladial (43), isolated from the brown alga Dilophus ligatus which displayed antimicrobial activity against Staphylcoccus aureus, Micrococcus luteus and Aeromonas hydrophyla (Figure 3.12).

Red algae, in particular the genus Laurencia (Rhodophyta), are unsurpassed as a source of halogenated sesquiterpenes. Chemical investigations into the genus Laurencia for secondary metabolites have been active since the 1970s. The most commonly occurring secondary metabolites are the

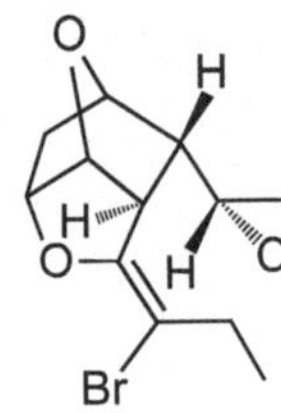

44

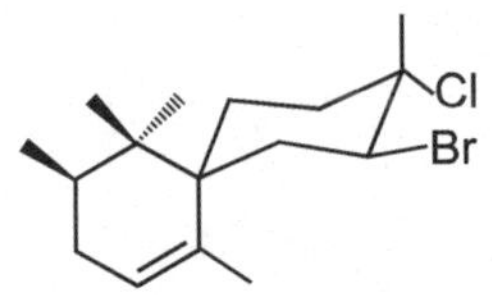

45

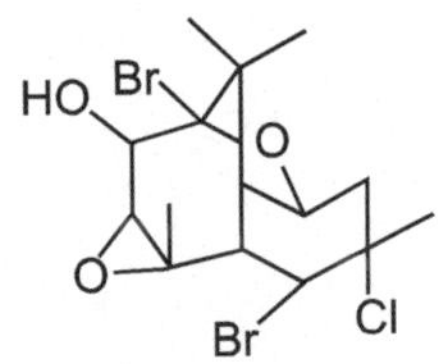

46

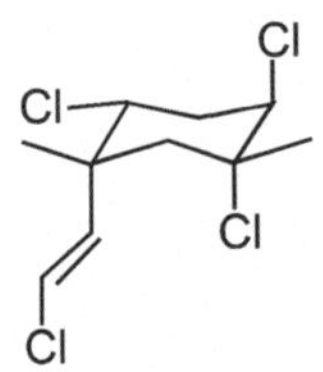

47

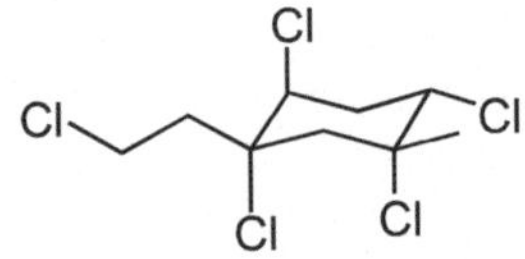

48

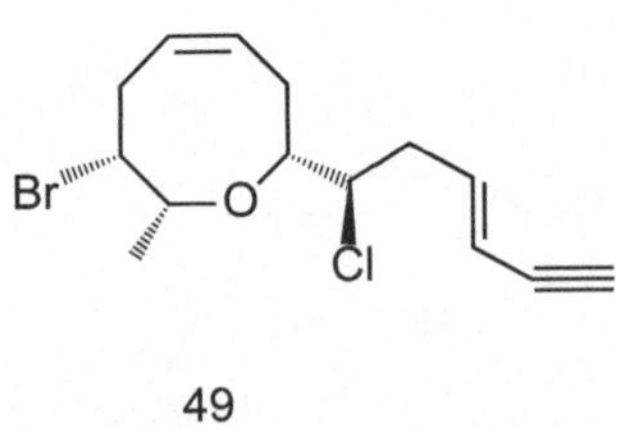

49

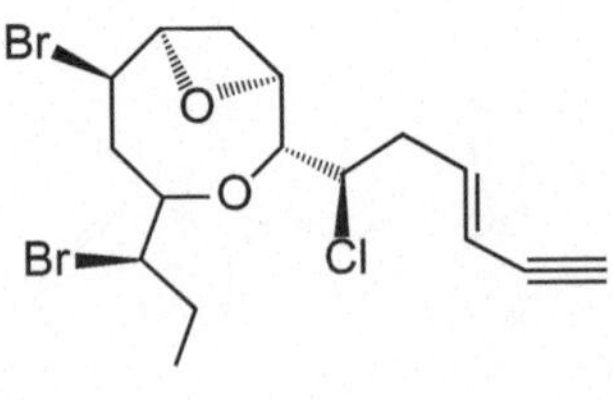

50

Fig. 3.13: Compound (44), Compound (45), Compound (46), 1a-(2-E-chlorovinyl)-2a, 4b, 5a-trichloro-1b, 5b-dimethylcyclohexane (47), 1b-(2-E-chlorovinyl-2b, 4a, 5a-trichloro-1a, 5b-dimethylcyclohexane (48), Laurepinnacin (49) and (Z)-laureatin (50).

(**Source:** Based on Review of Literature).

halogenated sesquiterpenes and diterpenes. Furthermore, this genus is unique in producing C15-acetogenins, for example those constituents which possess a terminal enyne such as 44. Other examples include the class of compounds known as the chamigrenes, which are halogenated terpenes possessing unique structures such as 45 and 46 (Figure 3.13). There have been many chamigrenes, which have been isolated to date from the genus Laurencia, which grows in many very different geographical areas.

Productivity in agriculture in the last half century has been as a result of advances in pest control due to synthetic chemical pesticides (SCPs). However, the search for new pesticides has been necessary due to the significant rise in the resistance to current control agents. It has been documented that between 1984 to 1990 resistance to synthetic chemical pesticides by insects and mites increased by 13%. As a result, a significant amount of research has focused on the isolation of insecticidal leads from marine algae. This has led to the isolation of over 40 active constituents. Some examples of natural insecticides include the isolation of 1α-(2-E-chlorovinyl)-2α,4β,5α-trichloro1β,5β-dimethylcyclohexane (47) and 1β-(2-E-chlorovinyl)-2β,4α,5α-trichloro-1α,5β-dimethylcyclohexane (48) which are cyclic polyhalogenated monoterpenes isolated from the Chilean red alga Plocamium cartilagineum (Figure 3.13). These compounds show insecticidal activity against the Aster leafhopper, Macrosteles fascifrons. Other examples include laurepinnacin (49), an acetylenic cyclic ether from the red alga Laurencia pinnata Yamada, and (Z)-laureatin (50) and related compounds from the red alga L. nipponica Yamada. These have all shown to display potent insecticidal activity against the mosquito larva, C. pipiens (Figure 3.13). 2.5. Natural Products from Marine Sponges Sponges (Porifera) are sessile organisms, which lack a nervous, digestive and circulatory system and maintain a constant water flow through their bodies to obtain food, oxygen and to remove wastes. All sponges are 'current' or 'filter' feeders and have few physical means of defense against predators. They are considered to be the first multicellular animals and have changed very little in approximately 500 million years. The first notable discovery of biologically active compounds from marine sources can be traced back to the reports of Bergmann on the isolation and identification of C-nucleosides, spongouridine (51) and spongothymidine (52) from the Caribbean sponge, Cryptotheca crypta in the early 1950s (Figure 3.14). These compounds were found to possess antiviral activity and the synthesis of structural analogues led to the development of cytosine arabinoside (Ara-C) as a clinical anticancer agent, together with (Ara-A) as an antiviral agent 15 years later. This was an important discovery since previously it was believed that for a nucleoside to possess biological activity, it had to have a deoxyribose or ribose sugar moiety. These investigations led to the identification of (Ara-C) as a potent antileukemic agent.

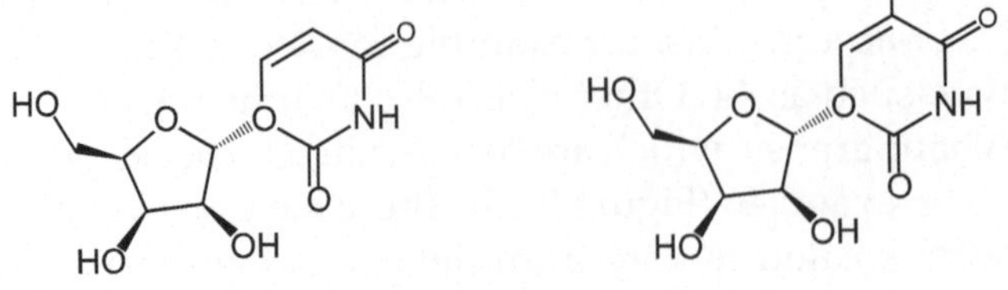

51 52

Fig. 3.14: Spongouridine (51) and Spongothymidine (52)

(**Source:** Based on Review of Literature).

Natural Products from other Marine Sources

The class of synthetic derivatives known as the bryologs, such as 53, are derived from bryostatin 1 (54), an antineoplastic compound isolated from the bryozoan, Bulgula neritina. Bryostatin 1 (54) has been isolated in sufficient quantities to permit more than 80 clinical trials to date, with 20 being completed at both phase I and phase II levels (Figure 3.15). It has displayed positive responses acting as a single agent with effects ranging from complete to partial remission. From 2007 to date there were four Phase I and eight Phase II clinical trials, all combination studies with biologicals or cytotoxins against multiple carcinomas. Currently, 54 is in two Phase I clinical

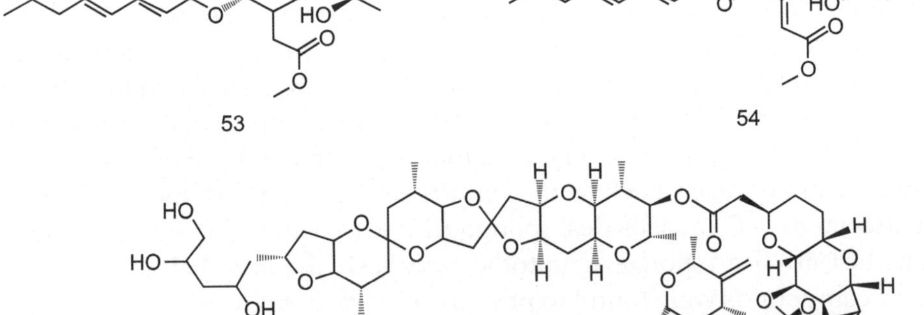

53 54

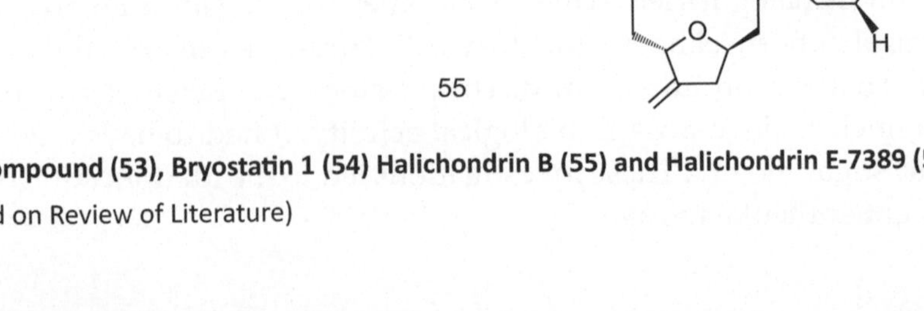

55

Fig. 3.15: Compound (53), Bryostatin 1 (54) Halichondrin B (55) and Halichondrin E-7389 (56)

(**Source:** Based on Review of Literature)

trials and is being assessed as an anti-Alzheimer's drug (Phase I trial approved). Halichondrin B (55) has been isolated from several sponges including, Halichondria okadai (Japan); Axinella sp. from the Western Pacific, Phakellia carteri from the Eastern Indian Ocean and from Lissodendoryx sp., off the East Coast of the South Island of New Zealand (Figure 3.15). Halichondrin B (55) has been successfully synthesized along with several structural analogues including Halichondrin E-7389 (56) which has been selected for further development and is currently in phase III clinical trials for the treatment of breast carcinoma (Figure 3.15).

Drug Discovery: Natural Product Chemistry Versus Combinatorial Chemistry

After the 'Golden Age of Antibiotics' and the worldwide incentive to discover new antibiotics many major pharmaceutical industries at the time initiated natural product discovery (NPD) programs which focused not only on antibacterial and antifungal targets but also on infectious diseases. These programs provided lead compounds for the treatment of cancer, microbial infections, hypercholesteremia and tissue rejection in organ transplantations. However, many of the larger pharmaceutical companies decommissioned their NPD programs during the 1990s and early 2000s. It was the advent of automated high throughput screening (HTS) which increased the momentum of biological testing and combinatorial chemistry began to be promoted as a better approach to creating "drug-like" compounds for HTS. As a result, many of the pharmaceutical companies disbanded or sold their collections of screening extracts as it was believed that traditional extract-based screening resulted in the continuous re-discovery of previously isolated compounds and that the structural complexity of natural products required total synthesis and derivatization which is both economically and synthetically problematic. Because of supply problems, the time required to develop a natural product from an extract hit to a pharmaceutical was deemed to be too long; HTS technologies rely on combinatorial chemistry to generate large compound libraries. In the past two decades "classical natural product chemistry" has largely been replaced by molecular target based drug discovery, utilizing large combinatorial libraries to obtain efficient "hits". Nevertheless advances in technology and sensitive instrumentation for the rapid identification of novel bioactive natural products and structure elucidation continues to improve the natural product discovery process. From the 1980s onwards it was thought that combinatorial chemistry would be the future source of numerous novel carbon skeletons and drug leads or new chemical entities (NCEs). This has clearly not been the case as there has only been one combinatorial NCE approved by the U.S Food and Drug Administration (FDA) in that time period, the kinase inhibitor sorafendib (57) (approved by the FDA, 2005) for renal carcinoma (Figure 3.16).

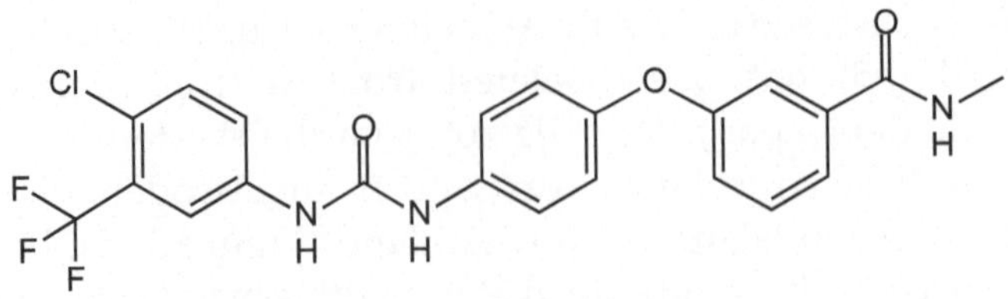

57

Fig. 3.16: Sorafendib (57)

(**Source:** Based on Review of Literature)

Combinatorial chemistry has indeed revolutionized the development of novel active chemical leads resulting in the synthesis of structural analogues. At the time, combinatorial libraries consisted of hundreds to thousands of new compounds, but during the late 1990s synthetic chemists realized that these libraries lacked the complexity of the intricate natural products synthesized by nature. The concept of diversity-oriented synthesis (DOS) was adopted in which synthetic chemists would synthesize compounds that resembled natural products (mimics) or that are based on natural product topologies. These compounds are currently being tested in a large number and variety of biological screens in order to determine their role (s) as leads to novel drug entities. Inspection of the rate of NCEs approvals demonstrates that natural products still contribute to or are involved in ~50% of all small molecule testing between the years 2000–2006. Though the pharmaceutical industry has expended a considerable amount of resources to both HTS and combinatorial chemistry overall of the 1184 NCEs covering all diseases/countries/sources between the years 1981–2006, 30% were found to be synthetic. It is also worth noting that 52% (total) of these compounds are either a natural product, a mimic or a chemical modification of an existing natural product pharmacophore.

Dereplication

A drug discovery program endeavors to search for (a) novel bioactive natural product(s), which possess(es) some form of potent biological activity. Nevertheless, the isolation of known and undesirable natural products with no chemical or pharmacological interest is inevitable. The process of identifying known compounds responsible for the activity of an extract prior to bioassay-guided isolation is referred to as dereplication. At present there are many advanced methodologies and protocols that distinguish novel entities from known natural compounds at an early stage of a drug discovery program or in a natural product isolation strategy. It is important to realize that the isolation of novel natural products was far more frequent during the 1970s and is steadily declining, although natural sources (e.g., plants, fungi, marine and microbial sources) are still regarded as inexhaustible sources for novel chemicals. As such, the time, effort and cost to find new chemical entities must be considered as their discovery has become far more infrequent. Furthermore, even the selection of new types of organisms (terrestrial and/or marine) tends to lead to the rediscovery of previously reported natural products as they are often present in more than one phylum or genera. It has been estimated that it takes $US 50,000 and three months of work to isolate and identify an active compound from a natural product source. Therefore, it is exceedingly important to recognize previously known compounds early on, not only for saving time and money, but to allocate resources to more profitable extracts. It is evident that natural product programs require more patience and perseverance for the identification of adequate lead compounds than programs strictly based on synthetic chemicals. This is also dependent on availability of bioassayguided fractionation, in-house screening, accessibility to higher field NMR and mass spectrometers, all of which are necessary to efficiently run such a program. Lead compounds arising from natural product discovery programs are structurally unique due to their co-evolution with target sites in biological systems. However, the speed at which lead compounds can be generated and progressively advanced is slower than corresponding synthetic drug discovery approaches. With the advent of new hyphenated spectroscopy technologies such as HPLC-MS, HPLC-NMR and HPLC-NMR-MS, further means of rapid compound identification and dereplication are now possible.

Dereplication Methods

Dereplication strategies generally involve a combination of bioassay, separation science, spectroscopic methods, and database searching and can be regarded as chemical or biological screening processes. There are a number of ways in which natural product programs approach dereplication, which is based upon availability of screening methods/instrumentation, time and the cost to identify possible "biological leads or novel compounds" from a crude extract.

Database Searching

There are many commercially available databases, which can assist in the dereplication process and will often reduce the time taken for structure elucidation of known compounds. The Chapman and Hall Dictionary of Natural Products; The Dictionary of Marine Natural Products (on-line) (subset of the Dictionary of Natural Products) containing over 30,000 compounds; MarinLit-The Marine Natural Products Database containing up to date bibliographic data on marine organisms with the number of references from 1,200 journals/ books and data for ~21,000 compounds; AntiMarin is a more recent database, in which the number of methyl groups, the number of sp3-hybridised methylene or methine protons, alkene, acetal, ether and formyl groups can be searched. SciFinder Scholar and SCOPUS is a research discovery tool (Chemical Abstracts on-line) and NAPRALERTTM is a database of all natural products, including ethnomedical information, pharmacological/biochemical information of extracts of organisms in vitro, in situ, in vivo, in humans (case reports, non-clinical trials) and clinical studies. Access to scientific databases such as the ones mentioned, is a fundamental and crucial step in a well-governed natural product program. Thorough and extensive literature searches are necessary when the following questions need to be addressed:

- Have there been any previous literature reports on the target organism (terrestrial or marine?)
- Is there potential to isolate novel compounds (geographical or seasonal variations?)
- What kind of compound classes has been isolated from the species and if not from the species, then the genus or family?
- Is there incomplete or poor NMR spectroscopic data for previously uncharacterized natural products?
- Are there any new biological activities for known compounds that have been overlooked?

It is fundamentally important to address these questions early as one of the most common issues that occurs is the time consuming process of isolating, purifying and determining the structure of a suspected novel compound and realizing that it has already been reported in the literature.

Hyphenated Instrumentation "Classical versus Hyphenated (on-line) Approaches"

Natural product extracts often contain a large number of constituents including those, which are challenging to separate. The combination of classical techniques such as Ultraviolet absorption Spectroscopy (UV), Infra-red spectroscopy (IR), Mass spectrometry (MS) and Nuclear Magnetic Resonance spectroscopy (NMR) often permits the unambiguous structure determination of pure compounds. In cases where the absolute configuration cannot be determined, synthesis or single-crystal X-ray analysis is utilized. As classical separation techniques are tedious and time consuming, the direct hyphenation of an efficient separation technique with powerful spectroscopic techniques can assist in the dereplication process. Such hyphenated systems (though not in widespread use) include HPLC-FTIR, which is useful for the detection of functional groups in major constituents of mixtures. HPLC-FTIR has been used by their designers but has not found wide application due to limitations in compatibility; that is, obtaining optimal separation together with sufficient detection. FIA-NMR involves a sample, which is injected as a plug into a fluid stream, which is then swept into the NMR detector coil. FIA-NMR uses the mobile phase as a hydraulic-push solvent to carry the injected sample from the injector port to the NMR flow cell. After the pump stops, the spectrometer acquires the scout scan to determine the location of solvent peaks and then acquires the solvent suppressed spectrum. After completion, a signal is sent to the solvent pump to flush the old sample from the NMR flow-cell. HPLC-NMR-MS is an advanced spectrometric hyphenated technique which is used in the dereplication of natural product extracts (typically plant extracts). Apart from its efficiency, the most important advantage of HPLC-NMR-MS is the unequivocal matching of the MS data to the NMR spectrum. Furthermore, as HPLC-NMR does not provide information about silent functional groups (e.g., hydroxyl and amino moieties) as a result of D2O exchange, these functionalities can be readily detected by MS techniques. Chemical and biological investigation for the search of novel bioactive natural products involves the extraction, isolation, purification and structure elucidation (classical natural product isolation methodologies), which can be challenging and/or time consuming. The extraction is normally the first step for both marine and terrestrial organisms. The choice of the extraction solvent followed by solvent partitioning or by trituration can result in many problems including the formation of artifacts. Further, homogenization and lyophilization with organic solvents can affect the nature and relative amounts of extracted secondary metabolites present. The application of HPLC-NMR to the crude extracts (NMR and UV profile from PDA HPLC detection) was found to be a powerful spectroscopic tool which had advanced in the last decade, in particular with the advent of higher field magnets and cryo-probes. In recent years the advances in microcoil HPLC-NMR and capillary NMR (CapNMR) has allowed for smaller quantities of samples to be analyzed in the order of 40–120 µL, this in combination with higher field magnets has greatly increased the sensitivity in profiling and dereplication natural product extracts. Microcoil HPLC-NMR is generally suited for on-line HPLC-NMR typically where components present in higher concentrations in an extract are separated and analyzed in a conventional HPLC-NMR system using either on-flow, stop-flow or time slicing experiments. Capillary NMR allows for the use of non-deuterated solvents in the off-line HPLC separation providing a broader range of solvents to be used and low costs. Isolated compounds are redissolved in deuterated solvents and injected into the CapNMR flow probe using volumes of approximately 6 µL with 1H-NMR spectra obtained for sample quantities in the order of 2–30 µg, thereby providing a substantial increase in sensitivity with the potential of identifying novel low level secondary metabolites. Apart from providing a "high-fidelity" snapshot of the constituents in the extract, the information acquired from both 1D and 2D NMR spectra may be sufficient to identify compound classes, therefore providing information which will allow rational decisions about the best method of fractionation or whether to further pursue the isolation. A number of recent publications have been reported in utilizing this approach. The technique and use of HPLC-NMR in natural products identification/characterization is well documented in the literature but applications of its uses have predominately dealt only with the chemical profiling of plants. Various modes of HPLC-NMR (predominantly on-flow and stop-flow modes) combine the resolving power of chromatography, which is interfaced with the structural insight provided by NMR. 4. Combining Natural Product Chemistry and Metabolomics Approaches in Drug Discovery. Systems biology is an emerging field encompassing tools in the post-genomics revolution such as transcriptomics, proteomics, glycomics and fluxomics with the ambition to characterize all gene and cell products including mRNA, proteins, glycan structures and metabolites in the most comprehensive manner. The objectives of metabolomics are to construct unbiased observations with highly reproducible analytical tools followed by data analysis to locate correlations between all available data. In the emerging field of metabolomics a single analytical technique capable of profiling all low molecular weight metabolites of a given organism does not exist. This emerging field combines analytical chemistry, biochemistry and sophisticated informatics allowing the analysis of thousands of small molecules (metabolites) in any biological system. Mass spectrometry hyphenated with gas chromatography (GC), liquid chromatography (LC) or capillary electrophoresis (CE) and nuclear magnetic resonance (NMR) spectroscopy are the leading analytical platforms. Both primary and secondary metabolites in tissues and biofluids are extracted utilizing unbiased crude extraction procedures aiming to efficiently extract all or most metabolites in their natural form prior to analysis in the solvents used. Since metabolite extracts are extremely complex, given the huge chemical diversity of metabolites they represent, there is no one single analytical platform and methodology, which is capable of analyzing all metabolites simultaneously. Multiple separation chemistries have to be employed to achieve the greatest comprehensiveness in the analysis. Due to the improvement in sensitivity, resolution and advances in instrumentation hundreds of compounds can be simultaneously analyzed with subsequent refined informatics tools developed to extract information from the resulting data, filtering algorithms to remove background noise, detection and integration of peaks throughout large data sets and normalization and transformation of resulting data matrices prior to any statistical analysis can now be achieved. The greatest bottleneck in metabolomics is the ability to identify the detected signals with respect to their chemical nature. Even now, about 60 to 80 % of all detected compounds are unknown and the metabolomic community has implemented many different initiatives to tackle the problem by creating large mass spectral or NMR spectral libraries. Many of these unknown structures (i.e., secondary metabolites) detected may be undiscovered natural product resources. Fingerprinting, footprinting, profiling or target analyses are common terms used in this field. Fingerprinting aims to take a "snapshot" of the organism where the signals cannot necessarily be used to detect/identify specific metabolites and depends strongly on the technique used. Metabolite profiling techniques require that signals can be assigned to a specific metabolite whether it is of a known or novel nature. The term target analysis aims to determine and quantify a specific metabolite of interest. There are few reports in the scientific literature, which discuss the unison of classical natural product chemistry approaches with metabolomics to identify novel bioactive natural products. These have generally focused on the study of plants. The identification of bioactive natural products from plants remains a multifaceted task because of their high chemical diversity and complexity. By measuring the metabolome of different extracts or fractions of a plant and combining these data with its corresponding biological activity, signals related to the compounds related to the displayed activity can potentially be determined. In one example, myxoprincomide (58), a novel NRPS/PKS natural product from Myxococcus xanthus DK1622 was identified by combining methods of targeted mutagenesis, liquid chromatography coupled to high resolution mass spectrometry (LC-HRMS), and a statistical data evaluation (Figure 3.17). Mutant and wildtype strains were grown in small-scale fermentation in quadruplicate, replicate extracts were analyzed by LCHRMS, and data were pretreated by using a compound finding algorithm, resulting in the definition of >1,000 molecular features per sample. Molecular features specifically missing in culture extracts from DK1622 mutant strains were identified using PCA to the preprocessed LC-MS datasets.

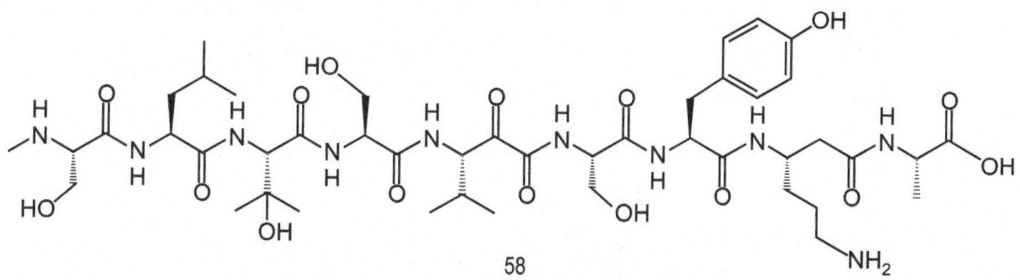

58

Fig. 3.17: Myxoprincomide (58)

(**Source:** Based on Review of Literature)

Five medicinal Panax herbs (ginseng species) were subjected to a metabolomic analysis using Ultra-Performance Liquid Chromatography-Quadrupole Time of Flight Mass Spectrometry (UPLCQTOFMS) and multivariate statistical analysis techniques. PCA of the analytical data explained that the five Panax herbs could be separated into five different groups of phytochemicals. PCA identified, ginsenoside Rf (59), 20(S)-pseudoginsenoside F11 (60), malonyl gisenoside Rb1 (61), and gisenoside Rb2 (62) which accounted for the variance which was identified through the loadings plot of the PCA, and tentatively by the accurate mass of TOFMS (Figure 18). The results and methodology demonstrated this method to be reliable for the rapid analysis of a group of metabolites present in natural products extracts. In the case of NMR of crude extracts, patterns can be visualized and interpreted which is generally combined with multivariate data analysis. This can be carried out in a comparative manner distinguishing differences between relatively similar extracts or it can be linked with a specific (generally in vitro) biological activity. Ultimately this enables the construction of a complex database of the metabolome. An NMR based metabolomics approach has recently been utilized in the study of Galphimia glauca, a Mexican plant which has been used in traditional medicine for the treatment of central nervous disorders. Six collections from the Mexican area demonstrated sedative and anxiolytic activities, with only two collections of G. glauca showing significant activity. 1H-NMR metabolomic profiling was conducted on all six extracts

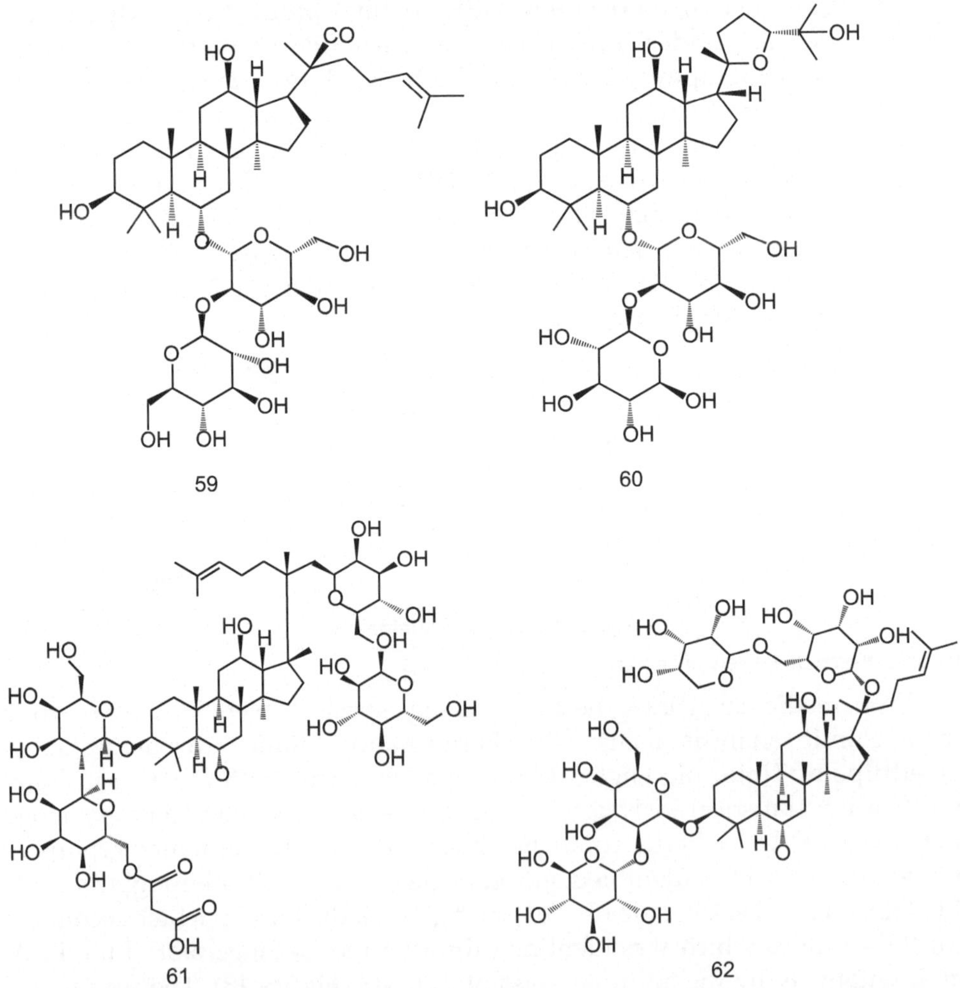

59 60 61 62

Fig. 3.18: Ginsenoside Rf (59). 20(S)-pseudoginsenoside F11 (60). Melonyl gisenoside Rb1 (61), and gisenoside Rb2 (62)

and was analyzed by partial least square-discriminant analysis (PLS-DA) using previous information on their bioactivities. The PLS-DA loadings plot demonstrated a signal strongly correlated with sedative and anxiolytic activities was found to be galphimine (63) (Figure 3.19). A targeted HPLC metabolomic approach was also conducted which provided evidence that the two collections possessing strong sedative and anxiolytic activities contained high amounts of galphimine while both other (less active) samples did not.

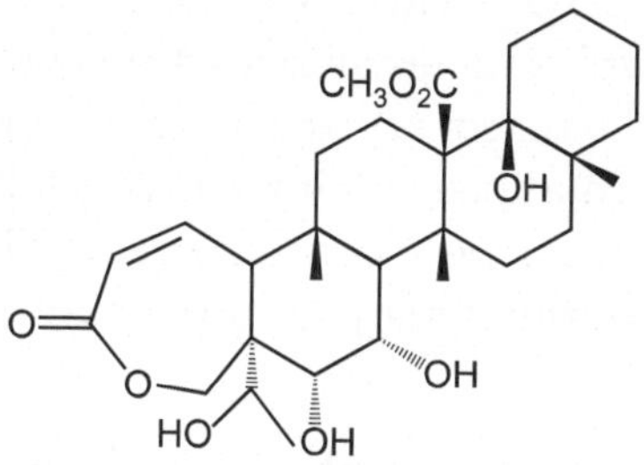

63

Fig. 3.19: Galphimine (63)

(**Source:** Based on Review of Literature)

Zhi and co-workers analyzed the effect of different antibiotics with different modes of action on various microbes. The results concluded that dihydrocucurbitacin F-25-O-acetate (64), a major constituent of the Chinese plant Hemsleya pengxianensis, showed antimicrobial activity. The metabolome of a Staphylococcus aureus culture treated with a plant extract, 64 and several known antibiotics were compared. PCA analysis revealed that 64 was the component responsible for the main antimicrobial activity on S. aureus in H. pengxianensis through its ability to inhibit cell wall synthesis, as in the case of vancomycin (Figure 3.20).

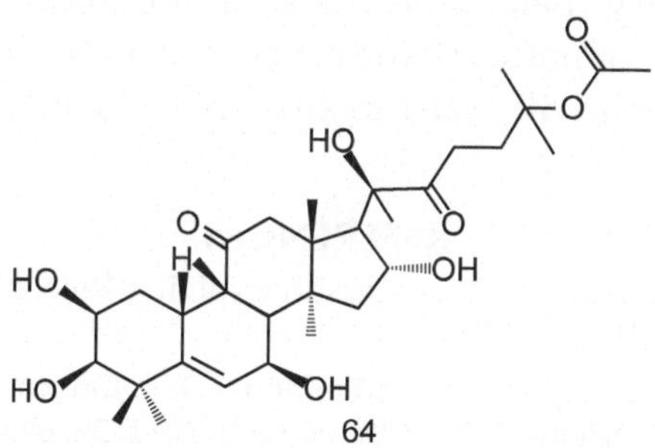

64

Fig. 3.20: Dihydrocucurbitcin F-25 O-acetate (64)

(**Source:** Based on Review of Literature)

NMR based metabolomics has many applications in plant science and can be used in functional genomics to differentiate plants from different origin, or after different treatments. Kim and co-workers describe the advantage of a NMR metabolomic analysis and the possibility of identifying metabolites by comparing NMR data with references or by structure elucidation using 2D-NMR. Deyrupa and co-workers also demonstrated the use of 2D-NMR spectroscopy to screen a library of biorationally selected insect metabolite samples for partial structures. This investigation enabled the detection of novel compounds in complex metabolite mixtures without prior fractionation or isolation. This led to the discovery and isolation of two families of tricyclic pyrones in Delphastus catalinae, a tiny ladybird beetle that is employed commercially as a biological pest control agent. The D. catalinae pyrones represent ring systems not previously found in nature.

Conclusions

In summary, we propose that a combination of metabolomics technologies with natural product discovery processes will be beneficial on multiple levels. Firstly, by increasing the number of identifications in our metabolomics data we may provide novel structures to be tested for bioactivity for any disease under investigation. Multi-parallel analysis using metabolomics technologies will also enhance and increase throughput of chemical characterization processes of many different species from natural resources. Secondly, as mentioned above, natural product chemists have collected a lifetime of compound libraries of active and also inactive pure compounds which can now be analyzed to construct mass spectral and NMR spectral libraries and therefore improve biological interpretations of metabolomics data. The advancements in analytical instrumentation and sophisticated hyphenation of separation techniques with high sensitive detectors have allowed for greater detection of small molecule compounds measurable in biological systems (i.e., primary and secondary metabolites) and undoubtedly will now be used to advance the discovery of natural product chemistry to identify potential novel drugs candidates which will assist in sustaining health and the fight against disease and illness.

REFERENCES

Mishra, B.B.; Tiwari, V.K. Natural Products: An Evolving Role in Future Drug Discovery. Eur. J. Med. Chem. 2011, 46, 4769–4807.

Rey-Ladino, J.; Ross, A.G.; Cripps, A.W.; McManus, D.P.; Quinn, R. Natural Products and the search for Novel Vaccine Adjuvants. Vaccine 2011, 29, 6464–6471.

Cragg, G.M.; Newman, D.J. Biodiversity: A Continuing Source of Novel Drug Leads. Pure Appl. Chem. 2005, 77, 7–24.

Haefner, B. Drugs from the deep: Marine Natural Products as Drug Candidates. Drug Discov. Today 2003, 8, 536–544.

Butler, M.S. The Role of Natural Product in Chemistry in Drug Discovery. J. Nat. Prod. 2004, 67, 2141–2153.

Hicks, S. Desert Plants and People, 1st ed.; Naylor Co.: San Antonio, TX, USA, p. 75.

Kinghorn, A.D.; Pan, L.; Fletcher, J.N.; Chai, H. The Relevance of Higher Plants in Lead Compound Discovery Programs. J. Nat. Prod. 2011, 74, 1539–1555.

Duke, J.A.; Duke, P.A.K.; du Cellier, J.L. Duke's Handbook of Medicinal Plants of the Bible; CRC Press Taylor and Francis Group: Boca Raton, FL, USA, 2008; p. 552.

Dillenius, J.J. Synopsis Methodica Stirpium Britannicarum, 3rd ed.; G. and J. Innys: London, UK, 1724; p. 482

Martin, M. A Description of the Western Isles of Scotland, 4th ed.; Macleod, D.J., Ed.; Stirling: Eneas Mackay: Cornhill, UK, 1934.

Lightfoot, J. Flora Scotica; Benjamin White: London, UK, 1977, Volume 2.

Beith, M. Healing Threads: Traditional Medicines of the Highlands and Islands Edinburgh; Polygon: Edinburgh, UK, 1999.

Svabo, J.C. Indberetninger fra en Reise I Færøe 1781 og 1782; Selskabet til Udgivelse af Færøske Kildeskrifter og Studier: Copenhagen, Denmark, 1959, p. 497.

Allen, D.E.; Hatfield, G. Medicinal Plants in Folk Tradition: An Ethnobotany of Britain and Ireland; Timber Press: Cambridge, UK, 2004; p. 431.

Swanton, E.W. Economic and folklore notes. Trans. Br. Mycol. Soc. 1915, 5, 408–409.

Swanton, E.W. Sussex County Magazine; T.R. Beckett: Eastbourne, UK, 1932, Volume 6, p. 709.

Hatfield, G. Country Remedies: Traditional East Anglian Plant Remedies in the Twentieth Century; Boydell Press: Woodbridge, UK, 2005.

Müller, K. Pharmaceutically relevant metabolites from lichens. Appl. Microbiol. Biotechnol. 2001, 56, 9.

Purvis, W. Lichens; Natural History Museum, London/Smithsonian Institution: Washington D.C., USA, 2000; p. 112.

MacFarlane, A.M. Gaelic names of plants: Study of their uses and lore. Trans. Gaelic Soc. Inverness 1929, 32, 1–48.

Cameron, J. The Gaelic names of plants (Scottish, Irish and Mnax) Collected and Artanged in Scientific Order, with Notes on Their Etymology, Uses, Plant Superstitions, etc., among the Celts, with Copious Gaelic, English and Scientific Indices; John Mackay: Glasgow, Scotland, UK, 1900; p. 160.

Vickery, R. A Dictionary of Plant-Lore; Oxford University Press: Oxford, UK, 1995.

Moloney, M.F. Irish Ethno-botany and the Evolution of Medicine in Ireland; Dublin, M.H., Ed.; Gill and Son: Dublin, Ireland, 1919.

Borlase, W. The Natural History of Cornwall; E. & W. Books: Oxford, UK, 1758.

Ó hEithir, R. Folk Medical Beliefs and Practices in the Aran Islands. Master's thesis, National University of Ireland, Galway, Ireland, 1983.

Dewick, P.M. Medicinal Natural Products: A Biosynthentic Approach, 2nd ed.; John Wiley and Son: West Sussex, UK, 2002; p. 520.

Maplestone, R.A.; Stone, M.J.; Williams, D.H. The Evolutionary Role of Secondary Metabolites— A Review. Gene 1992, 115, 151–157.

Colegate, S.M.; Molyneux, R.J. Bioactive Natural Products: Detection, Isolation and Structure Determination; CRC Press: Boca Raton, FL, USA, 2008; pp. 421–437.

Sarker, S.D.; Latif, Z.; Gray, A.I. Methods in Biotechnology: Natural Product Isolation; Satyajit D., Ed.; Human Press Inc: Totowa, NJ, USA, 2006; p. 528.

Der Marderosian, A.; Beutler, J.A. The Review of Natural Products, 2nd ed.; Facts and Comparisons; Seattle, WA, USA, 2002; pp. 13–43.

Aniszewski, T. Alkaloids—Secrets of Life. In Alkaloid Chemistry, Biological Significance, Applications and Ecological Role; Elsevier Science: Amsterdam, The Netherlands, 2007; p. 334.

Mann, J. Murder, Magic, and Medicine; Oxford University Press: New York, NY, USA, 1994; pp. 164–170.

Abraham, E.P.; Chain, E.; Fletcher, C.M. Further Observations on Penicillin. Lancet 1941, 16, 177–189.

Alder, A.L. The History of Penicillin Production; American Institute of Chemical Engineers: New York, NY, USA, 1970.

Lax, E. The Mold in Dr. Florey's Coat: The Story of the Penicillian Miracle; John Macrae/ Henry Hol: New York, NY, USA, 2004; p. 308.

Wainwright, M. Miracle Cure: The Story of Penicillin and the Golden Age of Antibiotics; Blackwell Scientific: Oxford, UK, 1990; p. 57.

Mann, J. The Elusive Magic Bullet: The Search for the Perfect Drug; Oxford University Press: New York, NY, USA, 1999.

Buss, A.D.; Waigh, R.D. Antiparasitic Drugs. In Burger's Medicinal Chemistry and Drug Discovery, 5th ed.; Wolff, M.E., Ed.; Wiley-Interscience: New York, NY, USA, 1995; Volume 1, pp. 1021–1028.

Fabbretti, A.; Gualerzi, C.O.; Brandi, L. How to Cope with the Quest for new Antibiotics. FEBS Lett. 2011, 585, 1673–1681

Zjawiony, J.K. Biologically Active Compounds from Aphyllophorales (Polypore) Fungi. J. Nat. Prod. 2004, 67, 300–310.

Stamets, P. Novel Antimicrobials from Mushrooms. Herbal Gram 2002, 54, 28–33.

Gwinn, K.D.; Schardl, C.L.; Friburg, A. Southern Regional Information Exchange Group (SRIEG-37) on the tall Fescue Endophyte. J. Prod. Agric. 1992, 5, 189–190

Tan, R.X.; Zou, W.X. Endophytes: A Rich Source of Functional Metabolites (1987 to 2000). Nat. Prod. Rep. 2001, 18, 448–459.

Petrini, O. Taxonomy of Endophytic Fungi of Aerial Plant Tissues. In Microbiology of Phyllosphere; Fokkema, N.J., van den Heuvel, J., Eds.; Cambridge University Press: Cambridge, UK, 1986; pp, 175–187

Newmsan, D.J.; Cragg, G.M. Natural Products as Sources of New Drugs over the last 25 years. J. Nat. Prod. 2007, 70, 461–477.

Martin, D.E.; Blum, R.; Wilton, J. Safety and Pharmacokinetics of Beririmat (PA-457) a Novel Inhibitor of Human Immunodeficiency Virus Maturation, in Healthy Volunteers. Antimicrob. Agents Chemother. 2007, 51, 3063–3066.

Kashiwada, Y.; Hashimoto, F.; Cosentino, L.M. Betulinic Acid and Dihydrobetulinic Acid Derivatives as Potent HIV agents. J. Med. Chem. 1996, 39, 1016–1017.

Yogeeswari, P.; Sriram, D. Betulinic acid and its Derivatives: A Review on their Biological Properties. Curr. Med. Chem. 2005, 12, 763–771.

Heider, D.; Verheyen, J.; Hoffman, D. Predicting Bevirimat Resistance of HIV-1 from Genotype. BMC Bioinformatics 2010, 11, 1–9.

Min, B.-S.; Nakamura, N.; Miyashiro, H.; Bae, K.-W.; Hattori, M. Triterpenes from the Spores of Ganoderma Lucidum and their Inhibitory Activity against HIV-1 protease. Chem. Pharm. Bull. 1998, 46, 1607–1612.

Lee, J.C.; Strobel, G.A.; Lobkovsky, E.; Clardy, J.C. Torreyanic Acid: A Selectively Cytotoxic Quinone Dimer from the Endophytic Fungus Pestalotiopsis Microspora. J. Org. Chem. 1996, 61, 3232–3233.

Li, C.; Johnson, R.P.; Porco, J.A. Total Synthesis of the Quinine Epoxide Dimer (+)-torreyanic Acid: Application of a Biomimetic Oxidation/Electrocyclization/Diels-Alder Dimerization Cascade. J. Am. Chem. Soc. 2003, 125, 5059–5106.

McRae, J.; Yang, Q.; Crawford, R.; Palombo, W. Review of the Methods used for Isolating Pharmaceutical Lead Compounds from Traditional Medicinal Plants. Environmentalist 2007, 27, 165–174.

Fellows, L.; Scofield, A. Chemical Diversity in Plants. In Intellectual Property Rights and Biodiversity Conservation—An Interdisciplinary Analysis of the Values of Medicinal Plants; University Press: Cambridge, UK, 1995.

Farnsworth, N.R.; Akerele, R.O.; Bingel, A.S.; Soejarto, D.D.; Guo, Z. Medicinal Plants in Therapy. Bull. WHO 1985, 63, 965–981.

Fabricant, D.S.; Farnsworth, N.R. The Value of Plants Used in Traditional Medicine for Drug Discovery. Environ. Health Perspect. 2001, 109, 69–75.

Cragg, G.M. Paclitaxel (Taxol): A Success Story with Valuable Lessons for Natural Product Drug Discovery and Development. Med. Res. Rev. 1998, 18, 315–331.

Cseke, L.J.; Kirakosyan, A.; Kaufmann, P.B.; Warber, S.L.; Duke, J.A.; Brielmann, H.L. Natural Products from Plants, 2nd ed.; CRC, Taylor and Francis: Boca Raton, FL, USA, 2006; p. 640.

Nicolaou, K.C.; Yang, Z.; Liu, J.J.; Ueno, H.; Nantermet, P.G.; Guy, R.K.; Claiborne, C.F.; Renaud, J.; Couladouros, E.A.; Paulvannan, K.; Sorensen, E.J. Total Synthesis of Taxol. Nature 1994, 367, 630–634.

Kedei, N.; Lundberg, D.J.; Toth, A.; Welburn, P.; Garfield, S.H.; Blumberg, P.M. Characterization of the Interaction of Ingenol 3-angelate with Protein Kinase C. Cancer Res. 2004, 64, 3243–3255.

Ogbourne, S.M.; Suhrbier, A.; Jones, B. Antitumour Activity of Ingenol 3-angelate: Plasma Membrane and Mitochondrial Disruption and Necrotic Cell Death. Cancer Res. 2004, 64, 2833–2839.

Kiviharju, T.M.; Lecane, P.S.; Sellers, R.G.; Peehl, D.M. Antiproliferative and Proapoptic of Triptolide (PG490), a Natural Product Entering Clinical Trials, on Primary Cultures of Human Prostatic Epithelial Cells. Clin. Cancer. Res. 2002, 8, 2666–2674.

Fidler, J.M.; Li, K.; Chung, C. PG490-88, a Derivative of Triptolide, Casues Tumor Regression and Sensitizes Tumors to Chemotherapy. Mol. Cancer. Ther. 2003, 2, 855–862.

Newman, D.J.; Cragg, G.M. In Drug Discovery, Therapeutics, and Preventive Medicine; Zhang, L., Fleming, A., Demain, A.L., Eds.; Humana Press: Totowa, NJ, USA, 2005; p. 74.

Holwell, S.E.; Cooper, P.A.; Grosios, J.W.; Lippert, J.W., III; Pettit, G.R.; Snyder, S.D.; Bibby, M.C. Combretastatin A-1 Phosphate, a Novel Tubulin-binding Agent with in-vivo anti-Vascular Effects in Experimental Tumors. Anticancer Res. 2002, 22, 707–712.

Kashman, Y.; Gustafson, K.R.; Fuller, R.W.; Cardellin, J.H., II; McMahon, J.B.; Currens, M.J.; Buckheist, R.W.; Hughes, S.H.; Cragg, G.M.; Boyd, M.R. The Calanolides, a Novel HIVinhibitory Class of Coumarin Derivatives from the Tropical Rainforest Tree, Calophyllum Lanigerum. J. Med. Chem. 1992, 35, 2735–2743.

Gustafson, K.R.; Cardellin, J.H., II; McMahon, J.B.; Gulakowski, R.J.; Ishitoya, J.; Szallasi, Z.; Lewin, N.E.; Blumberg, P.M.; Weislow, O.S.; Beutler, J.A.; et al. A Nonpromoting Phorbol from the Samoan Medicinal Plant Homalanthus Nutans Inhibits Cell Killing by HIV-1. J. Med. Chem. 1992, 35, 1978–1986.

Cox, P.A. Saving the Ethnopharmacological Heritage of Samoa. Pharm. Biol. 2001, 39, 33–40.

Davidson, R.N.; Den Boer, M.; Ritmeijer, K. Paromomycin. Trans. R. Soc. Trop. Med. Hyg. 2009, 103, 653–660.

Carroll, A.R.; Arumugan, G.; Quinn, R.J.; Redburn, J.; Guymer, G.; Grimshaw, P. Grandisine A and B, Novel Indolizidine Alkaloids with -Opioid Receptor Binding Affinity from the Leaves of the Human Australian Rainforest tree Elaeocarpus Grandis. J. Org. Chem. 2005, 70, 1889–1892.

Howes, M.-J.R.; Perry, N.S.L.; Houghton, P.J. Plants with Traditional uses and Activitities, Relevant to the Management of Alzheimer's Disease and other Cognitive Disorders. Phytother. Res. 2003, 17, 1–18.

Heinrich, M.; Teoh, H.L. Galanthamine from Snowdrop-the Development of a Modern Drug against Alzheimer's Disease from Local Caucasian Knowledge. J. Ethnopharmacol. 2004, 92, 147–162.

Deleu, D.; Hanssens, Y.; Northway, M.G. Subcutaneous Apomorphine: An Evidence-based Review of its use in Parkinson's Disease. Drugs Aging 2004, 21, 687–709.

Marris, E. Marine Natural Products: Drugs from the Deep. Nature 2006, 443, 904–905.

Haefner, B. Drugs from the Deep: Marine Natural Products as Drug Candidates. Drug Discov. Today 2003, 8, 536–544.

Alejandro, M.; Glaser, K.B.; Cuevas, C.; Jacobs, R.S.; Kem, W.; Little, R.D.; McIntosh, J.M.; Newman, D.J.; Potts, B.C.; Shuster, D.E. The Odyssey of Marine Pharmaceuticals: a Current Pipeline Perspective. Trends Pharm. Sci. 2010, 31, 255–265.

Rinehart, K.L.; Lithgow-Bertelloni, A.M. Novel Antiviral and Cytotoxic Agent, Dehydrodidemnin B. PCT Int. Pat. Appl. 1991, 15, 248086q.

Urdiales, J.L.; Morata, P.; De Castro, I.N.; Sanchez-Jimenez, F. Anti-proliferative Effect of Dehydrodidemnin B (DDB), a Depsipeptide Isolated from Mediterranean Tunicates. Cancer Lett. 1996, 102, 31–37.

Henríquez, R.; Faircloth, G.; Cuevas, C. In Ecteinascidin 743 (ET-743, Yondelis), Aplidin, and Kahalalide F. In Anticancer Agents from Natural Products; Cragg, G.M., Kingston, D.G.I., Newman, D.J., Eds.; Taylor and Francis: Boca Raton, FL, USA, 2005; p. 215.

Rinehart, K.L.; Holt, T.G.; Fregeau, N.L.; Stroh, J.G.; Keifer, P.A.; Sun, F.; Li, L.H.; Martin, D.G. Ecteinascidins 729, 743, 745, 759A, 759B, and 770: Potent Antitumor Agents from the Caribbean Tunicate Ecteinascidia Turbinata. J. Org. Chem. 1990, 55, 4512–4515.

Wright, A.E.; Forleo, D.A.; Gunawardana, G.P.; Gunasekera, S.P.; Koehn, F.E.; McConnell, O.J. Antitumor Tetrahydroisoquinoline Alkaloids from the Colonial Ascidian Ecteinascidia Turbinata. J. Org. Chem. 1990, 55, 4508–4512.

Manzanares, I.; Cuevas, C.; Garcia-Nieto, R.; Marco, E.; Gago, F. Advances in the Chemistry and Pharmacology of Ecteinascidins, a Promising New Class of Anticancer Agents. Curr. Med. Chem. Anticancer Agents 2001, 1, 257.

Cuevas, C.; Francesch, A. Development of Yondelis® (Trabectedin, ET-743). A Semisynthetic Process Solves the Supply Problem. Nat. Prod. Rep. 2009, 26, 322–337.

Alvarez-Miranda, M.; Rodriguez-Gonzalez, A.; Ptero, G.; Lacal, J.C. Characterization of the Mechanism of Action of ES-285, a Novel Antitumor Drug from Mactomeris Polynyma. Clin. Cancer Res. 2003, 9, Abstract C17.

Cuadros, R.; Montejo de Garcini, E.; Wandosell, F.; Faircloth, G.; Fernandez-Sousa, J.M.; Avila, J. The Marine Compound Spisulosine, an Inhibitor of Cell Proliferation, Promotes the Disassembly of Actin Stress Fibers. Cancer Lett. 2000, 152, 23.

Salcedo, M.; Cuevas, C.; Otero, G.; Sanchez-Puelles, J.M.; Fernandez-Sousa, J.M.; Avila, J.; Wandosell, F. The Marine Antitmor Compound ES 285 Activates EGD Receptors. Clin. Cancer Res. 2003, 9, Abstract C24.

Salcedo, M.; Cuevas, C.; Sanchez-Puelles, J.M.; Otero, G.; Sousa, J.M.F.; Avila, J.; Wandosell, F. ES-285, a Novel Antitumoral Compound, Interacts with EDG Receptors. Proceedings of American Association for Cancer Research 94th Meeting, Washington, 11–14 July, 2003, Abstract 3649.

Trimurtulu, G.; Ohtani, I.; Patterson, G.M.L.; Moore, R.E.; Corbett, T.H.; Valeriote, F.A.; Demchik, L. Total Structures of Cryptophycins, Potent Antitumor Depsipeptides from the Bluegreen Alga Nostoc sp. Strain GSV 224. J. Am. Chem. Soc. 1994, 116, 4729–4737.

Faulkner, D.J. Marine Natural Products. J. Nat. Prod. Rep. 2002, 19, 1–48.

Bhakuni, D.S.; Rawat, D.S. Bioactive Marine Natural Products, 1st ed.; Springer-Verlag: New Delhi, India, 2005; p. 404.

Baslow, M.N. Marine Pharmacology; A Study of Toxins and Other Biologically Active Substances of Marine Origin; Williams & Wilkins Co: Baltimore, MD, USA, 1969; p. 286

Yotsu-Yamashita, M.; Haddock, R.L.; Yasumoto, T. Polycavernoside A: A Novel Glycosidic Macrolide from the Red Alga Polycavernosa Tsudai (Gracilaria edulis). J. Am. Chem. Soc. 1993, 115, 1147-1148.

White, J.D.; Blakemore, P.R.; Browder, C.C.; Hong, J.; Lincoln, C.M.; Nagornyy, P.A.; Robarge, L.A.; Wardrop, D.J. Total Synthesis of the Marine Toxin Polycavernoside A via Selective Macrolactonization of a Trihydroxy Carboxylic Acid. J. Am. Chem. Soc. 2001, 123, 8593–8595.

Paquette, L.A.; Barriault, L.; Pissarnitski, D.; Johnston, J.N. Stereocontrolled Elaboration of Natural (-)-Polycavernoside A, a Powerfully Toxic Metabolite of the Red Alga Polycavernosa Tsudai. J. Am. Chem. Soc. 2000, 122, 619–631.

Ishitsuka, M.O.; Kusumi, T.K.H. Antitumor Xenicane and Norxenicane Lactones from the Brown Alga Dictyota Dichotoma. J. Org. Chem. 1988, 53, 5010–5013.

Faulkner, D.J. Marine Natural Products. Nat. Prod. Rep. 1988, 20, 269–309.

Tringali, C.; Oriente, G.; Piattelli, M.; Geraci, C.; Nicolosi, G.; Breitmaier, E. Crenuladial, an Antimicrobial Diterpenoid from the Brown Alga Dilophus Ligulatus. Can. J. Chem. 1988, 66, 2799–2802.

San-Martin, A.; Darias, J.; Soto, H.; Contreras, C.; Herrera, J.S.; Rovirosa, J. A new C15 Acetogenin from the Marine Alga Laurencia Claviformis. Nat. Prod. Lett. 1997, 10, 303–311.

Kimura, J.; Kamada, N.; Yoshikazu, T. Fifteen Chamigrane Derivatives from the red alga Laurencia Nidifica. Bull. Chem. Soc. Jpn. 1999, 72, 289-88292.

Elsworth, J.M. A New Chamigrane from Laurencia Glomerata. J. Nat. Prod. 1989, 52, 893–895.

Dias, D.A.; White, J.M.; Urban, S. Laurencia Filiformis: Phytochemical Profiling by Conventional and HPLC-NMR Approaches. Nat. Prod. Commun. 2009, 4, 157–172.

Duke, S.O.; Menn, J.J.; Plimmer, J.R. Pest Control with Enhanced Environmental Safety; ACS Symposium Series No. 514; Duke, S.O., Menn, J.J., Plimmer, J.R., Eds.; American Chemical Society: Washington, DC, USA, 1993.

Georghiou, G.P. Overview of Insecticide Resistance. In Managing Resistance to Agrochemicals: From Fundamental Research to Practical Strategies; Green, M.B., Le Baron, H.M., Moberg, W.K., Eds.; ACS Symp. Ser. 421. Am. Chem. Soc: Washington, DC, USA, 1990; pp. 18–41.

El Sayed, K.A.; Dunbar, D.C.; Perry, T.L.; Wilkins, S.P.; Hamann, M.T.; Greenplate, J.T.; Wideman, M.A. Marine Natural Products as Prototype Insecticidal Agents. J. Agric. Food Chem. 1997, 45, 2735–2739.

San-Martin, A.; Negrete, R.; Rovirosa, J. Insecticide and Acaricide Activities of Polyhalogenated Monoterpenes from Chilean Plocamium Cartilagineum. Phytochemistry 1991, 30, 2165–2169.

Fukuzawa, A.; Masamune, T. Laurepinnacin and Isolaurepinnacin, New Acetylenic Cyclic Ethers from the Marine Red Alga Laurencia Pinnata Yamada. Tetrahedron Lett. 1981, 22, 4081–4084.

Watanabe, K.; Umeda, K.; Miyakado, M. Isolation and Identification of three Insecticidal Principles from the Red Alga Laurencia Nipponica Yamada. Agric. Biol. Chem. 1989, 53, 2513–2515.

McConnell, O.; Longley, R.E.; Koehn, F.E. The Discovery of Natural Products with Therapeutic Potential; Gullo, V.P., Ed.; Butterworth-Heinemann: Boston, MA, USA, 1994; pp. 109–174.

Newman, D.J.; Cragg, G.M.; Snader, K.M. The Influence of Natural Products on Drug Discovery. Nat. Prod. Rep. 2000, 17, 215–234.

Chin, Y.-W.; Balunas, M.J.; Chai, H.B.; Kinghorn, A.D. Drug Discovery from Natural Sources. AAPS J. 2006, 8, 239–253.

Uemura, D.; Takahashi, K.; Yamamoto, T.; Katayama, C.; Tanaka, J.; Okumura, Y.; Hirata, Y. Norhalichondrin A: An Antitumor Polyether Macrolide from a Marine Sponge. J. Am. Chem. Soc. 1985, 107, 4796–4798.

Pettit, G.R.; Herald, C.L.; Boyd, M.R.; Leet, J.E.; Dufresne, C.; Doubek, D.L.; Schmidt, J.M.; Cerny, R.L.; Hooper, J.N.A.; Rutzler, K.C. Antineoplastic Agents. 219. Isolation and Structure of the Cell Growth Inhibitory Constituents from the Western Pacific Marine Sponge Axinella sp. J. Med. Chem. 1991, 34, 3339–3340.

Pettit, G.R.; Srirangam, J.K.; Herald, D.L.; Erickson, K.L.; Doubek, D.L.; Schmidt, J.M.; Tackett, L.P.; Bakus, G.J. Antineoplastic Agents. 251. Isolation and Structure of Stylostatin 1 from the Papua New Guinea marine Sponge Stylotella sp. J. Org. Chem. 1993, 58, 3222.

Litaudon, M.; Hart, J.B.; Blunt, J.W.; Lake, R.J.; Munro, M.H.G. Isohomohalichondrin B, a New Antitumour Polyether Macrolide from the New Zealand Deep-water Sponge, Lyssodendoryx sp. Tetrahedron Lett. 1994, 35, 9435.

Aicher, T.D.; Buszek, K.R.; Fang, F.G.; Forsyth, C.J.; Jung, S.H.; Kishi, Y.; Matelich, M.C.; Scola, P.M.; Spero, D.M.; Yoon, S.K. Total Synthesis of Halichondrin B and Norhalichondrin B. J. Am. Chem.Soc. 1992, 114, 3162–3164.

Baker, D.D.; Chu, M.; Oza, U.; Rajgarhia, V. The Value of Natural Products to Future Pharmaceutical Discovery. Nat. Prod. Rep. 2007, 24, 1225–1244.

Ojima, I. Modern Natural Products Chemistry and Drug Discovery. J. Med. Chem. 2008, 51, 2587–2588.

Nussbaum, F.V.; Brands, M.; Hinzen, B.; Weigand, S.; Habich, D. Antibacterial Natural Products in Medicinal Chemistry - Exodus or Revival? Angew. Chem. Int. Ed. 2006, 45, 5072–5129.

Luzhetskyy, A.; Pelzer, S.; Bechthold, A. The Future of Natural Products as a Source of New Antibiotics. Curr. Opin. Investig. Drugs 2007, 8, 608–613.

Newman, D.J. Natural Products as Leads to Potential Drugs: An Old Process or the New Hope for Drug Discovery? J. Med. Chem. 2008, 51, 2589–2599.

Ramakrishna, N.V.S.; Nadkarni, S.R.; Bhat, R.G.; Naker, S.D.; Kumar, E.K.S.V.; Lal, B. Screening of Natural Product Extracts for Antibacterial Activity: Early Identification and Elimination of known Compounds by Dereplication. Ind. J. Chem. 1999, 38B, 1384–1387.

Sashidhara, K.V.; Rosaiah, J.N. Various Dereplication Strategies using LC-MS for Rapid Natural Product lead Identification and Drug Discovery. Nat. Prod. Commun. 2007, 2, 193–202.

Cordell, G.A.; Shin, Y.G. Finding the Needle in the Haystack. The Dereplication of Natural Product Extracts. Pure Appl. Chem. 1999, 71, 1089–1094.

Brkljaca, R.; Urban, S. Recent Advances in HPLC-NMR and Applications for Natural Product Profiling and Identification. J. Liq. Chroma. Rel. Technol. 2011, 34, 1063–1076.

Blunt, J.W.; Munro, M.H.G. Dictionary of Marine Natural Products. Available online: http://dmnp.chemnetbase.com/ (accessed on 21 July 2009).

Buckingham, J. The Dictionary of Natural Products. Available online: http://dmnp.chemnetbase.com/ (accessed on 22 August 2011).

MarinLit. Available online: http://www.chem.canterbury.ac.nz/marinlit/marinlit.shtml (accessed on 23 June 2011).

Blunt, J.W.; Munro, M.H.G.; Laatsch, H. AntiMarin Database. Available online: http://www.chem.canterbury.ac.nz/marinlit/marinlit.shtml (accessed on 10 April 2012).

Lang, G.; Mayhudin, N.A.; Mitova, M.I.; Sun, L.; van der Sar, S.; Blunt, J.W.; Cole, A.L.J.; Ellis, G.; Laatsch, H.; Munro, M.H.G. Evolving Trends in the Dereplication of Natural Product Extracts: New Methodology for Rapid, Small-scale Investigation of Natural Product Extracts. J. Nat. Prod. 2008, 19, 1595–1599.

SciFinder Scholar. Available from: http://www.cas.org/SCIFINDER/SCHOLAR/ (accessed on 2 July 2011).

SCOPUS. Available online:http://www.scopus.com/home.url (accessed on 25 August 2011).

Napralert. http://www.napralert.org/ (accessed on 3 May 2011).

Urban, S.; Separovic, F. Developments in Hyphenated Spectroscopic Methods in Natural Product Profiling. Front. Drug Des. Discov. 2005, 1, 113–166.

Wolfender, J.-L.; Ndjoko, K.; Hostettman, K. Liquid Chromatography with Ultraviolet Absorbance-mass Spectrometric Detection and with Nuclear Magnetic Resonance Spectroscopy: A powerful Combination for the on-line Structural Investigation of Plant Metabolites. J. Chromatogr. A 2003, 1000, 437–455.

Wolfender, J.-L.; Queiroz, E.F.; Hostettman, K. The Importance of Hyphenated Techniques in the Discovery of New Lead Compounds from Nature. Expert Opin. Drug Dis. 2006, 1, 237–260.

Schroeder, F.C.; Gronquist, M. Extending the Scope of NMR Spectroscopy with Microcoil probes. Angew. Chem. Int. Ed. 2006, 45, 7122–7131.

Lewis, R.J.; Bernstein, M.A.; Duncan, S.J.; Sleigh, C.J. A Comparison of Capillary-scale LC-NMR with Alternative Techniques: Spectroscopic and Practical Considerations. Magn. Reson. Chem. 2005, 43, 783–789.

Dias, D.; Urban, S. Phytochemical Analysis of the Southern Australian Marine Alga, Plocamium Mertensii using HPLC-NMR. Phytochem. Anal. 2008, 19, 453–470.

Dias, D.A.; Urban, S. Application of HPLC-NMR for the Rapid Chemical Profiling of a Southern Australian Sponge, Dactylospongia sp. J. Sep. Sci. 2009, 32, 542–548.

Lin, Y.; Schiavo, S.; Orjala, J.; Vouros, P.; Kautz, R. Microscale LC-MS-NMR Platform Applied to the Identification of Active Cyanobacterial Metabolites. Anal. Chem. 2008, 80, 8045–8054.

Sun Lin, J.; Mahyudin, N.A.; Chamyuang, S.; Blunt, J.W.; Cole, T.; Lang, G.; Mitova, M.I.; van der Sar, S.; Munro, M.H.G. Less is more: Dereplication and Discovery using CapNMR Techniques. Proceedings of Manapro XII: 12th International Symposium of Marine Natural Products, Queenstown, New Zealand, Feb 4th–9th, 2007.

Clarkson, C.; Stærk, D.; Hansen, S.H.; Smith, P.J.; Jaroszewski, J.W. Discovering New Natural Products Directly from Crude Extracts by HPLC-SPE-NMR: Chinane Diterpenes Harpagophytum Procumbens. J. Nat. Prod. 2006, 69, 527–530.

Cogne, A.-L.; Queiroz, E.F.; Marston, A.; Wolfender, J.L.; Mavi, S.; Hostettmann, K. On-line Identification of Unstable Iridoids from Jamesbrittenia Fodina by HPLC-MS and HPLC-NMR. Phytochem. Anal. 2005, 16, 429–439.

Zschocke, S.; Klaiber, I.; Bauer, R.; Vogler, B. HPLC-coupled Spectroscopic Techniques (UV, MS, NMR) for the Structure Elucidation of Phthalides in Ligusticum Chuanxiong. Mol. Divers. 2005, 9, 33–39.

Roessner, U.; Beckles, D.M. Metabolite Measurements. In Plant Metabolic Networks; Junker, B., Schwender, J., Eds.; Springer: Heidelberg, Germany, 2009.

Roessner, U.; Nahid, A.; Hunter, A.; Bellgard, M. Metabolomics—The Combination of Analytical Chemistry, Biology and Informatics. In Comprehensive Biotechnology, 2nd ed.; Moo-Young, M., Ed.; Springer: Heidelberg, Germany, 2011; Volume 1, pp. 447–459

Beckles, D.M.; Roessner, U. Plant Metabolomics—Applications and Opportunities for Agricultural Biotechnology. In Plant Biotechnology and Agriculture: Prospects for the 21st Century; Altmann, A., Hasegawa, P.M., Eds.; Elsevier/Academic Press: Boston, MA, USA, 2011.

Rochfort, S. Metabolomics Reviewed: A New "Omics" Platform Technology for Systems Biology and Implications for Natural Products Research. J. Nat. Prod. 2005, 68, 1813–1820.

Cortina, N.S.; Krug, D.; Plaza, A.; Revermann, O.; Muller, R. Myxoprincomide: A Natural Product from Myxococcus Xanthus Discovered by Comprehensive Analysis of the Secondary Metabolome. Angew. Chem. Int. Ed. 2012, 51, 811–816.

Guoxiang, X.; Robert, P.; Mingming, S.; Zhaohui, X.; Aihua, Z.; Mingfeng, Q.; Xiangbao, L.; Zhong, L.; Wei, J. Ultra-performance LC/TOF MS Analysis of Medicinal Panax herbs for Metabolomic Research. J. Sep. Sci. 2008, 31, 1015–1026.

Politi, M.; Peschel, W.; Wilson, N.; Zloh, M.; Prieto, J.M.; Heinrich, M. Cannabis Water Extracts and Tinctures Analysed by NMR Spectroscopy; different Strategies to Reduce the Content of D9-THC. Phytochemistry 2008, 69, 562–570.

Verpoorte, R.; Choi, Y.H.; Kim, H.K. Ethnopharmacology and Systems Biology: A Perfect Holistic Match. J. Ethnopharmacol. 2005, 100, 53–56.

Wang, M.; Lamers, R.J.A.N.; Korthout, H.A.; Van Nesselrooij, J.H.J.; Witkamp, R.F.; Van der Heijden, R. Metabolomics in the Context of Systems Biology: Bridging Traditional Chinese Medicine and Molecular Pharmacology. Phytother. Res. 2005, 3, 173–182.

Cardoso-Taketa, A.T.; Pereda-Miranda, R.; Choi, Y.H.; Verpoorte, R.; Villarreal, M.L. Metabolic Profiling of the Mexican Anxiolytic and Sedative Plant Galphimia Glauca using Nuclear Magnetic Resonance Spectroscopy and Multivariate Data Analysis. Planta Med. 2008, 74, 1295–1301.

Biao-Yi, Z.; Yan Yu, Y.; Zeng-Liang, Y. Investigation of Antimicrobial Model of Hemsleya Pengxianensis W.J. Chang and its Main Active Component by Metabolomics Technique. J. Ethnopharmacol. 2008, 116, 89–95.

Kim, H.K.; Choi, Y.H.; Verpoorte, R. NMR-based Metabolomic Analysis of Plants. Nat. Protoc. 2010, 5, 536-549.

Deyrupa, S.T.; Eckman, L.E.; McCarthy, P.H.; Smedley, S.R.; Meinwald, J.; Schroeder, F.C. 2D NMR-spectroscopic Screening Reveals Polyketides in Ladybugs. Proc. Natl. Acad. Soc. USA 2011, 108, 9753–9758.

Phyto-chemicals and Ethanobotany **Pages 78-114**
Edited by: Pawan Kumar 'Bharti'
ISBN: 978-93-86841-93-3
Edition: 2019
Published by: Discovery Publishing House Pvt. Ltd., New Delhi (India)

4 Design and Biological Evaluation of Environmentally Safe Agrochemicals of Heterocyclic Ligands with Copper Surfactants Derived from Neem and Karanj Oils

[1]Dr. Shema Khan, [2]Dr. Rashmi Sharma, [3]Dr. Arun Kumar Sharma

ABSTRACT

The phenomenon of micellization of surfactants in the bulk phase, as well as their ability to be accumulated at an interface are of immense theoretical, applied and biological interests as indicated by large number of publication of papers and reviews in last three decades. Fungal toxicity of Neem and Karanj to several fungi which attack humans, including those that cause athlete's foot and ringworm, and Candida, an organism that causes yeast infections and thrush and also other fungus is a good step towards their more pharmacological role. Particular information about Copper (II) soaps, play a vital role in its selection in specific phenomena such as foaming, wetting, detergency, emulsification etc. and also in their use as herbicides, fungicides, pesticides and insecticides etc. Recently, the deeper understanding of the role of metal ion in bio-system had led to the awareness that metal complexing is useful in the treatment of bacterial, fungal and viral diseases. Copper soap have a tendency of complex formation with compounds containing donor atoms like N, S, O, Br, etc. as benzothiazole and other related compounds play significant role in biological activities due to the presence of nitrogen and sulphur atoms, which are responsible for their pharmacological activities. Coherence of biological activities of Copper soaps and other N and S containing compound stimulated our interest to extend the studies in their cumulative form as complexes. It is anticipated that it will generate new hopes in various industrial and pharmacological applications.

1 Department of chemistry, Govt. College kekri-305404 Raj. India
2 Department of chemistry, s.p.c. govt. college ajmer-305001 raj. india
3 Department of chemistry, Govt. P.g. college jhalawar-326001 raj. india

The present work highlights:

1. Synthesis of Copper (II) soaps derived from non - edible oils i.e. Neem & Karanj and their complexes with 2-amino-6–methyl Benzothiazole for comparative studies.
2. Spectral studies (IR and NMR) have been carried out to understand the structural insight of the soaps and complexes synthesized.
3. In order to understand their biological aspects with special reference to fungicidal activities, the study has also been done which may be of utmost use in the field of biochemistry.

Introduction

"the best of my knowledge, no plant material with greater activity against species, has yet been found." Dr. Martin Jacobson, United States, Department of Center in Beltsville, Madison, USA stated about Neem (*Azadirectaindica).*

The Neem tree is a member of the mahogany family, Meliaceae, it is today known by the botanical name *Azadirectaindica.* It is also called by the name Indian Lilac and Margosa Tree. The US Academy of science currently attaches very high importance to the Neem tree. The United Nations declared Neem as the "Tree of the 21st Century". All the development amply indicates the growing global importance of Neem. Fortunately over 60% of the entire Neem tree population is in India. Multitude of Uses and Remedies include all the parts of the Neem tree. [1-2]

Wood is moderately heavy, durable and resistant to insects attack. It exudes a gum known as East Indian Gum and yields essential oil. **Gum** is stimulant, demulcent and tonic and is used in silk dyeing. Its **bark** possesses astringent, anti-tumourial, moluscicidal, tonic and anti-periodic properties and used in cutaneous diseases. **Leaves** along with twigs mixed with other feeds are fed to cattle and camels. They possess carminative, helminthic, anti-leucodermic, anodyne and anti-ulceration properties. Their extracts exhibit mosquito larvicidal, antiviral, anticoagulant, antibacterial, anti-diabetic and anti-arrhythmic action. They yield an essential oil which shows antibacterial and antifungal properties. Its juice is insect repellent and control nematodes. The **Flowers** in dried form is eaten. It provides plenty of nectar. It is given in atonic dyspepsia and general debility. **Fruit** is used as a tonic, antiperiodic, purgative, emollient and antihelminticand is also useful in piles, urinary and cutaneous diseases. The **Seed** is composed of a shell and kernel (sometimes two or three kernels), each about half of the seeds weight. Its kernel possesses extraordinary gustatory and repellent properties against a number of pests. Kernel powder is used as important antifeeding agent and in hair preparations. The **Neem cake** is the main by product of Neem seeds. It contains 1.07-1.30 percent sulphur. This is one of the very useful fertilizers for our crop. This is both organic nitrogen manure and nitrification inhibitor. The **Neem Pellet**s can be use for soil insects such as rot mealy bugs, rot. Nematodes, grass grubs, carrot flies etc.

The Neem oil is a major non-wood product of Neem. The oil is greenish yellow to brown in color with fixed acrid bitter taste having disagreeable odour. The oil contains 0.427 percent Sulphur. The quantity of sulphur is reduced to 0.109 percent if the oil is agitated with alcohol.

The Oil is used in skin diseases, ulcers, rheumatism, leprosy, sprain metritis, ear trouble, dental and gum troubles and asthma. It exhibits antiseptic, anti-microbial and anti-fertility activities. Oil contains Nimbidin and nimbin as active principles. Nimbidin is toxic to parasitic nematodes, anti-diabetic, and analgesic, antipyretic, anti-helminthic and anti-fungal; its sodium derivative being potent diuretic, spermicidal and anti-inflammatory agent. Nimbin is antipyretic. Other constituents present in the oil are nimbinin; nimbandiol, tiglic acid, gedunin, meldenin, salannin, azadirone, vepinin, nimbinene, and salannol, some derivatives of these compounds and deacetyl-azadirachtinol possess insecticidal property. Nimbidol, a by-product of oil constituents exhibits anti-arthritic action.

Recently a process has been developed at Hyderabad to produce colorless and debittered Neem oil that can be used for edible purpose. This oil is most important for commercial point of view. The oil yield is sometimes as high as 50 percent of the weight of Kernel.

Oil can be converted to 'polyol' which may find use as a rocked-propellent fuel in place of polypropylene glycol. It can also be used in textile and rubber industry. Organic compounds of oil are being used with advantage to tan raw hides and skins.

Various Neem extracts are known to act on various insectsas the bodies of these insects absorb the Neem compounds as if they were the real hormones. It works in the following ways:

- Disrupting of inhibiting the development of eggs, larvae, or pupae.
- Blocking the moulting of larvae or nymphs.
- Disrupting mating and sexual communication.
- Repelling larvae and adults.
- Deterring females from laying eggs.
- Sterilizing adults.
- Deterring feeding.
- Blocking the ability to "swallow" (that is, reducing the motility of the gut);

Trails done in nurseries in New Zealand and overseas has found Neem oil to be effective in the control of whitefly, caterpillars, mites, scale and aphids. Some other remedies include:

- AIDS – The National Institutes of Health reports encouraging results as an AIDS preventative and possible cure using Neem extracts.
- Allergies – Neem inhibits allergic reactions when applied externally or eaten.
- Birth control (men) – In India and the United States, trails show Neem extracts reduced fertility in male monkeys without inhibiting libido or sperm production, making it potentially the first male birth control pill. Birth control (women) – Used as a vaginal lubricant, Neem oil was up to 100 percent effective in preventing pregnancy.
- Cancer/immune – Polysaccharides and lemuroids found in Neem bark, leaves, and seed oil increased immune responses, reduced tumors and cancers without side effects.
- Diabetes – Oral doses of Neem leaf extracts reduced insulin requirement by between 30% and 50% for non-ketonic, insulin fast and insulin-sensitive diabetes.
- External parasites – Neem quickly kills external parasites and it is safer than and as effective as standard treatments for head lice and scabies.
- Heart disease – Neem delays the coagulation of blood, calms erratic heart bets and helps reduce elevated heart rates and high blood pressure.
- Herpes – Recent test in Germany show that Neem extract are toxic to the herpes virus and can quickly heal cold sores.
- Hepatitis – Tests in the U.S. show Neem hampers the virus that causes hepatitis B.
- Fungal toxin – Neem is toxic to several fungi which attack humans, including those that cause athlete's foot and ringworm, and Candida, an organism that causes yeast infections and thrush.
- Insect repellent – Studies have shown that one Neem compound is a more effective insect repellent than the widely used synthetic chemical known as DEET (N,N,-diethyl-m-toluamide), a suspected carcinogen with long periods of use. Insecticide – Neem extracts have been approved by the U.S. Environment Protection Agency of use on food corps. It is non-toxic to birds, animals, beneficial insects or man and protects crops from over 200 of the most costly pests.
- Malaria – An active ingredient in Neem leaves, called irodin A, is toxic to resistant strains of malaria.
- Psoriasis – Neem seed oil and leaf extracts is suggested to be a cure for psoriasis. It relieves the itching and pain while reducing the scale and redness of the patchy lesions.
- Periodontal disease control – German researchers have proven Neem extract prevent tooth decay and periodontal disease.

- Ulcer relief – Neem extracts given significant protection from discomfort and speed the healing of gastric problems.

Neem is very good for skin because it contains natural ingredients with anti-fungal, anti-bacterial, antiseptic (germicidal), and anti-inflammatory properties. It has moisturizing, regenerative and restructuring properties, and is used to heal eczema, psoriasis, dry skin and dandruff.

Neem 3% and peppermint oil 0.1% acts as a very effective Neem Mouth wash. Neem has pharmacological action as Neem has antiviral antifungal, antibacterial properties (*streptococcus mutants* and *streptococcus faecalis* by inhibiting cell membrane synthesis).Neem can suppress oral carcinogenesis and can reduce the ability of some streptococci to colonize tooth surfaces and also inhibits the production of insoluble glucan which may affect plaque formation. The chemical application of Neem mouth wash is to prevent dental caries, treatment of toothache and gingivitis.

Like Neem tree **Karanj**is primarily valued for its seeds, leaves, shade and ornamental value. Its botanical name is ***Pongamia pinnata*, Synonym *P. glabra* .It is also known as Indian Beech, Pongam Oil Tree of Family Leguminosae. Derris indicaBennet (now the preferred name).Root** is used as a fish poison and in scrofulous enlargements. Its juice is used in ulcers, fistulous sores, teeth cleaning, and gonorrhea. **Seed** is valued as febrifuge, fish poison, expectorant and tonic. Its paste is applied in leprous sores, skin disease and rheumatic pains. **"It is suggestive that if you Love Neem properties, but hate the smell Try Karanja Oil".** Karanj has a wonderful, nutty aroma, without the somewhat sulphurous overtone that Neem has. Like Neem oil, it has insecticidal, antiseptic, anti-parasitic and cleansing properties. Our Karanj has a minimum karanjin content of 20,000 ppm. It has been used historically in the treatment of scabies, itch, herpes, eczema and sores. Like Neem, it can also be used in a garden spray. The seeds yield the Pongam or "Karanja" oil of commerce. Both seeds and oil are used in indigenous systems of medicine; the oil is also used for tanning, soap making and lighting purposes. The oil cake is a good fertilizer and can be used in poultry rations.

The oil known as "Pongam Oil" is used for leather dressing, soap and candle-making, lubrications and illumination. It is applied in scabies, rheumatism, herpes, and leucoderma and also given as stomachic and cholagogue. Non-fatty portion of oil contains active principles karanjin (1.25%) and Pongamol (0.85%).

Biodiesel was prepared from Crude oil of *Pongamia pinnata* and *Azadirachtaindica* by trans-esterification with methanol in the presence of KOH as catalyst.

Toxicity of non-edible seed oils like *Azadirachtaindica, Pongamia pinnata, Madhucalongifolia* and *Ricinuscommunis* seed oils (5, 10 and 20%) against sugarcane stalk borer (*Chiloauricilius*) has been determined under laboratory conditions.

Growth inhibiting effect of four non-edible oils (NEOs) at 1% i.e. Neem (*AzadirachtaIndica*), Karanj (*Pongamia pinnata*), Mahua (*MadhucaIndica* [*M. longifolia*] and eucalyptus (*Eucalyptus rostrata*), on castor semilooper, *Achaeajanata*, was also studied by feeding the larvae on treated castor leaves.

Evaluation of bio-efficacy of insecticide and seed oil combinations against *Plutellaxylostella*(the diamondback moth) on cabbage has also been studied.

Karanja, eucalyptus, Neem, palas(*Buteamonosperma*), citronella (*Cymbopogon sp.*) and annona(*Annona sp.*) were tested oils used against pulse bettle, *Callosobruchuschinesis* in stored gram (*Cicerarietinum*). Citronella and Neem oil at 2.5 and 5.0 ml/kg of seed effectively controlled C. chinensis population by reducing oviposition rate.

AN Introduction About Oils

Oils and fats are invaluable for human dietary regimen. They are not only a concentrated source of energy but also sources of essential fatty acids which in turn act as building blocks for fats and oils. The edible vegetable oils are a rich source of fatty acids which have diverse application in various fields of industries like textiles, paints, cosmetics, foods and pharmaceuticals – both in their natural form-and derivatives.

Natural fats are mixtures of mixed glycosides in which the three fatty acids etherifying glycerol differ from each other[9]. The available analysis of natural fats is usually based on an analysis of fatty acids rather than the actual mixed glycerides, which occur in the natural products. A complete description of a fatty acid molecule must include the length of the carbon chain, the number of double bonds and also the exact position of double bonds.

The simplest fatty acids are referred to as saturated fatty acids. They have no unsaturated linkage and cannot be altered by hydrogenation or halogenation. When double bonds are present, fatty acids are said to be unsaturated–monounsaturated (MUFA) if only one double bond is present, and polyunsaturated (PUFA) if they have two or more double bonds, generally, separated by a single methylene group.

Composition of the Fatty Acids IN Natural OILS

Saturated Fatty Acids

Commonly they have straight chains and even number of carbon atoms (4-30), they have the general formula $CH_3\ (CH_2)_n\ COOH$. The most common saturated fatty acids are as follows –

Systematic Name	Trivial Name	Shorthand Designation	Molecular Weight	Melting Point (^0C)
Butanoic	Butyric	4:0	88.1	−7.9
Hexanoic	Caproic	6:0	116.1	−3.4
Octanoic	Caprylic	8:0	144.2	16.7
Decanoic	Capric	10:0	172.3	31.6
Dodecanoic	Lauric	12:0	20.3	44.2
Tetradecanoic	Myristic	14:0	228.4	53.9
Hexadecanoic	Palmitic	16:0	256.4	63.1
Octadecanoic	Stearic	18:0	284.4	69.6
Eicosanoic	Arachidic	20:0	412.5	75.3
Docosanoic	Behenic	22:0	340.5	79.9
Tetracosanoic	Lignoceric	24:0	368.6	84.2

Fatty acids with 4-12 carbon atoms are found mainly in milk fats but the higher members are found in seed oils.

- Lauric acid (12:0) occurs extensively in Lauraceae seeds (*Laurusnobilis*) where it was discovered. It is dominant in cinnamon oil (80-90%) coconut oil (40-60%) and is found in Cuphea species.
- Myristic acid (14:0) is present in major amount in seeds of the family Myristicaceae (nutmeg butter 60-70%). Coconut and palm kernel oils are common sources of C_8-C_{14} fatty acids.
- Palmitic acid (16:0) was first purified by Chevreul. Palmitic acid is present in major proportions in cottonseed oil (20%), Palm oil (35-40%) ,Chinese vegetable tallow (60-70%), and Neem oil(15-20%).
- Stearic acid (18:0) is a major component acid of several familiar animal depot fats (tallows) where it occurs to the extent of 10-30%.Neem contains 14-15% of this acid.
- Arachidic acid (20:0) occurs in appreciable quantities in groundnutoil (3%) but larger amount are found in seeds of Sapindaceae. Neem contains3-4% and Pongam oil contains 2.2-4.7% of this acid.
- Behenic acid (22:0) was first reported as a constituent of bean oil (seeds of *Moringooleifera*). Pongam oil contains 4.2-5.3% of this acid. This fatty chain is present in nearly all seed oils but in amounts lower than 1%.
- Lignoceric acid (24:0) is present at trace levels in plant oils except in groundnut oil and notably in leguminous seed oil. Though in Neem oil it is 1.1-3.5%

Unsaturated Fatty Acids

A. Monoenoic Fatty Acids :

Chevreul discovered the monoenoic fatty acids. These monounsaturated normal acids are wide spread in the living world where they occur mostly as the cis-isomer. They have the general structure –

$$CH_3\ (CH_2)_X\ CH = CH\ (CH_2)_y\ COOH$$

They can have unique double bond in number of different positions, but the commonest are n-9 series, as oleic acid from olive oil. Some important monoenoic acids are given below –

Systematic Name	Trivial Name	Shorthand Designation	Molecular Weight	Melting Point (°C)
Hexadec-cis-9-enoic	Palmitoleic	16:1	254.4	0.5
Octadec-cis-9-enoic	Oleic	18:1	282.4	16.2
Eicos-cis-11-enoic	Gadoleic	20:1	310.5	-
Docos-cis-13-enoic	Erucic	22:1	338.6	33.4

- Oleic acid is the most common fatty acid. Olive oil has a 60-70% content of this acid; Pongam oil has 44.5-71.3% and Neem oil has 55-60% respectively of this acid[1-2].
- Erucic acid with 22 carbon atoms is found in high amounts (up to 50%) in seed oil of the Cruciferae such as Nostrutium, rape, mustard and of the Tropacolaceae.

B-Polyenoic Fatty Acids

The commonest polyenoic fatty acids are listed below –

Systematic Name	Trivial Name	Shorthand Designation	Molecular Weight	Melting Point (°C)
Octadeca-9, 12-dienoic	Linoleic	18:2 (n-6)	280.4	–5
Octadeca-6,9, 12-trienoic	γ-Linolenic	18:3 (n-6)	282.4	16.2
Octadeca-9,12,15- trienoic	α-Linolenic	18:3 (n-3)	278.4	–11
Eiocatadeca-5,8,11, 14-teraenoic	Arachidonic	20:4 (n-6)	304.5	–50

- Linoleic acid (18:2) is the most common polyunsaturated fatty acid in plants. It was isolated by Sacc[14-16]. Walnut, peanut, seeds of sunflower, grape, corn, sesame and Soya contain large amounts of this fatty acid.Neem oil and Pongam oil contains 7-10% and 10.8-18.3% respectively.
- Arachidonic acid (20:4) is a major constituent of membrane lipids (phospholipids) and is the principal precursorof hormone-like compounds known as prostaglandins (prostanoids)[17-18].
- Linolenic acid (18:3) is the major fatty acid of plant leaves, stems and roots.

Surface Active Agents

Surface active agents or surfactants are the compounds that have the potential or tendency to alter the properties of fluid interfaces i.e. they not only accumulate at surfaces, but also by their presence, change the properties of surfaces. They are the materials that are active at interfaces which can be between solid/liquid liquid/liquid or liquid/gas pairs of phases.

Surfactants are capable of making a transition from a state of molecular disintegration to a colloidal state, they lower the interfacial tension and therefore used as emulsifiers, detergents dispersing agents foaming agents, wetting agents penetrating agent etc. Surfactants are used as wood preventative, water proofing & repelling agent eg. Fish net protection and in various industries of rubber, paints & varnishes.

The surfactant molecule is typically composed of a strongly hydrophobic (water hating) as well as hydrophilic (water loving) moiety i.e. it share the property of amphipathy. Hydrophobic end is non-polar and hydrophilic a polar therefore the molecule has partially both properties and has a dual nature*. The hydrophilic portion (often includes anions or cations) of the surfactant monomer is referred to as the 'head' of the molecule. The hydrophobic part is typically an elongated hydrocarbon chain, referred to as the tail of the molecule therefore surfactant monomer is illustrated as a tadpole with a head and a tail.

On the basis of charge carried by the polar head group surfactants are classified as anionic, cationic non-ionic or amphoteric.

Anionic Surfactant $M^{n+} = Cu^{+2}$

Surfactants have also been classified as (a) anionic. (b) cationic, (c) nonionic. (d) zwitterionic, (e) polymeric, (f) polyelectrolyte, (g) gemini, (h) bola etc. Many text books and various research articles have discussed this classification.

Anionic surfactants bearing copper ion are gaining popularity on account of their utility in foaming, herbicide, fungicide. Many other copper compounds are employed as pesticides also. These copper containing surfactants play a vital role in various fields' paints varnishes, rubber industries, fish catching net protection, crop protection, stabilization of nylon threads, lubrication etc.

Micellar Features of Copper Surfactants

One of the most characteristic properties of amphiphilic molecules is their capacity to aggregate in solutions. The aggregation process depends upon the species and the condition of the system in which they are dissolved. In solutions of amphiphiles in either aqueous or non-aqueous solvents there is a tendency of grouping of molecules in which like is associated with like. The non-polar paraffin chains tend to associate together in fluid arrangement leaving the polar groups in association with the polar water molecules. These local groupingsfluctuate under the influence of thermal motion and come in equilibrium with the neighboring molecules. This transitory grouping is termed as micelle.

Ever since Mc-Bain proposed the presence of molecular aggregates in soap solutions on the basis of unusual changes in electrical conductivity observed with changing soap concentration, the structure of micellar aggregates has been a matter of discussion. He also suggested the lamellar and spherical forms co-exist. A simple form of micelle, recognized by Hartley was consisting of Spherical aggregates. It is however, a very mobile structure and on dilution of the solutions it dissociates extremely rapidly.

X-ray studies by Harpins et al suggested the sandwich/lamellar model[37]. Later Debye and Anacker proposed that micelles are rod shaped rather than spherical or disc like. The nature of micelles has been greatly clarified oweing to recent progress in research techniques as NMR, ESR, neutron scatterings and Quasi-electric light scattering.

The abrupt change in many physicochemical properties is seen in aqueous solutions of amphiphilic molecules or surfactants with the long hydrophobic chains when a specific concentration is exceeded. It is attributed to the formation of oriented colloidal aggregates. The narrow come range over has been called the critical micelle concentration (cmc) and these molecular aggregates that form above the cmc area are known as micelles. A variety of methods have been used to determine the cmc, with or without additives, in the surfactant solutions.

According to Corrin, the cmc is the total surfactant concentration at which a small and constant number of surfactant molecules are in the aggregated form. According to William et al,thecmc is the concentration of surfactant solute at which the concentration of micelles would become zero if the micellar concentration continued to change at the same rate as it does at a slightly higher concentration of the solute. By this definition, the cmc is the concentration at which the two straight lines of solution properties below and above the cmc intersect each other.

Micellestherefore,areofstatisticalcharacter.Incertainspecialcircumstances, however, micellar groupings show marked persistence and long range inter-micellar order. Nevertheless local change in conditions exampletemperature come or shearing will immediately alter this order.

The effects of temperature of electrolytes on the solubilization and cmc have been studied by Cutoff, stricks and also by Demchenko.

Many colloid chemical behaviour of Copper (II) soap surfactant in non-aqueous mixture of varying compositions has been investigated by Mehrotra et al& Mehta et al using viscometric and allied parameters. A number of solvents have been used to understand the micellar features of copper (II) soaps by viscosity surface, tension, parachor and electrical conductance. Membrane incorporating heavy metal soaps has been used to determine the concentration of surface-active ion by measuring membrane potential.

Malik, Popov and Mehrotra carried out the versatility of colorimetric &polaragraphic method for the determination of the metal content in Copper soaps. Malik reported polaragraphic behaviour of copper soaps in pyridine, o-toludine and dioxane. Further, the formation of Copper butyro complex was confirmed polarographically. By measuring the optical density of Copper soaps in $CHCl_3$, higher fatty acids were estimated.

X-ray spectro-chemical methods were applied to determine copper naphthenate in wood by Ayers & Yokolshii, Larant and Hattiandi and other workers carried out the differential thermal analysis of metal soaps. The molar susceptibility temperature variation of hydrated copper acetate soaps was studied and it was concluded that Curie & Weiss law are not obeyed by copper soaps. Gilmour suggested a covalent chelate structure for Copper laurate, based on magnetic measurements. Simultaneously Satake, Kishita and Martin examined structure of Copper stearate, oleate and their complexes.

The dipole moment of copper oleate in benzene was investigated by Banerjee & Palit. Fisel described the formation of the complex in electro chromatographic analysis of soaps in presence of bases. Kaufman and Fisel reported solid green complex of copper and oleic acid. Viscometric studies at various temperature apparent molar volume, ultrasound, surface tension and antifungal activities related with micellar features of copper soaps in various organic solvents have been studied by Sharma et al.

Structure and Applicantions

Schulman and Riely, with the help of X-Ray diffraction propounded the concept that the structure of Copper (II) soaps consists of closely packed uniform water sphere in oil or oil in water. It has been pointed out by Anacker that the molecular weight obtained for soap solutions is incompatible with the assumption of a spherical micelle. And according to Mc-Bain and Johnson, the spherical micelle concept is totally inadequate to account for the solubilization of hydrocarbons. In conformity with X-Ray diffraction data, Mc-Bain has postulated the existence of lamellar micelles. Shinoda has supported this on the basis of the results obtained from the effects of alcohols on cmc. Ooshika suggested that the change in cmc on addition of alcohol is due to lamellar micellar structure.

However, later Mc-Bain pointed out that it is not possible to account for all the properties of the soap solutions with only one kind of micelle; and he thus suggested the existence of both spherical ionic micelles and lamellar micelles.

Mc-Bain and co-workers suggested that soap solutions contain different proportions of the various micelles at different concentrations. It has been pointed out by Kolthoff and Stricks that different type of micelles with different solubilising power are formed, and that with increase in soap concentration greater number of micelles with greater solubilising power are formed.

Matuura investigated the IR spectra and X-Ray diffraction patterns of Copper oleate. Barclay and Kennard studied the crystal structure Copper formate by X-Ray technique. The IR spectra of Copper soaps, and Copper soaps with benzidine were also studies. Grantstudied the NMR spectra of Copper stearate.

Various other workers have studied different spectral techniques like IR, ESR, NMR and magnetic moment studies of various complexes containing Copper so as to determine their geometrical and structural aspects.

Souza et al investigated various edible (vegetable) oils and established their thermal stability and various other kinetic parameters. It was established from the TGA curves that the thermal decomposition of edible oils takes place in three steps corresponding to the thermal degradation of polyunsaturated, monounsaturated and saturated fatty acids, respectively. The various kinetic parameters evaluated included energy of activation, order of reaction and pre-exponential factor. The TGA/DTA analysis, so as to determine various kinetic parameters like energy of activation of edible oils were done by various other workers.

Various other scientists have done thermal analysis of various alkaline earth and transition soaps of fatty acids like laurate, caprate, caprylate, stearate and palmitate Kishita, Inoue and Kubo studied the structure of Urea complex of Copper alkanoates. Potts and Hadson used Copper soaps in the polymerization of vinyl derivatives of pyridine. Several workers described the uses of Copper soaps as stabilizers for nylon threads synthetic polyamide and polyesters. The protection of fabrics, nets, cordage etc. from fungi and decay by impregnating them in ammonical solution of Copper soaps was described by several workers. The effectiveness of Copper soaps s fungicides, bactericides, insecticides and herbicides were also studied.

Varkonyi and Sz'ell studied the water repellency of Copper (II) soaps, and it was observed that treating the heavy fabrics with Copper naphthenate formed waterproofing and water repellant coating. It was observed by Zahradniuket al.that Copper (II) soaps were more, effective for protection of stored sugar beets. It was pointed out by Leyland and Stanford, Gabhardt and by Pederson that oxidation of natural rubber increased rapidly by the addition of Copper stearate.

Bartleson and Hughes used Copper (II) soaps in lubricants, which were stable to oxidative deterioration. To decrease wear and tear or drawing dies, lubricant containing Copper (II) soap was observed to be more effective. Mattiello described the use of Copper (II) soap as driers for the preparation of paint, varnishes and other protective coating. It was observed that the addition of Copper (II) soaps to fuel oil reduced the smoke and fumes of burning oil.

The use of Copper linoleate as heavy-duty wood preservative, and many other biological activities of Copper Metal containing surfactants have also been studied.

Atkins suggested Copper oleate, Copper resinate, Copper naphthenate, mixed Copper (II) soap containing stearate with oleate, palmitate and laurate are the Copper (II) soaps used in preservation of fishing nets, canvas and also wood. These soaps are used with coal tar for better effect. Zinc naphthenate like Cupronil i.e. copper naphthenate is used for preservation which is even more active but the ions are less toxic.

Due to the presence of nitrogen and sulphur atom, the application of benzothiazole and its various derivatives as ulcer inhibitor, anti-glutamate, fungicidal agents, antibacterial, anti-tubercular agents, herbicidal agents, intermediates in agrochemical and pharmaceutical fields and their uses in diabetic complications have been reported recently by various workers[134-141].

Compounds (Ligands) Containing Nitrogen, Sulphur with their Applications

Benzothiazole and other nitrogen and sulphur containing compounds have been serving as the basis of a variety of drugs for over five decades. They constitute an important and interesting class of heterocyclics not only for synthetic investigations but also for their usefulness.

Copper (II) soaps have a tendency of complex formation with the compounds containing donor atoms like N, O, Br and S etc. Urea, thiourea and benzothiazole possess nitrogen and sulphur atoms which are responsible for their pharmacological activities.

Coherence of biological activities of Copper (II) soaps and benzothiazole and other N and S containing compounds stimulated our interest to extend the studies to their cumulative form as complexes. It is anticipated that it will generate new hopes in the pharmacological field.

Many nitrogen and sulphur containing compounds were synthesized and investigated for a wide range of pharmacological and biological activities. They have been used as tranquilizers anti-heliminthics, anti-inflammatory, neuroleptics, anti-histamines, sedatives, antipsychotics, anti-viral, fungicides. anaesthetics, bacteriocides, antimalarials etc. along with their activities.

One of the structural specificities considered responsible for such a wide spectrum of pharmacological activity in benzothiazole, is a fold along the nitrogen-sulphur axis. Structural resemblance applications have stimulated our interest to extend the synthetic and structural studies of benzothiazole complexes with a hope to obtain new compounds for therapeutic testing and better medicinal agents.

Recently work on poly-metallic complexes and transition metal complexes of heterocyclic ligands has been done; and their structure and biological characteristics have also been discussed. All these reference show that Copper soaps have a tendency for complex formation with compounds containing atoms like N, O, C1, S, Br etc..

Medved and Filliporic confirmed the formation of Copper butyro complex polarographically. Fisel explained the formation of complex in electro-chromatographic analysis of soaps in the presence of bases. Kaufman and Lissling prepared the solid green complex of one mole of Copper and four moles of oleic acid. Fisel described the formation of complexes of Copper di-stearate and di-palmitate with amines.

Various scientists synthesized the Copper (II) complexes with benzothiazole and its derivatives, which show moderate antimicrobial activity against gram positive bacteria and fungi. These complexes were found to possess fungicidal, herbicidal, anti-helminthic, insecticidal, pesticidal and nematicidal activity.

Experimental

All the chemicals used were of LR/AR grade. Solvent was purified according to standard procedures before use. Elemental analysis was done for soaps for their metal content following standard procedures.

Purification of Benzene

Benzene was dehydrated by storage over sodium wire for 2-3 days and by refluxing for about twenty hours, it was then distilled and redistillation was carried out azeotropically with ethanol (B.P. 80°C).

Extraction of Oils from Kernels

Neem and Karanj oils were extracted from their kernels respectively using petroleum ether and then purified. The fatty acid composition of these non-edible oils was confirmed through GLC of their methyl esters.

Synthesis of Soaps

Copper soap was prepared by refluxing the non-edible oils i.e. Neem (*Azadirectaindica*) and Karanj (*Pongamia pinnata*) oil (extracted from kernels and purified) with ethyl alcohol and 2N KOH solutions for 3-4 hours (DIRECT METATHESIS). The neutralization of excess of KOH present was done by slow addition of 0.5N HCl. Saturated solution of Copper Sulphate was then added to it, for conversion of neutralized potassium soap into their corresponding Copper soaps. Copper soap so obtained was then washed with warm water and 10% alcohol at 50°C and recrystallized using hot benzene.

Determination of Molecular Weights of Copper Soaps

Molecular weights of Copper soaps were determined from saponification value. The saponification equivalent or saponification value is a measure of the average length of the fatty acid that makes up a fat. The saponification equivalent (S.E.) is the amount of material saponified by one gram equivalent of potassium hydroxide, whilst the saponification value (S.V.) is the number of milligrams of KOH required to hydrolyze one gram of fat, indicating the number of ester groups in the fat; the two being related by the expression.

$$S.E. = \frac{56100}{S.V.}$$

Thus S.E. may be taken as average molecular weight of the oil. Value of S.E. is determined by experiment and from these values average molecular weights of Copper soaps are calculated. The copper soaps are abbreviated as follows:-

1. Copper – Neem soap (CN).
2. Copper – Pongamia soap (CP).

Spectral Studies

In order to study the structure of soaps, the Infra-red absorption spectra of compounds were obtained on a FTIR spectrophotometer, Shimadzu 821PC (4000-400 cm^{-1}) from sophisticated Analytical Instrument Facility, CDRI, Lucknow. Proton NMR spectra were also recorded at SAIF, CDRI, LUCKNOW on NMR spectrometers, Bruker DRX-300 at 300K using $C_6 D_6$ (deuterated benzene) as solvent for soaps.

Results and Discussion

IR Spectral Analysis[10]

(1) Copper (II) Neem Soap (CN)

The infrared spectral investigation of pure copper Neem soap (CN) shows absorption at 2925.6 cm^{-1} and 2855.1cm^{-1} corresponding to asymmetric and symmetric stretching of methylene ($-CH_2$) group with the overlapping of CH_3 (υ_{as} C-H) anti sym. at 2962 cm^{-1} and CH_3 (υ_s) sym. stretching at 2872 cm^{-1} respectively. The presence of absorption bands at 3020 cm^{-1} corresponds to olefinic =C-H stretch and the unconjungated C=C stretching peaks are very much distinguished at 1662.5 cm^{-1}. With these two medium bands at 3020 cm^{-1} and 1662.5 cm^{-1} a strong band occurring at 761.3 cm^{-1} confirms the cis nature of alkenes. This is the most characteristic vibrational mode of alkene and is the out of plane C-H bending vibration. These bands are usually strongest in the spectra of alkenes, and it is very clear in the spectra of Copper (II) Neem soap (CN). The absorption peak at 1416.5 cm^{-1} is representative of symmetric C-H deformation bands of = C-H group.

The absorption band near 1377 cm^{-1} arising from the symmetric bending of the methyl C-H bonds is very stable in position showing the methyl group in attached to another carbon atom and also the in-plane bending (δ_s) scissoring band of C-H of methylene group is very clear at 1462.5 cm^{-1}. It is veryclear that the C-H asymmetrical bending vibrations of methyl group (CH_3) generally overlaps the scissoring vibration of the methylene group therefore this peak may be taken for C-H asymmetrical bending vibration of $-CH_3$ group also.

The assigned to C-C stretching vibrations are weak and appear in the broad region of 1200-800 cm^{-1}.

The strong absorption band at 1592.8 cm^{-1} and 1217 cm^{-1} are due to carboxylate ion (COO^{-}), C-O anti-symmetric and symmetric stretching respectively. Also >C=O stretching is also observed at 1727.6 cm^{-1}. A small peak at 1340 cm^{-1} corresponding to $-CH_2$ twisting and wagging (According to Silverstein absorption of hydrocarbons due to methylene twisting and wagging vibration is observed in 1350-1150 cm^{-1}. These bands are generally appreciably weaker than those resulting from methylene scissoring. A series of bands in this region, arising from the methylene group is characteristic of the solid samples of long chain acids & esters as it is very clear from the Spectra of CN Soap) [10]. And also C-H rocking at 670.2 cm^{-1} has been observed. Copper–Oxygen (Cu-O) stretching bands have been distinguished at 480 cm^{-1}.

(II) Copper (II) Pongamia Soap (CP)

The absorption bands observed at 2927.6 cm^{-1} and 2855.7 cm^{-1} corresponds to asymmetric and symmetric stretching of methylene ($-CH_2$) group in the IR spectra investigation of Pure Copper Pongamia soap, with the overlapping of CH_3 anti symmetrical C-H (υ_{as}) at 2962 cm^{-1} and symmetrical C-H (υ_s) stretching at 2872 cm^{-1} respectively. The presence of absorption band at 3018.4 cm^{-1} corresponds to olefinic =C-H stretch and the unconjungated C=C stretching peaks are very much distinguished at 1655.8 cm^{-1} with these two medium bands at 3018.4 and 1655.8 cm^{-1} a strong band at 759.1 cm^{-1} confirms the cis-nature of alkenes. This out – of – plane C-H bending vibration of alkene is the most characteristic vibrational mode of alkene. As it is clear from the spectra of CP soap it usually is the strongest in the spectra of alkenes. The absorption peak at 1419.2cm^{-1} is representative of symmetric C-H deformation bands of =C-H group.

The absorption band near 1377.3 cm^{-1} is very stable in position arising from the symmetric bending of the methyl C-H showing that the methyl group is attached to another carbon atom. The in-plane bending (δ_s) scissoring band of C-H of methylene group is positioned at 1462.8 cm^{-1}. This peak may also be assigned to C-H asymmetrical bending vibration of methyl group as it generally overlaps the scissoring vibrations of methylene group.

The peaks 1609.3cm^{-1} and 1216.2cm^{-1} may be assigned to carboxylate ion COO^{-}, C–O anti-symmetric and symmetric stretching respectively. Also a very clear >C=O stretching is also observed at 1736 cm^{-1}. a small peak at 1345 cm^{-1}corresponds to CH_2 twisting and wagging and 669.2 cm^{-1} to C-H rocking. Copper – oxygen (Cu–O) stretching bands have been distinguished at 480 cm^{-1}.

NMR Spetcral Analysis

The ^{1}H NMR spectra of Cu (II) soaps of Neem and Pongamia were recorded in C_6D_6 as reference. They were examined to determine bonding and tautomerism present in the structure.

(I) Copper (II) Neem Soap (CN)

A perusal of the spectra of Copper (II) Neem Soap shows signal of aliphatic $-CH_3$ Proton attached to $-CH_2$-R group as a triplet at 0.904δ, 0.917δ & 0.999δ and CH_2 proton attached to CH_2-R group shows signal at δ1.277. The other signals observed are corresponding to $-CH_2$ attached to one C = C as a doublet 2.042δ & 2.091. Vinylic proton gave signal at δ5432. Proton on $-CH_2$ groups 'α' and 'β' carbon linked to $(-COO)_2Cu$ group. All the above peaks are due to the long chain fatty acid content (R) of the soap molecule $[(R\text{-}COO)_2\ Cu]$

(II) Copper (II) Pongamia Soap (CP)

The Copper (II) soap of Pongamia (CP) showed signal as a triplet at 0.918δ, 0.969δ 0.987δ and 1.290δ representing the aliphatic $-CH_3$ proton and CH_2 Proton attached to $-CH_2$-R group. While the peak at δ2.093 represents the proton of $-CH_2$ group attached to C=C group. Vinylic Proton gave signal at 5.474δ. The peaks at 2.233δ and 1.590δ corresponds to CH_2 proton on 'α' & 'β' carbon linked to $(-COO)_2Cu$ group. All the above peaks are due to the long chain fatty acid content (R) of the soap molecule $[(RCOO)_2Cu]$.

Synthesis of Complexes

Apart from synthesis of Neem & Karanj soaps, from application point of view (as benzothiazole and its derivatives/complexes are good antifungal agents) derivatives of these soaps i.e. their complexes of 2- amino-6-methyl-benzothiazole were synthesized specifically analysed against Candida species for their anti-fungal behaviour as a new approach and also against fungus like Alternaria alternata.

Preparation of Ligand

The synthesis of 2-amino-6-methyl-benzothiazole was synthesized using thiocyanation method as that had been reported in earlier works. 2-amino-6-methyl-benzothiazole was prepared by thiocyanation of para-substituted aryl amine, in the presence of thiocyanogen gas, which was generated in-situ by the reaction of cupric chloride and sodium thiocyanate. The purity of benzothiazole was checked by TLC in various non-aqueous solvent systems.

Synthesis of Complexes

The Purified Copper soap derived from non-edible oil i.e. Neem and Karanj were refluxed separately with ligand 2-amino-6-methyl-benzothiazole in 1:1 ratio. Ligand was dissolved in 2-3 ml of hot ethyl alcohol and Copper soaps were dissolved in 10-15 ml of Benzene separately and both solutions were added with stirring. The above reacting mixture was them refluxed for 3-4 hours with using water condenser. Further solid product so formed, was filtered hot, dried & recrystallized & purified. TLC using silica gel was used to check the purity of the complex. Their Molecular weights were determined as similarly as calculated for average molecular weight of soaps.

The complexes are abbreviated as follows:-

1. Copper – Neem benzothiazole complex (CNB).
2. Copper – Pongamia benzothiazole complex (CPB).

Results and Discussion

IR Spectral Studies of Complexes

(I) Copper Neem Benzothiazole Complex (CNB)

The absorption bands observed at 2926.2 cm^{-1} and 2856.4 cm^{-1} corresponds to asymmetric and symmetric stretching of methylene ($-CH_2$) group. The presence of absorption hands at 3020.1 cm^{-1} corresponds to olefinic =C-H stretch and the unconjungated C=C stretching peaks are very much distinguished at 1653.8cm^{-1} and with these two bands, a strong band occurring at 759.1cm^{-1} confirms the cis nature of alkenes being the strongest. The absorption band at 1416.9cm^{-1} is representative of symmetric C-H deformation of =C-H group.

The absorption band at 1374.1 cm^{-1} arising from the symmetric bending of the methyl C-H bond and 1468.3 cm^{-1} is in-plane bending (δ_s) scissoring band of C-H of CH_2 group.

The absorption bands at 1607.3 cm^{-1} and 1216.7 cm^{-1} are due to carboxylate ion (COO^-), C-O anti-symmetric and symmetric stretching respectively, also >C=0 stretching is observed at ~1725cm^{-1}. The C-H rocking of CH_2 group is observed at 670.2 cm^{-1} and Cu-O at 559.6 cm^{-1}. The increase in the stretch as compared to soap can be attributed to $NH_2 \rightarrow Cu$ complexation.

Apart from the absorption bands observed for pure Copper soap of Neem oil, the following bands were also observed corresponding to the ligand moiety.

The bands observed at 3399.4 cm^{-1} and 3331.4 cm^{-1} is attributed to N-H stretching i.e. ν_{as} NH and ν_s NH. The ν (C=N) stretch in the thiazole moiety in CNB complex show the stretch at 1532.1cm^{-1}.

The CN stretching (aryl tertiary) peaks are observed at 1308.2 cm^{-1}. The ϱ_r of NH_2 is also observed at 1100.6cm^{-1}.

The aromatic ring showing characteristics peaks between 3200-3000, at 1600 cm^{-1}, 1014.6 cm^{-1}, 928.1cm^{-1} and 815 cm^{-1} showing the features of =C–H stretching, C=C stretching, in-plane C–H bending, Out-of-plane C–H bending &ν(C–S–C) respectively.

(II) Copper Pongamia Benzothiazole Complex (CPB)

The perusal of the spectra absorption bands observed at 2926.7 cm^1 and 2855.1 cm^{-1} corresponding to asymmetric and symmetric stretching of methylene group. The presence of absorption bands at 3020 cm^{-1}corresponds to = C-H olefinic stretch and the unconjungated C=C stretching peaks are very much distinguished at 1661.5 cm^{-1} and with these a strong band at 759.5 cm^{-1} confirms the cis-nature of alkenes being the strongest. The absorption bands at

1375 cm^{-1} and 1466 cm^{-1} may be considered to be arising from the symmetric bending of C-H methyl and in–plane bending (δ_s) scissoring band of C-H methylene group respectively.

The absorption bands at ~1600 cm^{-1} and 1216 cm^{-1} are due to carboxylate ion (COO^-), C-O anti-symmetric and symmetric stretching respectively and main characteristic stretching of >C=0 at 1728 $cm^{-1}$is also observed, C-H rocking at 668.1, Cu-O at 574.9 cm^{-1} are seen.

Apart from the absorption bands observed for pure CP soap, the following bands were also observed corresponding to the ligand moiety.

The broad band observed at 3348.1 cm^{-1} is attributed to N-H stretching. The ν(C=N) stretch in the thiazoles moiety in CPB complex is seen at 1531.5 cm^{-1}. The CN aryl tertiary stretching peaks are observed at ~1310 cm^{-1} and ρ_r NH_2 at 1115.7 cm^{-1}.

The aromatic ligand rings features seen between 3200-3000 cm^{-1}, at 1626.6. 1031.4, 923.2 and 813.9 cm^{-1} corresponding to =C-H stretching, C=C stretch, in-plane C-H bending, out-of-plane C-H bending &ν(C-S-C) respectively.

Nmr Spectral Studies of Complexes

The ^1H NMR spectra of Cu (II) soaps of Neem and Pongamia were recorded in MeOD as reference.

(I) Copper Neem benzothiazole Complex (CNB)

A perusal of the spectra of Copper (II) Neem benzothiazole complex show an aliphatic $-CH_3$ proton attached to $-CH_2$-R group as a triplet 0.912δ, 0.897δ & 0.880δ and $-CH_2$ proton attached to $-CH_2$-R group at δ1.284.

The other signals observed are corresponding to $-CH_2$ attached to one C=C as a doublet 2.018δ & 2.096δ. Vinylic proton gave signal at 5.48δ and protons on CH_2, group 'α' & 'β' to $(-COO)_2Cu$ is showing peaks at 2.225δ and 1.49δ respectively. All the above peaks are due to the long chain fatly acid content(R) of the soap molecule $[(R\text{-}COO)_2Cu]$

The ligand moiety of the complex molecule is very much distinguished with the peaks of aromatic protons between 7.054δ and 8.166δ and Aromatic NH_2 protons between 3.413δ–3.466δ. The protons of methyl (CH_3) attached to aromatic ring is very clearly seen at 2.265δ.

(II) Copper Pongamia Benzothiazole Complex (CPB)

The NMR[10] spectra of CPB complex are also showing signals for both types of protons i.e. soap (fatty acid) and ligand moiety.

The triplet at 0.912δ, 0.987δ & 0.880δ refers to aliphatic -CH_3 proton attached to – CH_2-R group. The $-CH_2$ methyl proton attached to =CH_2-R at δ1.285.

The other signals observed are the doublet at 2.019δ & 2.029δ corresponding to$-CH_2$ attached to C=C. Vinylic proton showed signal at 5.338δ and the protons on $-CH_2$ group 'α' and 'β' to $(-COO)_2Cu$ are 2.122δ and 1.509δ respectively. All the above peaks are due to long chain fatty acid context (R) of the soap molecule.

Apart from the signals above the peaks between 7.059δ & 8.085δ are due the benzenoid protons (Aromatic). NH_2 protons (aromatic) is showing signal 3.344δ, 3.555δ & 3.596δ.

The signal of protons of the methyl group attached to aromatic ring is seen at δ2.267.

Fungicidal Analysis

Recently, the deeper understanding of the role of metal ion in bio-system had led to the awareness that metal complexing is useful in the treatment of bacteria, fungal and viral diseases. Most of the antimicrobial agents are obviously organic compounds, which behave as good-chelating agent. Their pathogenic activity is enhanced on complexing with various transition, inner transition and toxic metals.

The biological effect of their derivatives depends on the nature and structure of ligands and their metal complexes and also on the presence of particular element.

Many Coppercompounds are employed as pesticides either alone [as Cu (I) oxide and Cu (II) sulphate] or in mixture. Examples of the latter are the pesticide Cupronil which contains 35% Cu(II) Carbonate hydroxide, the fungicide Cuprozan containing 37.5% Cu(II) Chloride hydroxide and 15% Zineb (zinc ethylene–bis-dithiocarbamate), Bordeaux mixture a fungicide prepared by reacting Cu(II) sulphate with hydrated lime.

Nitrogenous ligands have been found to be effective against many metal enzymes, bacteria and number of fungi.

Large number of compounds containing nitrogen and sulphur atoms in the heterocyclic ring shows different types of activities. Some examples are given here possessing benzothiazole or similar structure containing nitrogen and sulphur atoms in the aromatic cyclic ring.

1. 8-methoxy-2-oxo-2H-Pyrimido [2,1-b] benzothiazole-3-carbonitrile: used as ulcer inhibitor.
2. 3-H-1, 2, 4-thiazole [3, 4-b] benzothiazole-3-one: used as a fungicide.
3. Thiazole derivatives: used as Pharmaceutical and agrochemical intermediates.
4. S-methylbenzo [1, 2, 3] thiadiazole-7-carbothioate derivative used against a range of fungal infections of crops.

Recently, Wood has developed metabolic antagonist theory of drug action and Fields led to the synthesis of several co-ordination compounds, which have been used for antibacterial and anti-tubercular activity.

Synthesized and evaluated biological activities of some new 2-arylamino-4-fluoroaryl thiazoles were found to possess fungicidal, herbicidal and anti-arthritic activities.

Berendset al synthesized and evaluated the biological activity of copper complexes with tridentate benzimidazolyl ligands. 2-alkoxy-4H-1, 3, 2-benzoxazaphosphorin-2-thiones (BOPS) were synthesized and their insecticidal activity against *Sodopteralitura* and *LaedelphaxStriatellus* was assessed by Yoshikawa et al.

Matevosyanet al and other studies the N- heterocyclic ligands and assessed their remarkable insecticidal activity. Number of heterocyclic derivatives proves to be very useful insecticides and used in crop protection.

Naim and Singh investigated the potential anti-helminthes activity of 2-acylamino-6-substituted benzothiazole. All the benzothiazole have been evaluated against *Ancylostomaceylanocum* in hamsters, *Hyrnenolepsis nana* in mice a *Litomosoidescarinii* in cotton rats.

Chaurasia at al studied anti-fungal activity of transition metal complexes of 6-methyl-2-amino benzothiazole. The CuL_2I_2, Cu L_4I_2, HgL_2I_2 and Hg L_4I_2 (where L = 2-amino-6-methyl benzothiazole) were screened for antifungal activity on *Aspergillus niger, Alternaria alternata, Curvulariaplunata* and *Penicilliumfumculorus* by employing Potato dextrose agar method at two dilutions (1:2143 & 1:5000). The results indicate that the activity of Cu (II) and Hg (II) complexes against *Alternaria alternata* is of very high order (100%) whereas that of *Aspergillus niger* is only 91 percent. Cu L_4I_2 Inhibits 100 percent and 85 percent of spore germination of *Penicilliumfumculorus, Culvulariaplunata* respectively

Thus on the basis of the foregoing studies, it becomes very clear that benzothiazole and their substituted derivatives have been found to be very active against variety of bacteria, fungi, herbs and insects.

Some medicated soaps have been prepared earlierwith the antifungal agent such as Clotrimazole, Bifonazole, Miconazole, Ketoconazole, Itraconazole, Econazole, Oxiconazole, Fluconazole, Sulconazole, Fenticonazole, Haloprogin, Nystatin, Tolnaftate, Griseofulvin, Amphotericin B etc..

It has also been established by several workers that chelation of the benzothiazole and there substituted derivatives enhances the biological and fungicidal activity.

The use of standard methodology for determination of antifungal activity of natural products against medical yeasts *candida* sp and *cryptococcus*sp. has been reported by many scientists earlier.

The N-donor ligand used during the present investigation is 2-amino-6-methyl benzothiazole, which has been very well reported to possess biocidal activity. Our continuing interest in the search for good fungicides and bactericides has led us to synthesize new complexes derived from Copper (II) Neem and Pongamia soaps with the above mentioned ligands and screen them for their fungicidal activities.

Sec. A: Antifungal Disk Diffusion Susceptibility Testing of Yeasts; approved Guideline (M 44-A, NCCLS, USA)

Experimental

The Method described here is intended for testing Candida Species and does not currently encompass any other genera and has not been used in studies of the yeast form of dimorphic fungi, such as *Blastomycesdermatiditis* or *Histoplasmacapsulatum*. Moreover testing of filamentous Fungi (i.e. moulds) is not addressed in current procedure.

Methodology for The Disk Diffusion Test

Reagents & Requirements

Media: Mueller – Hinton Agar No.2 + 2% Glucose + 0.5mg/ml Methylene Blue Dye (GMB) Medium: The agar medium had pH between 7.2 & 7.4 at room temperature after gelling. The sterilized media was poured in sterilized Petri-plates and after gel was set it was dried in an incubator with the lids ajar until moisture has evaporated (20-30 min). i.e. the surface of agar was kept moist but with no droplets on the agar surface or the Petri-dish cover and than kept for 24 hrs in other incubator at 37°C for sterility test.

Preparation of Mueller Hinton Agar (MHA)

1. MHA was prepared from a commercially available dehydrated MHA base according to the manufacturer's instruction.
2. 0.1gm of methylene blue dye was dissolved in 20ml of distilled water and warmed gently. 100 μl of this solution per litre of agar suspension was added. Then 20gms of glucose per liter of agar suspension was added and Autoclaved
3. Immediately after autoclaving, the agar solution was allowed to cool at 45 to 50°C in a water bath. Thereafter the freshly prepared and cooled medium was poured into flat bottomed glass Petri-plates on a horizontal leveled surface to give a uniform depth of approximately 4mm.
4. The agar medium was cooled to room temperature.
5. Plates were examined for sterility by incubating at 37°C for 24 hours.

Reference Strains for Quality Control: To Control the precision (repeatability) and accuracy (trueness) of the results obtained with disk diffusion test procedure, several quality control strains were obtained from a reliable source and were

1. *Candida albicans* ATCC 90028; 2. *Candida krusei* ATCC 6258

Strong Quality Control Strains

- The quality control strains were tested by the standard disk diffusion test procedure using the same materials and methods that are used to test clinical isolates.
- Quality control strains were stored in a way that minimizes the possibility of mutation in the organism.
- There are several methods for prolonged storage of reference strains. Yeasts were grown on slants of potato dextrose agar and then frozen at –70°C.
- Working quality control cultures were stored on sabouraud dextrose agar at 2 to 8°C and sub cultured each for three successive weeks.

A quality control strain can be used to monitor the precision (repeatability) and accuracy (trueness) of the disk test as long as there is no significant change in the mean zone diameter that cannot be attributed to a faulty methodology.

Dispensing Disk

1. Antimicrobial disks which were used as standard for quality control. a) Fluconazole b) Clotrimazole c) Amphotericin d) Ketoconazole
2. Prepared disks of the testing compounds.

To prepare the desks of testing compounds we required

1. Whattmann filter paper No. 2.
2. Sterile vials.

Firstly 6mm disks were punched and 100 disks per sterile vial plugged with cotton was kept in oven for sterilizing it. Number of vials was as many as per testing solutions of different conc. of solutions made. 0.5 ml of these solutions each is dispensed in sterile vials containing 100 disks, so as all the solution in absorbed by 100 disks.

Procedure

(A) Inoculation Preparation: Direct Colony Suspension Method

Steps for Preparation of the inoculum are as follows:-

(i) All organisms were sub-cultured onto sabouraud dextrose agar to ensure purity and viability. The incubation temperature throughout was between 38°C.

(ii) Inoculum was prepared by picking five distinct colonies of approximately 1 mm in diameter from a 24 hour old culture of Candida Species. Colonies were suspended in 5 ml of Sterile 0.145 mol/litre saline (8.5g/l NaCl 0.85% saline)

(iii) The resulting suspension was vortexed for 15 seconds and its turbidity was adjusted visually and also with a spectrophotometer by adding sufficient sterile saline or more colonies to adjust the transmittance to that produced by a 0.5 McFarland standard# at 625nm wavelength. This procedure will yield a yeast stock suspension of 1 X 10^6 to 1 X 10^5 cells per ml and produced semi-confluent growth with most Candida species isolates.

(Preparation of McFarland Nephlometry Standard (0.5)

To standardize the inoculum density for a susceptibility test, a BaSO4 suspension with turbidity equivalent to 0.5 McFarland standards or its optical equivalent was used as turbidity standard for inoculum.

Preparation

Required Reagents

(1) $BaCl_2.2H_2O$ 0.048M/lit or 1.175% (w/v)

(2) H_2SO_4 0.18M/Lit or % (v/V)

(3) Distilled water (DW) 200ml

Procedure

1. 100ml DW is taken in each two 250ml capacity sterile flasks.
2. In one flask, 1.175% $BaCl_2.2H_2O$ Solution is prepared.
3. From the other flask, 1ml of DW is discarded and 1ml pure H_2SO_4 is added to make a 1% (v/V) solution.
4. From the H_2SO_4 solution, 0.5ml is discarded and to the remaining 99.5ml, 0.5ml $BaCl_2.2H_2O$ solution is added drop by drop with a constant stirring
5. The solution thus prepared is now consisting of 0.5 standards of McFarland standards which is equivalent to 1.5×10^8 cells / ml.
6. The solution is distributed into 2-3 large (18 × 150mm) test tubes in approximately 4-6 ml amount
7. The transmittance of the solution at 625nm was between 0.08-0.1 and is standard.)

Inoculation of Test Plates

1. Optimally within 15 minutes after adjusting the turbidity of the inoculum suspension, a sterile cotton swab is dipped into the suspension. The swab was rotated several times and pressed firmly against and inside wall of the test tube above the fluid level. This removed excess fluid from the swab.
2. The dried surface of a sterile agar plate was inoculated by evenly streaking the swab over the entire agar surface. This procedure was repeated by streaking two more times rotating the place approximately

60° each time to ensure an even distribution of inoculum. As a final step, the rim of the agar was swabbed.

3. The lid was left ajar for 3-5 minutes, but no more than 15 minutes to allow for any excess surface moisture to be absorbed before applying the disks.

Application of Antifungal and Testing Disks to Inoculated Agar Plates

1. Antimicrobial disks and test disks were dispensed onto the surface of the inoculated agar plate. Each disk was pressed down to ensure its complete contact with the agar surface. The disks were placed individually and distributed evenly so that they are no closer than 24 mm from the center to center. Precaution was made that the disk should not move once it had come into contact with the agar surface as the drug/chemical diffuse almost instantaneously.
2. The plates were inverted and placed in an incubator set to 37°C (±2°C) with in 15 minutes after the disks were applied.

Results

Each plate was examined after 24 hours of incubation. The resulting inhibition zones were uniformly circular and as streaking was satisfactorily done there was a semiconfluient lawn of growth of the Candida species.

The plate was held a few inches above a dark non-luminated background illuminated with reflected light. The inhibition zone diameter was measured, the nearest whole millimeters at the point at which there is a prominent reduction in growth. This is highly subjective and experience results in greater accuracy (trueness) pinpoint micro colonies at the zone edge or local colonies within a zone are encountered frequently and should be ignored.

The compounds of concentration 0.5mg/disk marked on Petri plates are as under (Shown in Figures):

Neem oil: S_1

Pongamia oil: S_2

Copper Neem soap (CN): S_3

Copper Pongamia soap (CP): S_4

Copper Neem -2-amino-6-methyl benzothiazole complex (CNB): S_5

Copper Pongamia-2-amino-6-methyl benzothiazole complex (CPB): S_6

The results are expressed as diameter of inhibition zones of testing disks (Figure IB) and compared with the inhibition zone diameter of the standards antimicrobial agents (FigureIA) are given in Table 4.1.

Interpretation of Disk Diffusion Test Results

The strain is susceptible (s) which implies that an infection due to the strain may be appropriately treated with the dose of antimicrobial agent recommended for that type of infection and infecting species, unless otherwise contraindicated. The inhibition zones of test disks were compared with the inhibition zones of antimicrobial disks taken as standard.

When the concentrations of the agent / chemical cannot inhibit the strain than the stain in said to be Resistant (R).

Though the Neem and Pongamia oils and Copper soaps are good antifungal agents they show lesser activity than the Copper soap complexes of benzothiazole for *Candida species*, which suggests that these soap complexes of benzothiazole are more powerful antifungal agents. The presence of benzothiazole and other N, S etc. containing compounds are able to enhance the performance of copper soaps. The enhanced activity of complexes could possibly be explained on the basis of presence of donor atoms N and S as well as the structural compatibility with molecular nature of the toxic moiety.

The studies suggest that lower concentration (0.01mg/disk) and (0.1mg/disk) as well as higher concentrations (0.5mg/disk) of Neem oil, Pongamia oil, Copper (II) Neem soap and Copper (II) Pongamia soap do not show any inhibition zone i.e. the strains are resistant to them, at this concentration while Copper(II) Neem benzothiazole and Copper(II) Pongamia benzothiazole Complexes (Figure 4.2) at higher concentration showed inhibition zone resulting in the susceptibility of strains (*Candida albicans and Candida krusei).* It is suggestive that Candida species can be more susceptible with increase in concentration of Copper (II) Neem and Copper (II) Pongamia benzothiazole complexes. Their affectivity increases with their concentration. Thus it is evident that concentration plays a vital role in increasing the degree of inhibition. Fungicidal screening data revealed that at lower concentration the inhibition of growth is less as compared to the higher concentration of the complexes.And so the field is still open for further research.

The enhanced activity of newly synthesized complexes as compared to those of the ligand can possibly be explained on the basis of chelate formation, presence of donor atoms, basicity as well as the structural compatibility with molecular nature of the toxic moiety. Enhanced biological activity of complexes is in accordance with the chelation theory.

Suggesting that complexes are more effectively playing their role to check the growth of fungi (in the ternary system: complex + methanol + benzene these types of results have been reported earlier). Some recent studies about antimicrobial activities of newly synthesize 1, 4-benzothiazines possessing thiazolyl / imidazolyl moieties also support our studies.

Sec. B: Antifungal testing of *Alternaria alternata* suggested by Booth and Hawks worth

The general laboratory techniques followed in the course of this investigation are as suggested by Booth and Hawks worth.

1. **Sterilization of Glass-wares:** Glassware of Pyrex brand viz. test tubes, conical flasks, pipettes (micro and macro), glass rods and Petri-dishes were thoroughly washed after rinsing with chromic acid each time before sampling and were then sterilized in hot air oven at 160°C for 24 hours before use.

2. **Culture Media Used:** The culture media used for the growth of the organism of the present study was P.D.A. The following media were used in the present study.

Potatoes	—	200 gm
Dextrose	—	20 gm
Agar	—	200 gm
Distilled Water	—	1000 ml

200 gm of potatoes were cleaned, cut into pieces and boiled in about 1000ml of water of 2 hours. Then the contents were strained using muslin cloth. To this extract 20gm of dextrose, 20gm of agar were added in the flask, before sterilizing the medium.

3. **Preparation of Sample solutions:** The calculated amount of the testing material {Neem and Karanj oil (extracted from Kernels) & Copper (II) Neem soap and Copper (II) Karanj soap and their complexes} were weighed in a standard flask and the solutions of different concentration in benzene of varying composition were prepared.

4. **Test Organism:** The test organism used in the study i.e. *Alternaria alternata* was also isolated from its natural habitat, purified, characterized & identified. **Serial dilution method** was used.

5. **Fungicidal Testing:** Firstly 2mL of the fungal broth was poured in sterilized Petri-plates and than the sterilized P.D.A. media was poured and after the gel was set, it was dried with the lids ajar until moisture has evaporated i.e. the surface of agar was kept moist but with no droplets.Into these plates 5 ml of the diluted testing solution was aseptically transferred by rotating the Petri-plates in clockwise and anti clock wise direction 3-4 times and was allowed incubate at 25 + 1°C for 24 and 48 hours. After the period of incubation the plates were observed for the growth of fungus in different concentration of the testing solution used in the present study. The data were statistically analysed according to the following formula.

$$\%\ \text{inhibition} = (C - T)/C * 100$$

C = number of fungal colonies in control plate.

T = number of fungal colonies, in test plate.

Results and Discussion

Each plate was examined after 24 and 48 hours of incubation. The number of fungal colonies were counted using colony counter. The % inhibition was calculated according to the given formula above.

Complexes are better antifungal agents than soaps and Neem complex is more effective than Pongamia complex. (Figure II)

The enhanced activity of synthesized complexes as compared to those of the soap can be seen and possibly be explained on the basis of chelate formation, presence of donor atoms, basicity as well as the structural compatibility with molecular nature of the toxic moiety. Enhanced biological activity of complexes is in accordance with the chelation theory.

It is evident from the results that concentration plays a vital role in increasing the degree of inhibition. Fungicidal screening data revealed that at lower concentration the inhibition of growth is less as compared to the higher concentration of the complexes.And so the field is still open for further research and analysis can be made for longer period of incubation and the work can be extended. Earlier workers suggested that complexes are more effectively playing their role to check the growth of fungi.

Table 4.1: Antifungal Effect of Copper (II) Neem and Pongamia Soaps and their Complexes *Candida Albicans* and *Candida Krusei* (Expressed as Inhibition Zone in mm)

Disks (6mm)	Candida albicans (in mm)	Candida krusei (in mm)
Fluconazole	24	23
Amphotericin	42	33
Clotrimazole	26	15
Ketoconazole	36	35
0.01mg/disk, 0.1mg/disk and 0.5mg/disk of Copper Neem and Pongamia soap	N.Z	N.Z
0.01mg/disk of Copper Neem benzothiazole complex / Copper Pongamia benzothiazole complex	N.Z./N.Z.	N.Z./N.Z.
0.1mg/disk of Copper Neem benzothiazole complex / Copper Pongamia benzothiazole complex	8/N.Z.	8/N.Z.
0.5mg/disk of Copper Neem benzothiazole complex / Copper Pongamia benzothiazole complex	11/7	10/8

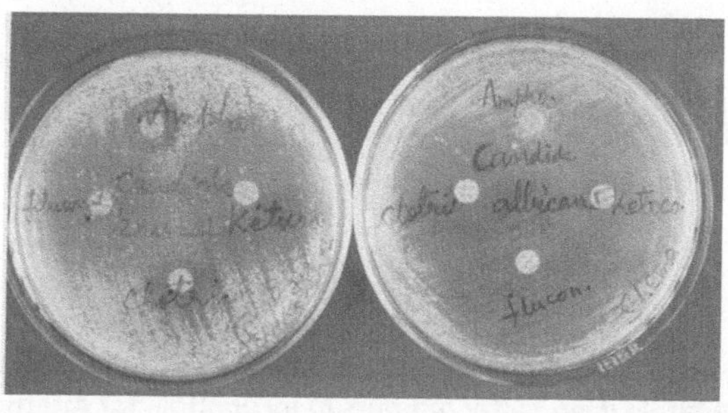

Fig. 4.1A: Inhibition Zones of Antimicrobial Discs for *Candida krusei (A) and Candida albicans (B)*

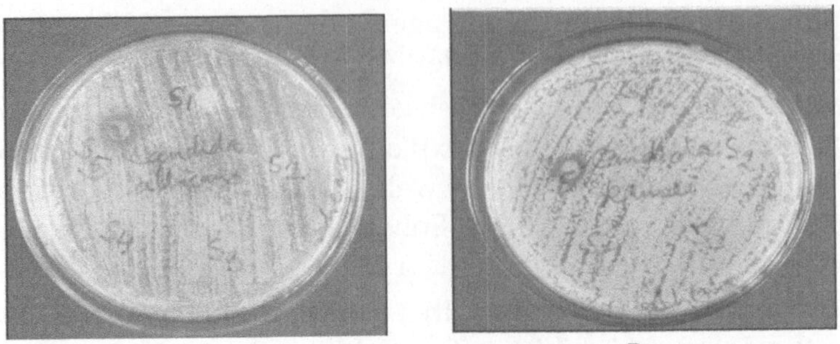

A B

Fig. 4.1B: Inhibition Zones of Copper–Neem–Benzothiazole-Complex (0.5mg/disk) for *Candida albicans (B) and Candida krusei (A)*

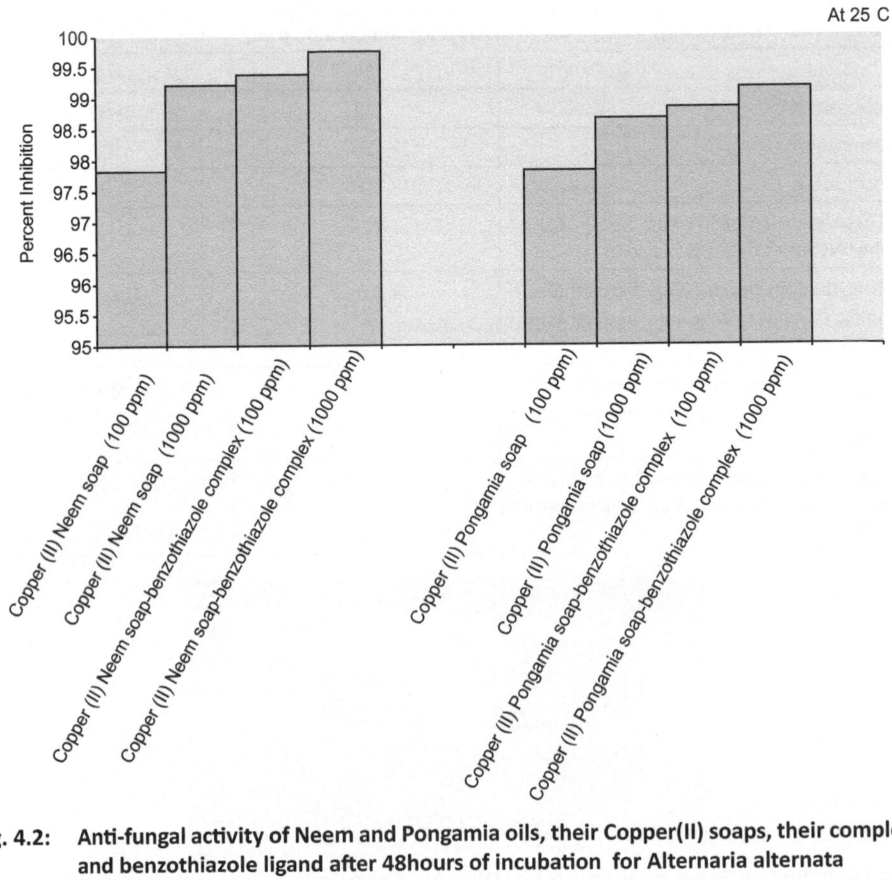

Fig. 4.2: Anti-fungal activity of Neem and Pongamia oils, their Copper(II) soaps, their complexes and benzothiazole ligand after 48hours of incubation for Alternaria alternata

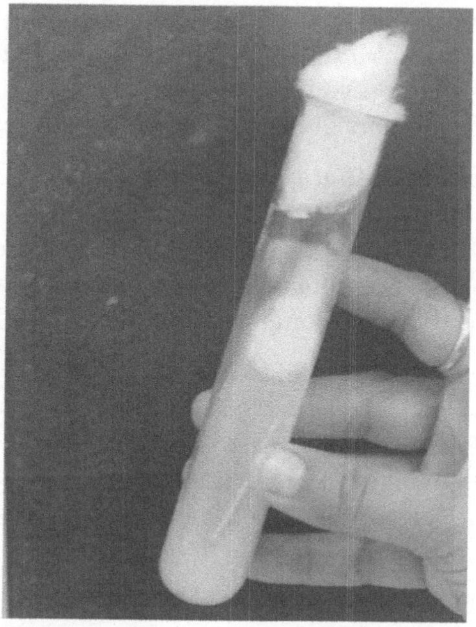

Fig. 4.3: Culture of test organism *"Alternaria alternata"*

Conclusion

Surface-active agents or surfactants are of great practical importance in our daily life, on account of their interesting behaviour at surfaces and interfaces. They not only accumulate at the surface, but also change the properties of surfaces.Synthesis of Copper (II) soaps and their Complexes derived from various non-edible oils will provide fundamental information regarding their colloido-chemical behaviour and fungicidal activities.Different methods were applied on Neem and Karanj oils; their Copper (II) soaps and also their Copper (II) soaps benzothiazole complexes to study their comparative fungicidal study. To find the biological activity different methods were used

Sec. A: Antifungal Disk Diffusion Susceptibility Testing of Yeasts; approved Guideline (M 44-A, NCCLS, USA)

The testing was done on two species of Candida i.e. *C.albicans* and *C.krusei.* Antimicrobial disks used were Fluconazole, Amphotericin, Clotrimazole and Ketoconazole. These antimicrobial disks were used as standard, as the strains of *Candida albicans* and *Candida krusei* are susceptible to them. The diameter of zones of testing disks was compared with the zone diameter of these standards antimicrobial agents.The studies suggest that lower concentration (0.01 mg/disk) and (0.1 mg/disk) as well as higher concentrations (0.5 mg/disk) of Neem oil, Pongamia oil, Copper (II) Neem soap and Copper (II) Pongamia soap do not show any zone i.e. the strains are resistant to them at this concentration while Copper (II) Neem benzothiazole and Copper (II) Pongamia benzothiazole complexes at higher concentration showed zone resulting in the susceptibility of strains (*Candida albicans and Candida krusei).* It is suggestive that Candida species can be more susceptible with increase in concentration of Copper (II) Neem and Copper (II) Pongamia benzothiazole complexes.

Sec. B: Antifungal testing of *Alternaria alternata* suggested by Booth and Hawks worth

Serial dilution method was used, using PDA as culture media. The result suggests that complexes are better antifungal agents than soaps and Neem complex is more effective than Pongamia complex.

REFERENCES

Tyagi P.D. : *Non conventional vegetable oils* (1991).

Srivastava, Ram Prakash : *Neem and Pest Management,* (2001).

AzamM.Mohibbe, WarisAmtul, NaharN.M. : *Biomass and Bioenergy* 29, (2005), 293-302.

Karmee S.K. and Chadha, Anju : *Bioresource Technology* 96(13), (2005), 1425-1429.

Rashid Mumtaj and Khan, M.A. : *Environment and Ecology, 24S (Special-2),* (2006), 243-248.

Jain, K.L., Jain H.K., Shekhawat K.S. : *Journal of Applied-Zoological –Researches,* 16(2), (2005), 192-194.

Kumar G.V.S., Sannaveerappanavar V.T. : *Mysore-Journal of Agriculture Science* 38(3),(2004), 302-305.

Biswas N.P., Biswas A.K. : *Journal of Interacademicia* 9(3),(2005),448-450.

Gunstone F.D. : *"An Introduction to the Chemistry of Fats and Fatty Acids". Chapmann and Hall Ltd., London* (1950).

Playfair L. : *Ann.*, 37, (1841), 152.

Fremy E. : *Ann.*, 36, (1840), 44.

Voelcker A. : *Ann.*, 64, (1848), 342.

Noller C.R. : *J Am. Chem. Soc.* 56, (1934), 156.

Sacc : *Ann.* 51, (1844), 213.

Hilditch T.P. : *J.Soc. Chem. Ind.* 58, (1934), 233.

Raphael R.A. : *Nature* 165, (1950), 235.

Shinowara G.Y. : *J. Biol. Chem.* 134, (1940), 331

Arens C.L. et al : *Biochem. J.* 37, (1943), I.

Jurij J., Hostynek H. and Oward I. : *Maibach Taylor & Fromics*5, (2006), 16.

Czeslawk and Kajdas : *Elsevier Ltd. Rolavel* 3, (2006), 38.

Ratomahenina A., Galzy P., Graitte J. and Pina M. : *Riv. ItalSostanze Grasse (Eng)*60(11), (1985), 673.

Singh, Verma S.B. Jordan J. Sossna R. : *Ger.Offen. D.E.* 3,703,258CI.4 Feb (1987) C.A. 110, 10119z, Jan (1989).

Atkins W.R.G. : *"The Preservation of Fishing Nets by Treatment with Copper soaps & Other Substances"*. Part 3,1936, 627 to 641.

Mukherji P. and Meysels K.J. : *Natl. Stand. Ref. Data. Ser. (U.S. Natl. Bur. Stand)* No. 36, (1971).

Moroi Y. : *"Micelles: Theoretical and Applied Aspects" Springer* (2005).

Rakshit, Amimesh Kumar : *J. Indian Chem. Soc.* 85, (2008), 1289-1300.

Adamson A.W. and Gast A.P., AndShaw D.J. : *Physical Chemistry of Surfaces* 6th*Edn. Willey New York,* 1997, &*Introduction to Colloid & Interface Chemistry* 2nd*Edn. Butterworths, London* 1978.

Rafalski L. and Zawadzki J. : *Pol. P L* 144,2 Aug (1985), 961 C.A. 112, Mar-Aug (1990), 1211535.

Crop K. : *KokaiTokkyoKohoJp*.59,18 Apr(1983) 193,129,C.A. 102, (1985), 168691z.

Filov V.A., Bandman A.L. and lvin B.A. : *"Harmful Chemical Substances"EillsHorwoodLmtd, Eng*.1,(1988), 66.

Reed P.D. : *J. Am. Perfumer Aromat*.76(3), (1961), 49-50.

Koeing A.E. : *J. Am. Chem. Soc*.36, (1914), 951.

Levy J. : *Fatty Acids: Their Ind. Appl*.(1968), 200-20.

Mc Bain J.W. : *Trans Faraday Soc.* 9, (1913), 99.

Hartle G.S. : *Aqueous Solutions of Paraffin Chain salts, Hermann, Paris,* (1936).

Mc Bain J.W. : *Colloid Chemistry, Theoretical and Applied (J. Alexander ed.)Reinhold New York* (1944).

Mattoon R.H. Stearns R.S. and Harpins W.D. : *J. Phys. Chem.* 15, (1947), 209.

Debye P. and Anacker E.W. : *J. Phys.Colloid Chem.* 5, (1951), 644.

Preston W.C. : *J.Phys. Chem.* 52, (1948), 84.

Kreschek G.C. : *Water: A Comprehensive Treatise, Aqueous solutions of Amphiphiles and Macromolecules (F. Franks, ed), Plenum Press, New York,*. 4, (1975), 96-98.

Shinoda K. : *Colloidal Surfactants, Chapter I Academic Press, New York* ,(1963).

Corrin M.L. : *J. Colloid Sci.* 3, (1948), 333.

Williams R.J., Phillips J.N. and Mysels K.J. : *Trans Faraday Soc.* 51, (1955), 728.

Kolthaff I.M. and Strieks W. : *J. Phys Colloid Chem.,* 52, (1948), 915-41 & 53, (1949) 424.

Demchenko P.A. : *DopovidiAkad. Nauk, UkrainUSSR*,(1959), 496-6, *Masloboino-Zhirovaya Prom.* 25(10), (1959), 22, *Ibid* 28(2) (1962), 23, *Kolloid-Zhur* 23(1961), 36-9, *Ukrain. KhimZhur* 23 (1962), 46-8, 203-5, *KolloidZh.* 24(1), (1962), 11-14, *J.Phys. Chem.* 36(1932), 1401-18, 1672-84, 2455-73.

Mehrotra K.N., Mehta V.P. and Nagar T.N. : *J. Prakt. Chem.Bd.* (1970), 312

Mehrotra K.N. Jain and M. : *Indian J. Chem.* 31(A), (1992) 452-6.

Malik W.U. and Ahemad S.I. : *J. Polarog. Soc.* 12(2), (1966), 50-58.

Malik W.U. and Haque R : *J. Analyt. Chem.* 189 ,(1962),179.

Popov A., Yanishlieva N. and Iuanova B. : *Maslo-Sapuena Prom. Byal*6(4), (1967), 13-19.

Mehrotra K.N., Mehta V.P. and Nagar T.N. : *J. Fur.Prakt. Chemic*.Bd. 313, Heft 4, (1971), 607-13.

Malik W.U. and Haque R. : *J. Am. Oil Chemists Soc.* 41(6), (1964), 168.

Malik W.U. and Ahemad S.I. : *Indian J. Chem.* 2(4), (1964), 168.

Ayers W.C. : *Analyt. Chem. Acta.* 15 (1956), 77-83

Yoklshi H. and Yogi S. : *Bunseki Kagaku,* 17(1),(1968),17-7.

Hattiandi G.S., Vold M.I. and Vold R.D. : *Ind.Eng. Chem.* 41, (1949), 2320-4.

Guha B.C. : *Proc. Roy. Soc. A*206, (1951), 353.

Foex G. and Karantases J. : *Compt. Rend.* 237, (1953), 982.

Figgis B.N. and Martin R.L. : *J. Indian Chem. Soc.* 35, (1956), 37.

Herron R.C. and Pink R.C. : *J. Indian Chem. Soc.* 52, (1956), 3938.

Gilmour A. and Pink R.C. : *J. Indian Chem. Soc.* (1953), 2198.

SatakeI. and Matuura R. : *Mem. Fac. Sci. Kyushu Univ. Ser.*C_5, (1962), 13-20.

Kishita M., Inoue M. and Kubo M. : **Nippon Kagaku Kaishi**84, (1963), 758.

Martin R.L. and Waterman H. : *J. Indian Chem. Soc.* (1957), 2545-51.

Mehrotra R.C. and Raj A.K. : *J. Inorg. Nucl. Chem.* 21 (¾), (1961), 311.

Kokot R. and Martin R.L. : *Inorg. Chem.* 3(9), (1964), 1306.

Martin R. and Whitelay A. : *J. Indian Chem. Soc.* (1952), 1394.

Banarjee B.C. and Palit S.R. : *J. Indian Chem. Soc.* 27, (1950), 385.

Fisel S. : *ZhurNeorgKhim* 5, (1955), 1090.

Kaufman H.P. and Lissling : *FetteU.Seiler* 55, (1953) 90-95.

Fisel S : *Acad, rep Popular Romaine FilialolajiStudicCareetaxistiint* 7(2), (1956), 13-17.

Mehta V.P. Talesara P.R. and Sharma R : *Indian J. Chem.* 39A, (2001), 383.

Mehta V.P. Telesara P.R. and Sharma R : *Indian J. Chem.* 40A, (2001), 399.

Sherwani M.R.K., Sharma R., Gangawal A. and Bhutra R. : *Indian J. Chem.* 42A, (2003), 2527.

Schulman J.H. and Riley D.P. : *J. Colloid Sci.* 3, (1948), 383.

Anacker E.W. : *J. Collid Sci.* 8, (1953), 402.

Mc Bain J.W. and Johnson K.E. : *J. Am Chem. Soc.* 66, (1944), 9.

Shinoda K. : *Bull. Chem. Soc. Jpn.* 26, (1953), 101.

Ooshika v. : *J. Colloid Sci.* 9, (1954), 254.

Mc. Bain J.W. : *"Frontiers in Colloid Chemistry" Vol. VIII, Inter science Publishers Inc.* (1950).

Mc. Bain J.W. and Huff H.M. : *J. Colloid Sci.* 4, (1949), 383.

Mc Bain J.W. and Mc Hon H. : *J. Am. Chem. Soc.*70, (1948), 3838.

Kolthoff I.M. and Stricks W. : *J. Physc. Colloid Chem.* 52, (1948), 915 & 53, (1949), 424.

Matuura R. : *Nippon Kagaku Kaishi*82, (1961), 1624.

Barclay G.A. and Kennard C.H.L. : *J. Indian Chem. Soc.*(1961), 3289.

Yoko Kurodo : *Nippon Kagaku Zasshi*86, (1965), 560.

Grant R.F. : *Can. J. Chem.* 42(4), (1964), 951.

Mehta V.P.., Hasan M. Mathur S.P. and Rai G.L. : *Tenside Surf. Det.* 16, (1979), 2.

Manhas B.S., Kalia S.B. and Sardana A.K. : *J. Indian Chem. Soc.*83, (2006), 652.

Reddy R.K., Reddy K.M. and Mahendra K.N. : *Indian J. Chem.* 45A, (2006), 377.

Lal R.A., Basumalary D., Chakraborty J., Bhumik S. and Kumar A. : *Indian J. Chem.*45A, (2006), 619.

Patel R.N., Singh N. and Gundla Y.L.N. : *Indian J. Chem.*45A, (2006), 614.

Mijanuddin M., Gangopadhyay S., Mondal S., Mukherji M. and Ali M. : *Indian J. Chem.*45A, (2006), 858.

Ali A., Salunke S. Gawali, Rao P. and Linares J. : *Indian J. Chem.*45A, (2006), 853.

ErdenI., Demirhan N. and AvciataU. : *Indian J. Chem.*45A, (2006), 1395.

Sharma V.K. and Shrivastava S. : *Indian J. Chem.*45A, (2006), 1368.

Souza A.G., Santos J.C.O., Conceicao M.M., Dantas Silva M.C. and Prasad S. : *Brazilian J. Chem. Engg.*21(2), (2004), 265.

Souza A.G., Conceicao M.M. and Macedo R.O. : *An. Assoc. Bras. Quim* 47, (1998), 361.

Santos J.C.O. Santos A.V. Souza A.G., Prasad S. and Santos I.M.G. : *J. Food. Science* 67(4), (2002), 1393.

Santos J.C.O., Santos A.V. and Souza A.G. : *Europ J. Pharm Sci.* 13 (Supp.1) (2001), 523.

Santos J.C.O., Santos M.G. Conceicao M.M. et al : *J. Thermal Anal. Colorimetry*75(2), (2004), 419.

Rasheed A. and Bhobe R.A. : *J. Indian Chem. Soc.* 53, (1976), 442.

Adeoson S.O. : *J. Therm. Anal.* 14(3), (1978), 235.

Kambe H. Ozania T. Onoue M. and Igarashi S. : *Bull. Chem. Soc. Jpn.* 35, (1962), 81.

Mehrotra K.N., Saroha S.P.S. and Kachhwaha R. : *Tenside Surf. Det.* 18(1), (1981), 28.

Mehta V.P., Heda L.C. and Gupta R : *Asian J. Chem.* 4(4), (1992), 791.

Kishita M., Inoue M. and Kubo M. : *Nippon Kagaku Zassshi*84, (1963), 758.

Potts M.F. and Hadson P.H. : *U.S.*, 2, (1956), 159,767.

Imperial Chemical Industries Ltd. : *Brit.* 1, 033, (Cl. C08g), (1966) 999.

Marsh B.P. : *Ind.Eng. Chem.* 36, (1944), 176-81.

Samsonova O.A. : *TekStil. Prom* (1/2), (1943), 15-18.

Singh H., SrivasatavaU.K., Shukla S.N. and Upadhayaya M.K. : *Indian J. Chem.* 31(A), (1992), 472-474.

Varkonyi B. and Sz'ell T. : **ActaUniv.SzagadiensisActa Phys. et. Chem.**, 5, (1959), 73.

DurenFabrikChemisch B.H : *Ger.* 1, 062, (1959), 664.

Zahradniuk J., Schmidt L. and Havranek A. : *ListyCukrov*83(9), [Czech] (1967), 193-7.

Leyland B.N. and Standford R.L. : **Trans. inst. Rubber Ind.** 35, (1959), 25-44.

Gebhardt H.L. : *Foundray* 74, (1946), 110-12, 198, 200, 202, 204, 206.

Pedersen L.H. : *Acta. Chem. Scand.* 4,(1950), 487-507.

Bartleson D.J. and Hughes C.E. : *U.S.* 2, (1951) 542, 560.

Yokouldev V.M., Pershina N.Y., Bekrenev A.N. and Masalkina C.N. : *Polytechnic Ins. SamaraU.S.S.R.* Su 1, [CICIoMI 73/00], (1992) 715-835, Appl. 4, 084, 08 Jan. (1990), 747.

Mattiello J.J. : *Protective and Decorative Coatings*, Wiley, New York, Vol. 1 ,(1941).

ESSO Research and Engg. Co. : *Fr.*I 381, (CI.C. 109), (1964), 305,381.

Reddy K.H., Reddy P.S. and Bahu P.R. : *Transition Met. Chem.* 25, (2000), 154.

Kriza A., Spinu C. and Plemiceanu M. : *J. Indian Chem. Soc.* 76, (2000), 82.

Malik A.K., Kaul K.N., Lark B.S., and Rao A.L.J. : *Bibliographic Citation, Pesticide - Science India* 53:1, (1998), 104-106.

Agnihotri N.K., Singh V.K. and Singh H.B. : *Bibliographic Citation, Talanta- OxfordIndia*45:2, (1998), 331-34.

Goff M.D., Sumack R.L., Tilt K.M. and Hagan A.K. : *Bibliographic Citation, J.ofArboriculture, U.S.A.* 22:5, (1996), 201-205.

Buick T.A., Stall W.M., Kostewicz S.R. and Smith K. : *Bibliographic Citation, Hort Science, U.S.A.*25:11, (1990), 1407-1408.

Demes H., Gaudchau M and Burow R.F. : *Bibliographic Citation, Pesticide - Science Germany*38:2-3, (1993), 278-280.

Soyez J.L. : *Brighton Crop Protection Conference Pests and Diseases. France* Vol. 1, (1992), 451-456.

Sarricolea M.L., Villa-ElizagaI. and Lopez J. : *Bibliographic Citation, Biology of the Neonate, Spain*63:1, (1993), 14-25.

Villa – ElizagaI., Sarricolea M.L. and Lopej Z. : *Bibliographic Citation, 8th International Symposium on Trace Elements in man and animals, Spaim.* 23, (1993), 558-561.

Blenis P.V., Nadeav L.B. Knowles N.R. and Logue G. : *Bibliographic Citation, Hort Science* 32(6), (1997), 1077-1084.

MezzinaElisabetta, FrennaVincenza and Chimchi Stefano : *Magn. Reson. Chem.* 34(12), (1996), 1019-1024.

Salman Salman R. : *Spectrosc. Lett.* 29(8), (1996), 1573-1577.

StetinovaJarmila and Krublora Marcela : *Khim. Geterotsikl. Soedin.*C (0), (1995), 1402-4.

Kutty N., Go-Palari and Bhatt A.R. : *J. Inst. Chem. (India)* 67(1), (1995), 22-3.

AotsukaTomoji, Abe Naoki and Ashizawa Naoki : *[Grelan Pharmaceutical Co. Ltd. Japan] Eur. Pat.* Appl. EP 714 893 (CI. C07D277/64) (1966) Jp Appl. 94/317, 809,(1994), 41.

Tanabe Yoo, Yoshida Yoshihiro and Okumura Hitorni. : *Heterocycl. Jp*,45(8), (1997), 1579-88.

CustelceanuRadu, Silberg I.A. and FarcasSorin I. : *Heterocycl. Commun, Rom*3(4), (1997), 317-22.

Malik A.K., Kaul K.N., Lark B.S. and Rao A.L.J. : *Bibliographic Citation, Pesticide- Science, India,* 53:1, (1998), 104-106.

Kumar N. and Kachroo Kant P.L. : *J. Indian Chem Soc.* VII, 98, (1980), 1.

Mukherjee G.N. and Das A. : *J. Indian Chem Soc.* 78, (2001), 78.

Singh N. Sangwan N.K. and Dhindsu K.S. : *PestManag. Sci.* 56, (2000), 284.

Mehrotra K.N. Mehta V.P. and Nagar T.N. : *Cellulose Chem. Technol* 1, (1973), 38.

Ojha K.G., Jaisinghani N. and Tahiliani H. : *J. Indian Chem. Soc.* 79, (2002), 191.

Gupta A., Sharma R. and Prakash L. : *J. Indian Chem. Soc.* 74, (1994), 635.

Gupta R.R. : *"Phenothiazines and 1, 4-benzothianizes: Chemical and Biomedical Aspects", Elsevier, Amsterdam* (1988).

Valli G., Sivakolunthu S. Muthusubramanian S, and Sivasubramanian S. : *J. Indian Chem. Soc.*77, (2002), 252.

Kulkarni K.G. and Fingerman M. : *Gen. Pharmacol.* 17(6), (1986), 671.

Vishwavidhyalaya, GourHar Singh and ChaurasiaSunitaShrivastavaSavitri : *Indian Drugs* 28, (1991), 474-6 .*Chem, Abst* 116, (1992), 15347f.

Sawhney S.S., Phindsa S.S. and Vir D. : *J. Indian Chem. Soc.*65(9), (1988), 643.

Burch E.A. and Ayd. F.J. : *J. Clin. Psychiatry* 44, (1983), 242.*Chem. Abst.* 99, (1983), 133118.

Koland F.P. : *IRCS Med. Sci. Libr. Compound* 9(6), (1981), 546 *Chem. Abst.* 95,(1981), 9085.

Marvini F.P. : *Mech. Ageing Dev.* 36(3), (1986), 295.

Shukla I.C. : *J. Inst. Chem. (India)* 62(4), (1990), 159-60.*Chem. Abst.* 114, (1991), 1503075.

Raknew N. : *Farmatsi (Sofia)*, 37(3), (1987) ,10.

Vorontsov Y.V., Lerner I.M. and Shchelkunov E.L. : *Farmacol. Toksikol.*, 43(1) (1980) 81 *Chem. Abst.* 92, (1980), 157547.

Schacht E., Vandorpe J., Dejardin S., Lemmouchi Y. and Seymour L. : *Biotechnology and Bioengineering* 52, (1996), 102.

Schacht E. Dejardi S. and Lemmouchi Y. : *Bioactive and Compatible Polymers* 13, (1998), 4.

Morgan R.J. Eaddy L.B., Solie T.N. and Turbes C.C. : *Lab. Anim.* 15, (1981), 281. *ChemAbst* 95, (1981), 214987.

Dave A.M., Bhatt K.N., Vandania N.K. and Trivedi P.B. : *J. Indian Chem. Soc.*, 65(5), (1988), 365.

Pinto A.C. Dasilva R.S. and Hollins R.A. : *J. Heterocycl. Chem.*, 16(5), (1979), 1085 *Chem. Abst.* 92, (1980), 58705.

Thirumalaikumar M., Sivakolunthu S., Punuswamy A and Sivasubramanian S. : *Indian J. Chem.* 58A, (1999), 720.

Sastry C., Reddy V., Ram B. Jogibhukta M., Krishnan V.S.H. Singh A.N., Reddy J.G., Chaturvedi S.C., Rao S.P. and Shridher D.R. : *Indian J. Chem.* 28B, (1989), 52.

Jogibhukta M., Krishnan V.S.H., Singh A.N., Rao K.S., Sridher D.R .Rastogi K. and Jain M.L. : *Indian IN* 158, (1987) 841*ChemAbst*. 107, (1978), 154344.

Gupta R.R. Kumar R. and Gautam R.K. : *J. Fluor. Chem.* 28(4) (1985) 381, C.A. : 105 (1986) 6467r

Mitsuaki T. and Masanori W. : *KokaiTokkyoKohoJpn.* 02, (1988), 7, 101,068 C.A. 113, (1990), 73019.

Ishige S., Usni H. and Sacki K. : *Geroffen* 2, (1977), 704,724,C.A.: 87, (1977), 144134.

Fengler G., Arlt D., Grohe K., Zeiler H.J. and Metzger K. : *Ger.Offen* 3, (1984), 125, 229,C.A.: 101, (1984), 7176.

Filacchioni G., Nacci V. and Stegfancich G. : *Farmaco. Ed Sci.*, 31(7), (1976)478, C.A.: 85, (1976), 143048.

Mahapatra B.B. and Ray Puspa : *J. Indian Chem. Soc.* 79, (2002), 536.

Patel R.N., Kumar and Pandeya K.B. : *Indian Chem. Soc.* 39A, (2001), 1124.

Kriza A., Reiss A. Blejoice S. Brujan L. and Stanica N. : *J. Indian Chem. Soc.* 77, (2000), 488 & 76, (1999), 406.

Mahapatra B.B. and Mishra R.R. : *J. Indian Chem. Soc.* 78, (2001), 395.

Patel R.N., Patel A.P. and Pandeya K.B. : *J. Indian Chem. Soc.* 76, (1999), 362.

Man P.S. Shirodhar S.G. and Chondhekar T.K. : *J. Indian Chem. Soc.* 79,(2002), 376.

Mishra V. : *J. Indian Chem. Soc.* 79, (2002), 374.

BhaveN.S., Bahad P.J., Sorrparote P.M. and Aswar A.S. : *J. Indian Chem. Soc.* 79, (2002), 342.

Kaur M.P. Kanungo B.K. and Sandhu J.S. : *J. Indian Chem. Soc.* 79, (2002), 46.

Medved A. and Filliporic I. : *Croat. Chem. Acta* 35, (1963), 51-9.

Fisel S. : *Zhur. Neorg. Khim.* 5, (1955), 1090.

Kaufman H.P. and Lissling : *FetteU.Seifen* 55, (1953), 90-5.

Fisel S. : *Acad. Rep. Popular Romaine FilialalajiStudicCareetaxiStiint* 7(2), (1956), 13-17 & 6(3/4),(1955), 295-326.

Chandra Sulekh and SharmaS.D. : *J. Indian Chem. Soc.* 79, (2002), 495.

Hussain Reddy K. and Radhakrishnan Reddy M. : *J. Indian Chem. Soc.* 79, (2002), 219.

Kumar Devendra and Sharma R.C. : *J. Indian Chem. Soc.* 79, (2002), 284.

Singh Bihari, Singh G.P., Kumar Madanjeet, Kumar Brajesh and KumariPriya : *J. Indian Chem. Soc.* 79, (2002), 278.

Pal. S. Das. D., Chattopadhyay P. Sinha C. and Panneerselvam K. : *Lu. T-H Polyherdon*19, (2002), 1263.

Gad : *Arch. Anat. Physiol.*, (1978), 181.

Mc Bain J.W. and Green A.A. : *J. Am. Chem. Soc.* 68, (1946), 1731-36 .

Mc Bain J.W and Morrill R.C. Jr. : *J. Am. Chem. Soc.* 63, (1941), 670 and Ind.Eng. Chem.,34,(1942),0115.

Mc Bain J.W. and Laing M.E. : *J. Am. Chem. Soc.* 58,(1936), 2610.

Lawarence A.S.C. : *Trans Faraday Soc.* 5(70),(1935),2*Ann. Reports (Chem., Soc. London),* 37, (1940), 102, J.Phys. *Colloid Chem.* 52, (1948), 1504.

Mc Bain J.W. and Morrill R.C. Jr. : *J. Phys. Chem.* 46, (1942), 10.

Von Hann F.V. : *Kolloid,* 2, (1932) 62, 202.

Lindan G. : *Naturwiss,* 20, (1932), 396.

Winsor P.A. : *Trans Faraday Soc.* 44,(1948),376, 382, 387, 390.

Chatterjee B.K. and Palit S.R. : *J. Indian Chem. Soc.* 39, (1962) ,571.

Relph C.L. : *J. Colloid Interface Sci.* 21(3), (1966), 266.

Jain A.K. and Singh R.P.B. : *J. Colloid Interface Sci.*77(1), (1980), 274.

Dobry A. : *J. Phys. Chem.* 58, (1950), 576.

Nobel R.W., Scalan T.J. and Eisher A. : *J.Am. Oil. Chem. Soc.* 35, (1962), 31-2.

Matuura R. and Nagasue K : *Mem. Fac. Sci. Kyusha Univ. Ser. C* $_3$, (1958), 49-54.

Nelson S.M. and Pink R.C. : *J Indian Chem. Soc.* (1952), 1744.

Wolf J.P. : *Olegineucu,* 5, (1950), 20.

Mehrotra R.C. and Rai A.K. : *J. Inorg. Nucl. Chem.* 21 (¾), (1961), 311.

Mehta V.P., Hasan M. and Mathur S.P. : *An. Quim* 74, (1978), 1016.

Phyto-chemicals and Ethanobotany **Pages 115-137**
Edited by: Pawan Kumar 'Bharti'
ISBN: 978-93-86841-93-3
Edition: 2019
Published by: Discovery Publishing House Pvt. Ltd., New Delhi (India)

5

Polyamine
A Mysterious Modulator Involved in Plant Responses to Stress

[1]Prasann Kumar, [2]Shweta Pathak

ABSTRACT

Polyamines (PAs) are omnipresent biogenic amines that have been ensnared in differing cellular capacities in broadly disseminated life forms. In plants, mutant and transgenic plants with changed movement pointed to their inclusion with diverse abiotic and biotic stresses. Besides, microarray, transcriptomic and proteomic approaches have illustrated key capacities of distinctive PAs in signaling systems in plants subjected to abiotic and biotic stresses, in any case the precise atomic instrument remains puzzling. Here, we contend that PAs ought to not be taken as it were as a defensive particle but or maybe like a double-faced atom that likely serves as a major zone for advance investigate endeavors. This audit summarizes later progresses in plant polyamine inquire about extending from transgenic and mutant characterization to potential components of activity amid natural stresses and infections.

Keywords: Agriculture, Biotic, Cadmium, Density, Energy, Forage

Introduction

Plants being sessile need to adapt with persistent natural changes with fitting physiological, formative and biochemical changes (Mahajan and Tuteja, 2005). Abiotic stresses speak to the essential cause of edit misfortune around the world with diminishments of more than 50% (Alcázar et al., 2006; Hussain et al., in press-a). It is assist anticipated that these stresses will gotten to be more strongly and visit with climate alter. On the other hand, the ever expanding world populace, assessed to be 10 billion by 2050, will witness genuine nourishment deficiency by that time (Bartels and Hussain, 2008). To check these stresses, plants are equippedwith a huge set of defensemechanisms (Bartels and Sunkar, 2005). The amassing of a few useful substances such as consistent moo atomic weight natural osmolites: aminoacids, sugars, sugar alcohols,

[1] Department of Agronomy, School of Agriculture. Lovely Professional University, Jalandhar, Punjab, 144411, India

[2] Department of Plant Physiology, I.Ag. Sci., BHU., Varanasi, 221005, U.P., India

and betaines (Kuznetsov and Shevyakova, 1999; Hussain et al., in press-b) and defensive proteins is an necessarily component of the physiological and biochemical reaction beneath stretch conditions (Hussain et al., in press-c). These solutes ensure cell turgor and restorewater status of cells by keeping up cellular water potential as well as acting as chaperones to stabilize films or foragers of ROS.

Among the different classes of compatible solutes, polyamines stand as one of the most effective against extreme environmental stress. Polyamines (PAs) are low molecular weight aliphatic nitrogen compounds positively charged at physiological pH (Groppa and Benavides,2008) that are found in awide range of organisms from bacteria to plants and animals (Alcázar et al., 2006). Polyamine (tetraamine spermine) was first reported more than 300 years ago in human spermatozoa (van Leeuwenhoek, 1678). The success of PAs in nature compared to other compatible solutes can be explained by their peculiar functions. These amines have been thoroughly investigated due to their role in a variety of regulatory and cellular processes such as cell division and elongation, root growth, flower and fruit development, replication, transcription, translation, membrane and cell wall stabilization, chromatin organization, ribosome biogenesis and programmed cell death (Bais and Ravishankar, 2002; Evans and Malmberg, 1989; Galston et al., 1997; Igarashi and Kashiwagi, 2000; Kusano et al., 2007a,b; Liu et al., 2006; Paschalidis and Roubelakis-Angelakis, 2005a,b; Thomas and Thomas, 2001;Walden et al., 1997; Zhao and Yang, 2008). PAs are also implicated in a wide range of diverse environmental stresses (Bouchereau et al., 1999; Kasukabe et al., 2004; Kumar et al., 1997; Liu et al., 2007)which includes drought (Nayyar et al., 2005; Yamaguchi et al., 2007; Yang et al., 2007), salinity (Duan et al., 2008; Kuznetsov and Shevyakova, 2010), low temperature (Cuevas et al., 2008; Imai et al., 2004; Nayyar, 2005), oxidative stress (Rider et al., 2007) and metal toxicity (Groppa and Benavides, 2008; Groppa et al., 2003; Wang et al., 2007; Shevyakova et al., 2010). It is well-documented that PAs are present in all compartments of the plant cell, including the nucleus, which indicates their role in the control of diverse fundamental cellular processes (Bouchereau et al., 1999; Kaur-Sawhney et al., 2003). Plant polyamines are preferentially detected in actively growing tissues. However, concentration of Pas may vary markedly depending on plant species, organ and tissue and also on the developmental stage. Their biological activity is attributed to cationic nature therefore PAs interact with negatively charged macromolecules such as DNA, RNA, proteins and phospholipids. These reversible ionic interactions lead to the stabilization of macromolecules. These findings have been discussed in detail in several recent articles (Groppa and Benavides, 2008; Kaur-Sawhney et al., 2003; Kusano et al., 2008; Liu et al., 2006; Pang et al., 2007).

Within the past decade, in any case, examinations into plant PAs at a atomic level have driven to segregation of a number of qualities encoding Dad biosynthetic proteins from a assortment of plant species (Bagni and Tassoni, 2001; Ge et al., 2006; Hanzawa et al., 1997, 2000, 2002; Janowitz et al., 2003; Malmberg et al., 1998; Piotrowski et al., 2003). In later a long time, atomic and genomic thinks about with mutants and transgenic plants having no or changed activity of chemicals included within the biosynthesis of PAs have contributed to distant better; a much better; a higher; a stronger; an improved">a much better understanding of natural capacities of PAs in plants. In any case, the exact parts of Pas stay tricky. Right now, transcriptomic and proteomic approaches are being utilized to encourage pick up an understanding in PAs functionresearch. These examinations will encourage unraveling atomic capacities of polyamines. In this survey, we examine how PA digestion system is included in plant reactions to both biotic and abiotic stresses. We moreover look at later propels in putative instruments whereby polyamines offer assistance plants to bargain with natural variances. At last, we talk about clear inconsistencies between a few harmful impacts of polyamines on plant advancement and the part of PAs in reaction to stress.

Biosynthesis of Polyamine in Plants

The PA biosynthetic pathway has been completely explored in numerous living beings counting plants and surveyed in detail (Alcázar et al., 2005; Bagni and Tassoni, 2001; Bortolotti et al., 2004; Hanfrey et al., 2001; Illingworth et al., 2003; Kakehi et al., 2008; Knott et al., 2007; Kusano et al., 2007b; Martin-Tanguy, 2001; Minguet et al., 2008; String et al., 2007; Rambla et al., 2010; Teuber et al., 2007; Wallace et al., 2003). Briefly, the biosynthesis of polyamine in plants has been welldocumented, covering decarboxylation of ornithine or arginine, catabolized by ornithine or arginine decarboxylases (ODC, ADC) individually to surrender diamine putrescine (Put). The coming about halfway agmatine synthesized from arginine is in this way changed over to Put, by agmatine iminohydrolase (AIH) and N-carbamoylputrescine amidohydrolase (CPA). Spermidine (Spd) and spermine (Spm) are shaped by the consecutive expansion of aminopropyl bunches to Put and Spd separately fromdecarboxylated S-adenosylmethionine (SAM) by SAM decarboxylase (Kusano et al., 2007a; String et al., 2007).

Polyamine-related Genes in Plants

Accessibility of the total genome grouping for Arabidopsis has encouraged the utilize of genomic approaches for distinguishing proof and segregation of qualities encoding PA biosynthetic proteins (Liu et al., 2007). All genes within the PA biosynthesis pathway of plants have been uncovered in different plant species and Arabidopsis (Ge et al., 2006; Illingworth et al., 2003; Janowitz et al., 2003). In Arabidopsis, there are six proteins mindful for PA biosynthesis encoding 10 genes: ADC-encoding qualities (ADC1and ADC2—Watson andMalmberg, 1996; Watson et al., 1997); SPDS (SPDS1 and

SPDS2—Hanzawa et al., 2002) and SAMDC (SAMDC1, SAMDC2, SAMDC3, SAMDC4—Franceschetti et al., 2001; Hashimoto et al., 1998; Urano et al., 2003, 2004). Essentially, Spm synthase, thermospermine synthase, agmatine iminohydrolase and N-carbamoylputrescine amidohydrolase are represented by single genes (Hanzawa et al., 2000; Janowitz et al., 2003; Knott et al., 2007; Panicot et al., 2002; Piotrowski et al., 2003). In differentiate to ADC1,which is constitutively communicated in all plant tissues, ADC2 is mindful to abiotic stresses such as dry season and injuring (Peréz-Amador et al., 2002; Soyka and Heyer, 1999). Be that as it may, qualities dependable for PA biosynthesis in plants but for ODC have as it were been characterized in Arabidopsis. A few thinks about found that the Arabidopsis genome needs ODC (Allen, 2002; Hanfrey et al., 2001; Urano et al., 2003).

Polyamine and Plant Response to Abiotic Stresses

A few considers have appeared that polyamine amassing happens abiotic stresses counting drought, saltiness, extraordinary temperature, paraquat, hypoxia, UV-B, overwhelming metals, mechanical injuring and herbicide treatment (Groppa and Benavides, 2008 and references in that; Throb et al., 2007). Consequently, tall cellular levels of polyamines relate with plant resilience in a wide cluster of natural stresses. Be that as it may, the physiological centrality of polyamine amassing remains tricky and must be uncovered whether these reactions are due to stress-induced damage or a defensive reaction to abiotic push.

Polyamine Metabolism under Abiotic Stress Conditions

The part of polyamine in abiotic push resilience to begin with came beneath seriously investigation after an increment in Put due to K+ lack was detailed decades back. As a result, analysts broadly explored changes in PA, when plants are uncovered to single or combined stresses (Camacho-Cristóbal et al., 2004; Kuthanová et al., 2004; Liu et al., 2006; Moment and Pua, 2002; Shen et al., 2000; Urano et al., 2003). Polyamine biosynthesis pathway and the foremost chemicals of this pathway are beneath complex metabolic and formative control and such control is fundamental for effective control of cell digestion system. In Arabidopsis, differential expression of ADC (ADC1 and ADC2) has been detailed beneath stretch conditions. In reality, ADC2 expression is emphatically initiated by a few abiotic stresses like dry season, tall saltiness, mechanical damage, potassium lack (Alcázar et al., 2006; Armengaud et al., 2004; Hummel et al., 2004; Peréz-Amadoret al., 2002; Urano et al., 2003), whereas ADC1 is primarily initiated by cold (Hummel et al., 2004). Essentially, the expression design of SPMS takes after that of ADC2 coming about in polyamine aggregation beneath lack of hydration and tall saltiness (Alcázar et al., 2006; Urano et al., 2003). Be that as it may, SPDS2 has constitutive expression beneath diverse stresses in differentiate to SPDS1 which shows expanded expression beneath lack of hydration. On the other hand, expression of SAMDC1 and SAMDC2 are emphatically initiated by cold and SAMDC2 has slight acceptance in expression beneath salt push (Vergnolle et al., 2005). The expression designs of CPA, AIH and ACL5 are not influenced by any stretch (Alcázar et al., 2006). Dad biosynthesis chemicals (ODC, ADC and SAMDC) are controlled at transcriptional, translational and post-translational levels (Hu et al., 2005); it is curiously to note that these proteins are at first synthesized as an inert forerunner (proenzyme), which are afterward subjected to post-translational preparing coming about in develop chemicals (Xiong et al., 1997). For case, an amassing of Puthas been recognized in reaction to natural changes concomitant with ADC2 and ADC1 up-regulation. In any case, Put collection and acceptance of downstream qualities included in Spdand Spm biosynthesis (SAMDC2, SPDS1, SPMS) did not influence the substance of both polyamines. This might be due to the translational or post-translational direction of SAM decarboxylase, which could be a key chemical in polyamine biosynthesis. Essentially, Hu et al. (2005) found that a 5′-untranslated grouping plays a central part in both transcriptional and post-transcriptional control of SAMDC quality expression. Beneath push conditions, the level of Dad in plant organs may too be directed by its debasement. Cellular Dad is controlled by catabolic pathway (Bagni and Tassoni, 2001; Cona et al., 2006), which comprises of two amine oxidases, doamine oxidase (DAO) and polyamine oxidase (PAO). The function of DAO is to convert Put into Pyrroline, ammonia and H_2O_2.

PAO oxidizes Spd to Pyrroline, 1,3-diamine propane (DAP), H_2O_2 and Spm to aminopropylpyrroline, DAP and H_2O_2 (Cona et al., 2003, 2006; Martin-Tanguy, 2001; Sebela et al., 2001). Capell et al. (2004) found that rice produces high levels of Spd and Spm until 3 days after drought stress but the level sharply dropped after 6 days, probably because of the action of PAO. It is well-known that ABA contents increase under drought, salinity and other abiotic stresses (Christmann et al., 2005). ABA induces the expression of a plethora of genes involved in defense against these abiotic stresses (Yamaguchi et al., 2007). It is established that genes involved in PA biosynthesis are also inducible by ABA (Alcázar et al., 2006; Kasinathan and Wingler, 2004; Urano et al., 2004). Alcázar et al. (2006) also showed that the dehydration inducible expression of ADC2, SPDS1 and SPMS is an ABA-dependent response because up-regulation of these genes is not observed in ABA deficient (aba2) and insensitive (abil) mutants. Moreover, it is further revealed that stress (DRE and LTR) and ABA responsive elements (ABRE and/or ABRE related motifs) are present in the promoters of these genes. Furthermore, microarray analysis has revealed that most of the genes involved in PA metabolism in Arabidopsis respond to a range of abiotic stresses such as drought (Öztürk et al., 2002); wounding or methyl jasmonate treatment (Peréz-Amador et al., 2002; Sasaki et al., 2001). However, the use of microarray technology for unraveling molecular mechanisms underlying PA effects on abiotic stress tolerance is in its infancy.

Plant Stress Tolerance Modulated by Polyamine Treatment

Stress-derived changes in cellular polyamines give clues on their conceivable suggestion in stretch but don't give prove of their part in checking stretch. Classical approaches utilizing exogenous PA application/mutant/use of inhibitors of proteins included in PA biosynthesis pathway speak to an great demonstrate to test various hypotheses and to reply crucial organic questions inferred from pathway control (Alcázar et al., 2006; Bhatnagar et al., 2002; Liu et al., 2007). Exogenous application of polyamines, which is anticipated to extend levels of an endogenous polyamine, has been endeavored some time recently or amid push (Navakouidis et al., 2003; Wang et al., 2007). There's a huge body of prove to propose that exogenous application of PAs seem, in changing degrees, (1) protect plant cell film keenness, (2) switch development or minimize development restraint caused by stretch, (3) direct expression of osmotically responsive qualities, (4) decrease superoxide radical and H2O2 substance, (5) decrease aggregation of NA+ and Cl particles totally different organs, and (6) increment exercises of antioxidant chemicals (Ali, 2000; Iqbal and Ashraf, 2005; Afzal et al., 2009; Ndayiragiji and Lutts, 2006; Tang and Newton, 2005; Yiu et al., 2009; Zhang et al., 2009). Be that as it may, the defensive impacts of person PAs are to some degree distinctive. The reason for such a disparity may be due to contrasts in assimilation, transport and utilization among plant species. These discoveries recommend that exogenous PA application acts as an elicitor of qualities included in abiotic stretch reactions (Gill and Tuteja, 2010). In another approach, treatment with Dad biosynthesis inhibitors, such as x-difluoromethylarginine (DFMA), x-difluoromethylornithine (DFMO), and D-arginine, to decrease endogenous PA brought about in stresssensitive phenotypes. Be that as it may, this impact is switched by the concomitant application of exogenous polyamine (He et al., 2002; Navakouidis et al., 2003). The impacts of these inhibitors are variable, extending from hindrance to incitement or no impact depending on the inhibitor soundness and specificity, formative organize, plant framework tried and presence of productive compensatory components (Kaur- Sawhney et al., 2003).

Another hereditary approach utilized for analyzing organic capacities of polyamine digestion system in push reaction is the utilize of mutants lacking in polyamine biosynthesis (Kaur-Sawhney et al., 2003; Urano et al., 2004; Watson and Malmberg, 1998). Watson et al. (1998) disconnected EMS mutants of Arabidopsis with decreased ADC action, spe-1 and spe-2. These mutants are lacking in Dad collection and displayed diminished salt resilience compared with the wild sort (Kasinathan and Wingler, 2004). On the other hand, the

ADC2 knockout mutant (adc2-1) appeared no self-evident phenotype alter beneath typical development conditions and was more touchy to salt stretch, which can be somewhat switched by exogenous application of Put (Urano et al., 2004). These comes about clearly uncovered that ADC2 could be a key gene and Put inferred from the ADC pathway was imperative in stretch reaction. As of late, a imperfect part for Spm in abiotic stresses such as dry season and saltiness was set up by the Arabidopsis acl5/ spms mutant, imperfect for Spm generation. This mutant displayed a delicate phenotype beneath dry spell and saltiness stresses but recuperated when treated with Spm (Yamaguchi et al., 2006, 2007). Taken together, point by point characterization of mutants, flawed in other PA genes, ought to help in decoding the exact mode of activity of PA genes in reaction to abiotic stresses.

Plant Abiotic Stress Tolerance Modulated by Engineering the Polyamine Synthesis Pathway

Later progresses in molecular science with accentuation on hereditary designing and accessibility of PA biosynthesis genes makes it conceivable to assess and give a effective methodology to recognize the conceivable part of PAs in stretch reaction (Groppa and Benavides, 2008). A common marvel watched is that PAs can change their titres in reaction to different sorts of natural stresses such as water stretch (Capell et al., 2004; Kasukabe et al., 2004; Ma et al., 2005), moo and tall temperatures (Hummel et al., 2004; Imai et al., 2004; Melody et al., 2002) and saltiness (Liu et al., 2006; Maiale et al., 2004; Roy et al., 2005). In arrange to get principal data on the part of Pas amid push, plant PAs have been tweaked by the over-expression/ down-regulation of adc/odc/samdc qualities (Kakkar and Sawhney, 2002; Minocha and Sun, 1997; Thu-Hang et al., 2002). Over-expression of Dad biosynthetic qualities like adc (Capell et al., 1998; 2004; Roy and Wu, 2001), odc (Kumria and Rajam, 2002), samdc (Roy and Wu, 2002; Waie and Rajam, 2003) and spd syn (Franceschetti et al., 2004; Kasukabe et al., 2004, 2006) in plants like O. sativa, N. tabacum, A. thaliana and I. batatas has expanded resilience to different abiotic stresses. There are a few reports on making transgenic plants harboring polyamine biosynthetic qualities in an endeavor to upgrade push resilience. Transgenic work is based on the perceptions that AtADC2 transcripts connects with the amassing of free Put beneath distinctive abiotic stresses in plants (Urano et al., 2004).

For illustration, in a later consider, transgenic rice plants communicating the Datura stramonium adc (arginine decarboxylase) quality created higher levels of Put beneath dry season push than wild sort plants, which driven to higher levels of Spd and Spm and moved forward dry season resilience; transgenic plants shown less chlorophyll misfortune and leaf action, spe-1 and spe-2. These mutants are insufficient in PA aggregation and shown diminished salt resistance compared with the wild sort (Kasinathan and Wingler, 2004). On the other hand, the ADC2 knockout mutant (adc2-1) appeared no self-evident phenotype alter beneath ordinary development conditions and was more delicate to salt push, which can be in part switched by exogenous application of Put (Urano et al., 2004). These comes about clearly uncovered that ADC2 could be a key quality and Put inferred from the ADC pathway was critical in stretch reaction. As of late, a inadequate part for Spm in abiotic stresses such as dry season and saltiness was set up by the Arabidopsis acl5/ spms mutant, flawed for Spm generation. This mutant displayed a delicate phenotype beneath dry spell and saltiness stresses but recouped when treated with Spm (Yamaguchi et al., 2006, 2007). Taken together, point by point characterization of mutants, imperfect in other PA qualities, ought to help in decoding the exact mode of activity of PA qualities in reaction to abiotic stresses. In differentiate, wild-type Datura stramonium display expanded endogenous Put levels on the onset of drought stretch but this Put level isn't sufficient to trigger the transformation of Put into Spd and Spm (Capell et al., 2004). Another case is the presentation of the Tritordeum SAMDC (S-adenosylmethionine decarboxylase) quality into rice, which come about in a three to four-fold increment in Spd and Spm levels in changed plants, which at that point had ordinary development and advancement indeed beneath NaCl stretch (Roy and Wu, 2002). In another illustration, Waie and Rajam, 2003, watched that transgenic tobacco plants over-expressing a human SAMDC quality had higher Spd and Put levels and displayed resilience to dry season and salt push. Franceschetti et al. (2004) moreover appeared that over-expression of Arabidopsis SAMDC in tobacco plants come about in expanded SAMDC action, aggregation of dcSAM, irritation of PA levels and transgenic plants displayed numerous stretch resilience. As of late, Peremarti et al. (2009) created transgenic rice plants constitutively communicating heterologous SAMDC quality from Datura stramonium to dismember the parts of Put from higher polyamines Spd and Spm. Both transgenic and wild sort plants appeared indistinguishable side effects when uncovered to dry season push but transgenic plants recuperated much more rapidly on re-watering. Additionally, transgenic carrot lines over-expressing mouse odc, which changes over ornithine to diamine putrescine were able to resist salt and osmotic push over brief period (Minocha and Sun, 1997). In another set of tests, ADC communicating transgenic rice plants delivered higher levels of Put, Spd and Spm and displayed dry spell resilience. Advance, it has been proposed that Put may reflect the sub ideal development conditions whereas Spd and Spm may offer assistance detoxifying free radicals (Larher et al., 2003). These comes about affirmed the inclusion of polyamines in dry season stretch and assist credited person parts to Put, Spd and Spm. Interests, presentation of a single polyamine biosynthesis quality has been appeared to bestow resilience to different stresses. Illustrations of these are when Kasukabe et al. (2004, 2006) and Wi et al. (2006) found wide range resistance to abiotic stresses—drought, chilling, solidifying, saltiness and oxidative stress—by over-expression of SPDS (Spermidine synthase) from Curcurbita ficifolia in Arabidopsis, sweet potato (Ipomoea batatas) or tobacco. A cDNA microarray examination between chilled clears out of a transgenic line and wild sort uncovered that qualities encoding translation variables such as WRKY, B-box zinc finger proteins, NAM proteins, DREB2B and NAC space proteins are up-regulated in transgenic plants. Wen et al. (2008) illustrated that overexpression of an apple MdSPDS1 quality in European pear significantly expanded resistance to different stresses by modifying PA levels. Additionally, Prabhavathi and Rajam (2007) illustrated that transgenic eggplant harboring the oat ADC quality shown expanded resistance to dry season, saltiness, moo and tall temperature and overwhelming metals. These information illustrated that a transgenic approach including PA biosynthetic qualities may be a great methodology to progress edit resistance to different abiotic stresses to meet the necessities of a challenging worldwide environment.

Polyamine and Plant Stress Response: Potential Mechanism of Action

Polyamine

A compatible solute in higher plants Metabolic acclimation via the accumulation of compatible solutes is regarded as a basic strategy for the protection and survival of plants under abiotic stresses (Bartels and Hussain, 2008). Compatible solutes are non-toxic molecules, serve in turgor maintenance and stabilize macromolecular structures under unfavorable conditions (Bohnert and Shen, 1999; McNeil et al., 1999). The notion of PA as a compatible solute is controversial in plants and needs further investigation. However, stress-induced PAs are often considered better stabilizers than others for protecting biomolecules and preventing the membrane system from denaturing under stress conditions (Liu et al., 2007). PAs share many properties, for example, hydropholicity, protection of macromolecules, active oxygen scavengers, maintenance of cellular pH etc., which are close to those of proline and other compatible solutes (Liu et al., 2007; Wi et al., 2006). However, the concentration of stress-induced PAs is lower than proline and other solutes, which suggests that PAs are not compatible solutes. On the other hand, Duhazé et al. (2002) showed that products of PA catabolism, like β-alanine, can convert into β-alanine betaine which is required for osmoregulation in some halophytes. Proline is one of the most common osmolytes in stressed plants(Bartels and Hussain, 2008; Delauney and Verma, 1993; Sharma and Dietz, 2006; Urano et al., 2009). Polyamine catabolism is closely related to proline accumulation in response to stress conditions (Aziz et al., 1998; Bouchereau et al., 1999). Öztürk and Demir (2003) showed that exogenous PA increases activity of peroxidase (POD) and catalase (Cat), along with proline production. PA metabolism is unique in that Put, proline and GABA share a common substrate, glutamate, and these metabolites often respond similarly to abiotic stresses (Seki et al., 2007; Sharma and Dietz, 2006; Simon-Sarkadi et al., 2005, 2006). There is no evidence yet about the mechanism of their coordinated accumulation (Radukina et al., 2007). However, it is possible that a common signal triggers all three sub-pathways in a coordinated manner. Ornithine is a key intermediate in the biosynthesis of both Put and proline (Coruzzi and Last, 2000; Roosens et al., 2002; Slocum, 2005) and is a possible candidate for a regulatory role in coordinating biosynthesis of these metabolites (Mohapatra et al., 2010). Similarly, a hierarchical accumulation of PAs in different

transgenic tissues/organs has been observed (Lepri et al., 2001) which suggest that PAs might act as compatible solute in specific organs, cells or organelles.

Polyamine and Antioxidant Response

Reactive oxygen species (ROS) production is a common plant response under both abiotic and biotic stresses (Miller et al., 2008). ROS is characterized by the accumulation of toxic molecules T2, H_2O_2, and OH in tissues which are capable of causing damage to plant cell membranes and macromolecules (Apel and Kirt, 2004). Plants have several antioxidant strategies (Rea et al., 2004) like ROS-scavenging enzymes such as superoxide dismutase (SOD) (Aronova et al., 2005), different peroxidases (POD; Hiraga et al., 2000), catalase (Cat), and glutation reductase (GR; Bartels and Hussain, 2008). PAs may be related to their multi-faceted nature, which includes working as an antioxidant, a free radical scavenger and a membrane stabilizer (Larher et al., 2003; Velikova et al., 2000). The generation of ROS is tightly linked to catabolic processes of PAs, by PAO (Cona et al., 2006) which is associated with plant defense and abiotic stress responses (Liu et al., 2005). Verma and Mishra (2005) demonstrated that positive effects of Put on Brassica juncea seedlings under NaCl stress are evident from reduced H_2O_2 and lipid peroxidation. Similarly, Put increased activity of antioxidant enzymes and carotenoids in leaf tissues of salt stressed Brassica. Based on these results, they concluded that PAs may exhibit antioxidant properties under some conditions. Conclusive evidence regarding antioxidant roles of PAs were provided Nayyar and Chander (2004), who observed that exogenous application of PAs reduced H_2O_2 levels and molandialdehyde (MDA) content, and raised the antioxidant level in 15-day-old chickpea plants subjected to drought and cold stress for 4 days. PAs are also involved in inhibition of DNA oxidative degradation by OH as shown by an in vitro experiment. TotalDNA fromM. Crystallinum is degraded, when incubated with an OH generating system and addition of Spm suppressed DNA damage (Kuznetsov and Shevyakova, 2007). At the same time, some reports have demonstrated that PA conjugates are more efficient compared to parent compounds with stronger protective antioxidant activities (Edreva et al., 2007). Nevertheless, it can be concluded that plants not only accumulate free PAs to function as scavengers of free radicals but also produce their conjugates which are more efficient antioxidants (Edreva et al., 2007).

Polyamine: A Signal Molecule during Stress Response

In contrast to the trustworthy establishment of the role of PA in plant defense against abiotic (Bartels and Hussain, 2008) and biotic (Walters, 2003 and references therein) stresses, few reports recently indicated that PAs may act as cellular signals in intrinsic talk with hormonal pathways including ABA (Alcázar et al., 2010a,b; Gill and Tuteja, 2010). It is well-known that ABA concentrations increase under water and salt stress as well as other abiotic stresses (Christmann et al., 2005). It is also well-documented that ABA induces the expression of multiple genes involved in abiotic stress tolerance (Bartels and Hussain, 2008; Bartels and Souer, 2003), e.g. PA biosynthesis genes in Arabidopsis (Kasinathan and Wingler, 2004; Urano et al., 2004). Exogenously applied ABA helped further to identify the possible roles of ABA in modulation of PA metabolism at the transcriptional level by up-regulating ADC2, SPDS and SPMS under stress conditions in plants (Alcázar et al., 2006; Hanfrey et al., 2001; Hanzawa et al., 2002; Peréz- Amador et al., 2002; Urano et al., 2003). Similarly, a plethora of data on the analysis of mutant plants and transcript profiling suggest a positive feedback mechanism between Put and ABA, which permits a fresh insight that both Put and ABA reciprocally promote each other's biosynthesis under stress to increase plant adaptive potential (Cuevas et al., 2008, 2009; Urano et al., 2003, 2009; Yamaguchi et al., 2006). PA catabolism produces H2O2whichwas often consideredmostly as a toxic metabolite. Only recently, our notions about H2O2 changed dramatically to a signalmolecule, capable of diffusion fromthe site of its production to neighbouring cells and tissues, resulting in activation of a defensive response (Neill et al., 2002). Similarly, PAs like Spm and Spd are regarded as potent inducers of nitric oxide (NO) in plants (Tun et al., 2006). Reports showing NO as a signaling molecule in plants appeared as late as 1998 (Delledonne et al., 1998). These reports provoked an intensification of research on the role of NO in plants. In plant cells, several pathways coexist for NO-mediated signals including cyclic nucleotides, Ca^{2+} ions, protein kinases and others. Moreover, wheat plants subjected to drought had much higher ABA synthesis in roots in the presence of NO and ROS, which suggests synergistic action of ROS and NO (Zhao et al., 2001). Also, the accumulation of NO proved necessary for ABA-induced closure of stomata in Vicia faba (Garia-Mata and Lamattina, 2002). Important clues about the functional cooperation between ABA, H_2O_2 and NO are also confirmed by a recent reportwhich found that ABA-induced stomatal closure in Arabidopsis is dependent not only on NO but also on H_2O_2 (Bright et al., 2006). Recently, An et al. (2008) reported that PAs are involved in ABA-induced stomatal regulation under abiotic stresses. ABA, H_2O_2, NO and PAs are multifunctional molecules implicated in numerous physiological and biological responses during stress responses (Grün et al., 2006; Neill et al., 2003). Evidence obtained so far is being compiled, showing the involvement and interaction of ABA, H_2O_2, NO and PAs during stress responses by a complex network. Recently, Alcázar et al. (2010 a,b) suggested a synergistic interplay between aforesaid molecules for abiotic stress tolerance in plants. However, whether or not the unique roles of these molecules in plants are attributable is still a matter of debate. 4.4. Polyamine: Regulation of ion channel and Ca^{2+} homeostasis Recently, it was found that PAs could substantially affect ion channel conductivity in plants (Kusano et al., 2007a). At physiological pH, PAs are positively charged molecules, which interact with negatively charged proteins including ion channels. PAs are also potent blockers of fast and slow vacuolar channels, including calcium channels (Brüggemann et al., 1999; Dobrovinskaya et al., 1999a; 1999b). The effect of PAs on ion channels is proportional to its charge (Spm + 4NSpd + 3NPut + 2) at both whole cell and single channel level, thus indicating a direct blockage of the channel by PAs (Brüggemann et al., 1998). These findings are in agreement with reports from animal literature, suggesting that PAs can block or modulate several types of cation channels (Bowie et al., 1998; Gomez and Hellstrand, 1999; Huang and Moczydlowski, 2001; Lu and Ding, 1999; Oliver et al., 2000; Williams, 1997a,b). As in the animal system, ion channels have been identified as PA targets in plants blocking inward rectifying K^+ and Na^+ channel and mediating additional aspects of ion fluxhomeostasis in cell type specific manner (Liu et al., 2000; Zhao et al., 2007). Furthermore, Garufi et al. (2007) suggested that PA may regulate the activity of numerous ion channels indirectly by affecting plasma membrane potential via activation of H^+-ATPase through enhancement of interactions with 14-3-3 proteins. Consistent with the above data, it has been reported that Pas including spermine inhibit stomatal opening and induce closure by regulating KAT-1 like voltage-dependent inward K^+ channel of Vicia faba guard cells. Similarly, exogenously applied PAs ameliorate the detrimental effects of salinity by reducing NaCl-induced K^+ efflux through non-selective cation channels, a major route of Na+ uptake into plant cells (Demidchik and Tester, 2002; Shabala et al., 2007). Yamaguchi et al. (2006) showed that acl5/spms mutant plant is hypersensitive to KCl and also Ca^{2+} deficient. The overall phenotype of mutant plants resembles transgenic plants over-expressing AtGluR2 and CAX1, which encode a Ca^{2+} influx channel at the plasma membrane and a vacuolar Ca^{2+}/H^+ exchanger, respectively (Hirschi, 1999; Kim et al., 2001). Similarly, mutant plants lose more water than wild type plants due to failed stomatal closure upon onset of drought (Yamaguchi et al., 2007). This phenomenon may again be explained by the impairment in Ca^{2+} homeostasis. It is documented that changes of free Ca^{2+} in the cytoplasm of guard cells are responsible for stomatal movement (Allen and Sanders, 1996; Peiter et al., 2005; Rob et al., 2005). On the other hand, spermine produced as a result of drought stress may modulate Ca^{2+} permeable channels, resulting in increased cytoplasmic Ca^{2+} concentration to trigger stomatal closure. Collectively, these results indicate that the absence of spermine may cause deregulation of Ca^{2+} trafficking, resulting in a lack of proper adaptation to high NaCl and drought stresses (Kusano et al., 2007a,b). Taken together, this data points to a possible link between PAs, Ca^{2+} homeostasis and stress responses which should be further explored.

Polyamine and Programmed Cell Death (PCD)

In plants, programmed cell death (PCD) can occur following both pathogen attack and environmental fluctuations (Reape and McCabe, 2008). For example, UV-C activate PCD in Arabidopsis (Danon et al., 2004) and PCD can also be activated in tobacco by infection with Pseudomonas syringae pv. phsaeolicola (del Pozo and Lam, 1998). Polyamines are considered essential for cell growth and survival (Hanfrey et al., 2001; Thomas and Thomas, 2001) and homeostasis (Mittler and Shulaev, 2003). PAs have also been involved in regulation of PCD, apoptosis (Schipper et al., 2000). There is substantial literature available indicating the involvement of PAs in apoptotic cell death in plants (Desiderio et al., 1995; Ha et al., 1997; Lindsay and Wallace, 1998). Furthermore, PA degradation seems to be important, leading to apoptosis in plants. In fact, Crowley and Walters (2002) observed an increase in PA catabolism by DAO and PAO in cells undergoing apoptosis which resulted in hypersensitive response in tobacco (Yoda et al., 2003). Similarly, Yoda et al. (2003; 2006) demonstrated that cell death caused by TMV infection is partially mediated by H_2O_2 production through PA catabolism. Hydrogen peroxide has long been considered to be a causative element for apoptotic cell death in Plants.

Apoptosis in plants follow similar interactions between PAs and components of PCD as described for animals. In numerous plant diseases, hypersensitive response (HR) is triggered when the host recognizes a pathogen affecter destined to suppress immunity (Jones and Dangl, 2006). It has been suggested that HR represents a form of PCD in plants (Greenberg et al., 1994; Walters, 2003) and PAs have been implicated in a prominent role in this process. HR involves inducing localized cell death at the point of infection, thus limiting the progression of the pathogen. Similarly, PAs also affect conformation and function of specific proteins by forming covalent linkages mediated by the activity of transglutamines (TGase) enzymes (Griffin et al., 2002). TGase activity has also been demonstrated in plants (Della Mea et al., 2004). TGase activity is elevated, when apoptosis is induced in animals, and similar enhanced activity has also been shown during HR in tobacco/TMV interactions (Del Duca et al.,

2007). However, further investigations are required for conclusive evidence of PAs involvement in PCD in plants.

Polyamine and Plant Responses to Biotic Stresses

Despite continued interest in polyamine metabolism in plants subjected to abiotic stresses (Bartels and Hussain, 2008), work on polyamine metabolism in plant-pathogen interactions relatively lags behind (Walters, 2000). Mostly, plant defense mechanisms against pathogen attack are triggered by a stimulus preceding the pathogen attack that reduces disease. The stimulus can boost the concentration of accessible defense compounds that include the assembly of new defensive structures and chemicals (Baileya et al., 2005). PA metabolism has long been known to distort in plant cells responding to insightful changes in plants interacting with fungal (Asthir et al., 2004; Greenland and Lewis, 1984), viral pathogens (Torrigiani et al., 1997; Walters, 2003) and mycorrhizae (Walters, 2000). Nevertheless, much progress has been achieved regarding PA and plant diseases (Walters, 2000, 2003). For example, spermine (Spm) not only plays a role as a mediator in defense signaling against pathogen (Takahashi et al., 2003, 2004) but is also important for resistance to virus infection (Yamakawa et al., 1998).

Polyamine: Elicitor of the Plant Defense Response

The coordination of internal processes in plants and their balance with the environment are connected with the excitability of plants cells. Yamakawa et al. (1998) reported that Spm accumulated in the apoplast of cells after lesion formation is an endogenous inducer of the expression of both pathogen-related (PR) proteins and resistance against TMV via salicylic acid (SA)-independent signaling pathway in tobacco plants. Later, it was known that Spm stimulates activity of (i) two important mitogen-activated protein kinases (MAPKs) involved in plant defense; wound-induced protein kinase (WIPK) and SAinduced protein kinase (SIPK) and (ii) defense gene expression (Takahashi et al., 2003, 2004). Later, using a similar experimental system, it was discovered that exogenously applied spermine to tobacco leaves provokes a pathway involving mitochondrial dysfunction, activation of MAPKs, increased expression of hypersensitive response (HR) marker genes, induced defense responses and HR-like cell death (Mitsuya et al., 2007, 2009; Uehara et al., 2005). However, the mechanismof PAs as an elicitor of plant defense response requires further research. In soil, root development and acquisition of root architecture as well as root functions greatly rely on interactions of root tissues with the surrounding biotic environment, especially microorganisms. However, little is known about the interactions between plants and mycorrhizae, and the role of PAs in symbiotic relationships is less studied (Kytoviita and Sarjala, 1997). It has been shown that externally applied Put in arbuscular mycorrhizae increases the colonization frequency in pea roots (El-

Ghachtouli et al., 1995, 1996). A possible role of PAs in arbuscular mycorrhizal infection was, therefore, postulated. Later, Kytoviita and Sarjala (1997) showed that ectomycorrhizal symbiosis result in increased free Put levels in mycorrhizal roots of Scots pine. However, they found differences in PA levels between symbiotic and non-symbiotic roots and suggested that PA could create a carbon sink for symbionts, resulting in attraction of photoassimilates (Niemi et al., 2002). Further, a high content of total free PAs in association with arbuscular mycorrhiza and Lotus glaber plants was detected compared to non-mycorrhizal plants (Sannazzaro et al., 2007). This relationship also increased PA levels in both plants and mycorrhizae. The modulation of PA pools in symbionts could help to resist host defense responses induced at the start of the association. However, the roles of PAs in the plant–mycorrhizal associations remain elusive and await further research. Although long known for their pharmacology effects, there has been little investigation of defense responses of polyamine during pathogenic infection. We are now beginning to understand their role in plant biotic stresses through molecular biology and modern biochemical approaches (Mehta et al., 2002; Walters, 2003). Early efforts found that in compatible interactions between barley and Puccinia hordei (brown rust fungus), polyamines particularly spermidine accumulate in infected leaves (Greenland and Lewis, 1984). Polyamine accumulation has also been reported in leaves of barley following infection by powdery mildew fungus (Blumeria graminis f. sp. hordei) (Walters and Wylie, 1986; Walters et al., 1985). The presence of PA in both plants and pathogenic fungi makes it difficult to identify their respective contribution to PA accumulation in infected organs. However, themost exciting and farreaching development in this area is the possibility of control of fungal plant diseases through specific inhibition of polyamine biosynthesis (Galston and Weinstein, 1988; Walters, 1989). Similarly, PA inhibitors like DFMO, MGBG and CHA resulted in complete inhibition of microcycle conidiation at 5 mM levels (Khurana et al., 1996). In relation to biotic stress responses and in order to identify regulatory components of the pathway involved in the hypersensitive response (HR) induced by tobacco mosaic virus (TMV) in tobacco plants, new developments are in the pipeline. Tobacco ZFT1 is a spermine-responsive gene encoding a zinc finger type transcriptional repressor, and is involved in spermine-signaling pathway (Uehara et al., 2005). Interestingly, tobacco plants over-expressing ZFT1 are more resistant to TMV compared with control plants (Mitsuya et al., 2007; Uehara et al., 2005). Another important observation regarding PA implication in the signaling pathway involved in biotic stress response has been postulated. Accumulation of H_2O_2 as a result of PA catabolism and nitric oxide due to induction by spermine/spermidine plays an important signaling role in plant–pathogen interactions (Romero-Puertas et al., 2004; Tun et al., 2006; Walters, 2003; Yamasaki and Cohen, 2006). These studies suggest that manipulation of key factors present upstream of polyamine biosynthesis or in the polyamine-induced signaling pathway could render the host plant resistant to biotic stresses. Some recent studies explored another layer of complex polyamineinduced signaling pathway. Rhee et al. (2007) described that the polyamine adaptive response appears to be shared between pathogen (prokaryote) stringent responses and host (eukaryote) unfolded protein responses (UPR). AtbZIP60 belongs to the basic leucine zipper protein family and is a key transcription factor involved in Arabidopsis UPR. An orthologue of AtbZIP60 has been identified in tobacco (NtbZIP60) via screening of spermine-responsive genes (Tateda et al. 2008). It is further confirmed that AtbZIP60 is responsive to spermine and is also involved in modulation of UPR-responsive genes in Arabidopsis (Iwata and Koizumi, 2005). However, further research may highlight the cross-talk between spermine function and UPR/ stringent response.

Concluding Remarks and Future Perspectives

We are as it were fair starting to comprehend the impact of PAs, and later inquire about on polyamine digestion system has built a solid case for assist thinks about towards cautious examination of PA qualities included in natural stresses. Tall throughput investigation counting advanced natural disciplines like electrophysiology, microarray, transcriptomics, proteomics, metabolomics approaches will too be accommodating to get it the association of the PA biosynthetic pathway in abiotic and biotic stretch resistance. Besides, biotechnological enhancement of trim abiotic and biotic stretch resistance at the atomic level is in advance. Hereditary control of polyamine digestion system has as of now given important data with respect to their part in stretch reaction. The exploitation of information revealed using plant models and the transfer of knowledge to a wide range of crop species for breeding purposes are current challenges for improvement of plant tolerance using the PA pathway. However, intelligent engineering of regulatory circuits involved in stress response requires detailed knowledge of signaling hierarchies and the impact of metabolic changes involved in this response. However, it is reasonable to assume that a thorough comparative analysis of the expression and function of PA genes and other genes involved in stress tolerance will be useful. Alternative approaches also include the use of PA as an external application which can also be administered for increasing tolerance to various stresses. In the long run, PA can be exploited in the same way as farm chemicals to mitigate stress-induced injury for crop protection. However, evidence from field level studies is still lacking. Some striking evidences of exogenous application of PA to counteract environment stresses are expected to promote its extended application to other crops. Nevertheless there are two main areas that need further investigation. Firstly, although there is a strong correlation between the presence of PAs and better tolerance to environmental stresses, intensive research at the molecular level is needed on signaling function. Secondly, current understanding of plant resistance to pathogens is that PA synthesis is stimulated by a plant–pathogen interaction. However, the role of PA in resistance to pathogens requires further research. Hence, research on PA and stress tolerance is at an interesting stage and has set the stage for intensive research to understand an array of functions of these relatively simple molecules.

REFERENCES

Afzal I, Munir F, Ayub CM, Basra SMA, Hameed A, Nawaz A. Changes in Antioxidant Enzymes, Germination Capacity and Vigour of Tomato Seeds in Response of Priming with Polyamines. Seed Sci Technol 2009;37:765–70.

Alcázar R, García-Martínez JL, Cuevas JC, Tiburcio AF, Altabella T. Overexpression of ADC2 in Arabidopsis Induces Dwarfism and Late-flowering through GA deficiency. Plant J 2005;43:425–36.

Alcázar R, Marco F, Cuevas JC, Patron M, Ferrando A, Carrasco P, Tiburcio AF, Altabella T. Involvement of Polyamines in Plant Response to Abiotic Stress. Biotechnol Lett 2006;28:1867–76.

Alcázar R, Altabella T, Marco F, Bortolotti C, Reymond M, Knocz C, Carrasco P, Tiburcio AF. Polyamines: Molecules with Regulatory Functions in Plant Abiotic Stress Tolerance. Planta 2010a;231:1237–49.

Alcázar R, Planas J, Saxena T, Zarza X, Bortolotti C, Cuevas J, Bitrian M, Tiburcio AF, Altabella T. Putrescine Accumulation Confers drought Tolerance in Transgenic Arabidopsis Plants over-expressing the Homologous Arginine Decarboxylase2 gene. Plant Physiol Biochem 2010b;48:547–52.

Ali RM. Role of Putrescine in Salt Tolerance of Atropa Belladonna Plant. Plant Sci 2000;152:173–9.

Allen KD. Assaying Gene Content in Arabidopsis. Proc Nat Acad Sci USA 2002;99: 9568–72.

Allen GJ, Sanders D. Control of Ionic Currents Guard Cell Vacuoles by Cytosolic and Luminal Calcium. Plant J 1996;10:1055–69.

Altabella T, Tiburcio AF, Ferrando A. Plant with Resistance to Low Temperature and Method of Production thereof. 2009; Spanish Patent Application WO2010/004070.

An Z, Jing W, Liu Y, Zhang W. Hydrogen Peroxide Generated by Copper Amine Oxidase is Involved in Abscisic acid-induced Stomatal Closure in Vicia faba. J Exp Bot 2008;59: 815–25.

Apel H, Kirt H. Reactive Oxygen Species: Metabolism, Oxidative Stress and Signal Transduction. Annu Rev Plant Biol 2004;55:373–9.

Armengaud P, Breitling R, Amtmann A. The Potassium-dependent Transcriptome of Arabidopsis Reveals a Prominent Role of Jasmonic Acid in Nutrient Signaling. Plant Physiol 2004;136:2556–76.

Aronova EE, Shevyakova NI, Sretsenko LA, Kuznetsov VIV. Cadaverine-induced Induction of Superoxide Dismutase Gene Expression in Mesembryanthemum crystallinum L. Dokl Biol Sci 2005; 403:257–9.

Asthir B, Spoor W, Duffus CM. Involvement of Polyamines, Diamine Oxidase and Polyamine Oxidase in Resistance of Barley to Blumeria Graminis f. sp. Hordei. Euphytica 2004;136:307–12.

Aziz A, Martin-Tanguy J, Larher F. Stress-induced Changes in Polyamine and Tyramine Levels can Regulate Proline Accumulation in Tomato Leaf Discs Treated with Sodium Chloride. Plant Physiol 1998;104:195–202.

Bagni N, Tassoni A. Biosynthesis, Oxidation and Conjugation of Aliphatic Polyamines in Higher Plants. Amino Acids 2001;20:301–17.

Baileya A, Strema D, Baea H, Myolob G, Guiltinan J. Gene Expression in Leaves of Theobroma cacao in Response to Mechanical Wounding, Ethylene, and/or Methyl Jasmonate. Plant Sci 2005;168:1247–58.

Bais HP, Ravishankar GA. Role of Polyamines in the Ontogeny of Plants and their Biotechnological Applications. Plant Cell Tissue Organ Cult 2002;69:1-34.

Bartels D, Hussain SS. Current Status and Implications of Engineering Drought Tolerance in Plants using Transgenic Approaches. CAB Reviews: Perspectives in Agri, Vet Sci, Nutri Natur Sci, 3. ; 2008. p. 020.

Bartels D, Souer E. Molecular Responses of Plants to Dehydration. In: Madhava KV, Editor. Plant Responses to Abiotic Stress. Berlin: Springer; 2003. p. 8-38.

Bartels D, Sunkar R. Drought and Salt Tolerance in Plants. Crit Rev Plant Sci 2005;24: Bhatnagar P, Minocha R, Minocha S. Genetic manipulation of the Metabolism of Polyamines in Poplar Cells: the Regulation of Putrescine Catabolism. Plant Physiol 2002;128:1455–69.

Bohnert HJ, Shen B. Transformation and Compatible Solutes. Sci Hortic 1999;78:237–60.

Bortolotti C, Cordeiro A, Alcázar R, Borrell A, Culiañez-Macià FA, Tiburcio AF, Altabella T. Localization of Arginine Decarboxylase in Tobacco Plants. Plant Physiol 2004;120:84–92.

Bouchereau A, Aziz A, Larher F, Martin-Tanguy J. Polyamines and Environmental Challenges: Recent Development. Plant Sci 1999;140:103–25.

Bowie D, Lange GD, Mayer ML. Activity-Dependent Modulation of Glutamate Receptors by Polyamines. J Neurosci 1998;18:8175–85.

Bright J, Desikan R, Hancock JT,Weir IS, Neill ST. ABA-induced NO Generation and Stomatal Closure in Arabidopsis are Dependent on H_2O_2 synthesis. Plant J 2006;45:113–22.

Brüggemann L, Pottosin I, Schönknecht G. Cytoplasmic Polyamines Block the Fast Activating Vacuolar Cation Channel. Plant J 1998;16:101–5.

Brüggemann L, Pottosin I, Schönknecht G. Selectivity of the Fast Activating Vacuolar Cation Channel. J Exp Bot 1999;50:873–6.

Camacho-Cristóbal JJ, Lunar L, Lafont F, Baumert A, González-Fontes A. Boron Deficiency Causes Accumulation of Chlorogenic Acid and Caffeoyl Polyamine Conjugates in Tobacco leaves. J Plant Physiol 2004;161:879–81.

Capell T, Escobar C, Liu H, Burtin D, Lepri O, Christou P. Over-expression of Oat Arginine Decarboxylase cDNA in Transgenic Rice (Oryza Sativa L.) Affects Normal Development Pattern in Vitro and Results in Putrescine Accumulation in Transgenic Plants. Theor Appl Genet 1998;97:246–54.

Capell T, Bassie L, Christou P.Modulation of the Polyamine Biosynthetic Pathway Intransgenic Rice Confers Tolerance to Drought Stress. Proc Nat Acad Sci USA 2004;101:9909–14.

Cheng L, Zou Y, Ding S, Zhang Y, Yu X, Cao J, Lu G. Polyamine Accumulation in Transgenic Tomato Enhances the Tolerance to High Temperature Stress. J Integr Plant Biol 2009; 51:489–99.

Christmann A, Hoffmann T, Teplova I, Grill E, Müller A. Generation of Active Pools of Abscisic Acid Revealed by in VivoImaging of Water Stresses Arabidopsis. Plant Physiol 2005;137:209–19.

Cona A, Cenci F, Cervelli M, Federico R, Mariottini P, Moreno S, Angelini R. Polyamine Oxidase, a Hydrogen Peroxide-producing Enzyme, is up-regulated by Light and Down-regulated by Auxin in the Outer Tissues of the Maize Mesocotyle. Plant Physiol 2003;131:803–13.

Cona A, Rea G, Angelini R, Federico R, Tavladoraki P. Functions of Amine Oxidases in Plant Development and Defence. Trends Plant Sci 2006;11:80–8.

Coruzzi G, Last R. Amino acids. In: Buchanan B, Gruissem W, Jones R, editors. Biochemistry and Molecular Biology of Plants. American Society of Plant Physiologists MD; 2000. p. 358–410.

Crowley T, Walters DR. Polyamine Metabolism in An Incompatible Interaction between Barley and the Powdery Mildew Fungus, Blumeria Graminis f. sp. Hordei. J Phytopathol 2002;150(11–12):1–7.

Cuevas JC, Lopez-Cobollo R, Alcázar R, Zarza X, Koncz C, Altabella T, Salinas J, Tiburcio AF, Ferrando A. Putrescine is involved in Arabidopsis Freezing Tolerance and Cold Acclimation by Regulating Abscisic Acid Levels in Response to Low Temperature. Plant Physiol 2008;148:1094–105.

Cuevas JC, Lopez-Cobollo R, Alcázar R, Zarza X, Koncz C, Altabella T, Salinas J, Tiburcio AF, Ferrando A. Putrescine as a Signal to Modulate the Indispensable ABA increase under Cold Stress. Plant Signal Behav 2009;4:219–20.

Danon A, Botari VI, Gordon A, Mailhac N, Gallois P. Ultraviolet-C overexposure Induces Programmed Cell Death in Arabidopsis, which is Mediated by Caspase-like Activities and which can be Suppressed by Caspase Inhibitors, p35, and Defender against Apoptotic death. J Biol Chem 2004;279:779–87.

Del Duca S, Betti L, Trebbi G, SeraWni-Fracassini D, Torrigiani P. Transglutaminase Activity Changes during the Hypersensitive Reaction, a Typical Defense Response of Tobacco NN Plants to TMV. Plant Physiol 2007;131:241–50.

del Pozo O, Lam E. Caspases and Programmed Cell Death in the Hypersensitive Response of Plants to Pathogens. Curr Biol 1998;8:1129–32.

Delauney AJ, Verma DPS. Proline Biosynthesis and Osmoregulation in Plants. Plant J 1993; 4:215–23.

Della Mea M, Caparros-Ruiz D, Claparols I, SeraWni-Fracassini D, Rigau J. AtPng1p: The First Plant Transglutaminase. Plant Physiol 2004;135:2046–54.

Delledonne M, Xia Y, Dixon RA, Lamb C. Nitric Oxide Functions as a Signal in Plant Disease Resistance. Nature 1998;394:585–8.

Demidchik V, Tester M. Sodium Fluxes through non-selective Cation Channels in the Membrane of Protoplasts from Arabidopsis Thaliana roots. Plant Pgysiol 2002;128:379–87.

Desiderio MA, Grassilli E, Bellesia EE, Salomoni P, Franceschi C. Involvement of Ornithine Decarboxylase and Polyamines in Glucocorticoid-induced Apoptosis of Rat Thymocytes. Cell Growth Differ 1995;6:505–13.

Dobrovinskaya OR, Muñiz J, Pottosin II. Asymmetric Block of the Plant Vacuolar Ca^{2+} Permeable Channel by Organic Cations. Eur Biophys J 1999a;28:552–63.

Dobrovinskaya OR, Muñiz J, Pottosin II. Inhibition of Vacuolar ion Channels by Polyamines. J Membr Biol 1999b;167:127–40.

Duan JJ, Li J, Guo SR, Kang YY. Exogenous Spermidine Affects Polyamine Metabolism in Salinity-stressed Cucumis Sativus Roots and Enhances short-term Salinity Tolerance. J Plant Physiol 2008;165:1620–35.

Duhazé C, Gouzerh G, Gagneul D, Larher F, Bouchereau A. The Conversion of Spermidine to Putrescine and 1,3-deaminopropane in the Roots of Limonium Tataricum. Plant Sci 2002;163:639–46.

Edreva AM, Velikova VB, Tsonov TD. Phenylamides in Plants. Russ J Plant Physiol 2007; 54:289–302.

El-Ghachtouli N, Paynot M, matin-Tanguy J, Dorandi D, Gianinazzi S. The Effect of Polyamines on Endomycorrhizal Infection ofwild-type Pisumsativum, cv Frisson (nod +myc+) and two Mutants (nod+myc- and nod-myc+). Mycorrhiza 1995;5:189–92.

El-Ghachtouli N, Paynot M, matin-Tanguy J, Dorandi D, Gianinazzi S. Effect of Polyamines and Polyamine Biosynthesis Inhibitors on Spore Germination and Hyphal Growth of Glomus mosseae. Mycol Res 1996;100:597–600.

Evans PT, Malmberg RL. Do Polyamines have Roles in Plant Development? Ann Rev Plant Physiol Plant Mol Biol 1989;40:235–69.

Franceschetti M, Hanfrey C, Scaramagli S, Torrigiani P, Bagni N, Burtin D, Michael AJ. Characterization of Monocot and Dicot Plant S-adenosyl-L-methionine Decarboxylase Gene Families including Identification in the mRNA of a Highly Conserved Pair of Upstream Overlapping Open Reading Frames. Biochem J 2001;53:403–9.

Franceschetti M, Fornale S, Tassoni A, Zuccherelli K, Mayer MJ, Bagni N. Effects of Spermidine Synthase Overexpression on Polyamine Biosynthetic Pathway in Tobacco Plants. J Plant Physiol 2004;161:989-1001.

Galston AW, Weinstein LH. Control of Phytopathogen by Inhibitors of Polyamine Biosynthesis. Adv Exp Med Biol 1988;250:589–99.

Galston AW, Kaur-Sawhney R, Altabella T, Tiburcio AF. Plant Polyamines in Reproductive Activity and Response to Abiotic Stress. Bot Acta 1997; 110:197–207.

Garia-Mata C, Lamattina L. Nitric Oxide and Abscisic Acid cross talk in guard cells. Plant Physiol 2002;128:790–2.

Garufi A, Visconti S, Camoni L, Aducci P. Polyamines as Physiological Regulators of 14-3-3 Interactionwith the Plant Plasmamembrane H+ -ATPase. Plant Cell Physiol 2007;48: 434–40.

Ge C, Cui X, Wang Y, Hu Y, Fu Z, Zhang D, Cheng Z, Li J. BUD2, Encoding an Sadenosylmethionine Decarboxylase, is required for Arabidopsis Growth and Development. Cell Res 2006;16:446–56.

Gill SS, Tuteja N. Polyamines and Abiotic Stress Tolerance in Plants. Plant Signal Behav 2010; 51:26–33.

Gomez M, Hellstrand P. Endogenous Polyamines Modulate Ca^{2+} Channel Activity in Guinea-pig Intestinal Smooth Muscle. Pflugers Arch 1999;436:445–51.

Greenberg JT, Guo A, Klessig DF, Ausubel FM. Programmed Cell Death in Plants: A Pathogen-Triggered Response Activated Coordinately with Multiple Defense Functions. Cell 1994;77:551–63.

Greenland AJ, Lewis DH. Amines in Barley Leaves infected with Brown Rust and their Possible Relevance to Formation of 'Green Islands'. New Phytol 1984;96:283–91.

Griffin M, Casadio R, Bergamini CM. Transglutaminases: Nature's Biological Glues. Biochem J 2002;368:377–96.

Groppa MD, Benavides MP. Polyamines and Abiotic Stress: Recent Advances. Amino Acids 2008;34:35–45.

Groppa MD, Benavides MP, Tomaro ML. Polyamine Metabolism in Sunflower and Wheat leaf discs under Cadmium or Copper Stress. Plant Sci 2003;16:481–8.

Grün S, Lindermayr C, Sell S, Durner J. Nitric Oxide and Gene Regulation in Plants. J Exp Bot 2006;57:507–16.

Ha HC, Woster PM, Jager JD, Casero RAJ. The Role of Polyamine Catabolism in Polyamineanalogue-induced Programmed Cell Death. Proc Natl Acad Sci USA 1997;94: 11557–62.

Hanfrey C, Sommer S, Mayer MJ, Burtin D, Michael AJ. Arabidopsis Polyamine Biosynthesis: Absence of Ornithine Decarboxylase and the Mechanism of Arginine Decarboxylase Activity. Plant J 2001;27:551–60.

Hanzawa Y, Takahashi T, Komeda Y. ACL5: an Arabidopsis Gene Required for Internodal Elongation after Flowering. Plant J 1997;12:863–74.

Hanzawa Y, Takahashi T, Michael AJ, Burtin D, Long D, Pineiro M, Coupland G, Komeda Y. ACAULIS5, an Arabidopsis Gene required for Stem Elongation, Encodes a Spermine Synthase. EMBO J 2000;19:4248–56.

Hanzawa Y, Imai A, Michael AJ, Komeda Y, Takahashi T. Characterization of the Spermidine Synthase-related Gene Family in Arabidopsis Thaliana. FEBS Lett Hashimoto T, Tamaki K, Suzuki K, Yamada Y. Molecular Cloning of Plant Spermidine Synthases. Plant Cell Physiol 1998;39:73–9.

He L, Nada K, Kasukabe Y, Tchibana S. Enhanced Susceptibility of Photosynthesis to low temperature Photohibition due to Interruption of Chill-induced increase of Sadenosylmethionine Decarboxylase Activity in Leaves of Spinach (Spinacia Oleracea L.). Plant Cell Physiol 2002;43:196–206.

He L, Ban Y, Inoue H, Matsuda N, Liu J, Moriguchi T. Enhancement of Spermidine Content and Antioxidant Capacity in Transgenic Pear Shoots Overexpressing Apple Spermidine Synthase in Response to Salinity and Hyperosmosis. Phytochem 2008;69:2133–41.

Hiraga S, Ito H, Yamakawa H, Ohtsubo N, Seo S, Mitsuhara I, Matsui H, Honma M, Ohashi Y. An HR-induced Tobacco Peroxidase Gene is Responsive to Spermine, but not to Salicylate, Methyl Jasmonate, and Ethephon. Mol Plant-Microbe Interact 2000;13: 210–6.

Hirschi KD. Expression of Arabidopsis CAX1 in Tobacco: Altered Calcium Homeostasis and increased Stress Sensitivity. Plant Cell 1999;11:2113–22.

Hu WW, Gong H, Pua EC. Molecular Cloning and Characterization of S-adenosylmethionine Decarboxylase Genes from Mustard (Brassica Juncea). Plant Physiol 2005;124: 25–40.

Huang CJ, Moczydlowski E. Cytoplasmic Polyamines as Permeant Blockers and Modulators of the Voltage-gated Sodium Channel. Biophys J 2001;80:1262–79.

Hummel I, Gouesbet G, El Amrani A, Ainouche A, Couee I. Characterization of the two Arginine Decarboxylase (Polyamine Biosynthesis) Paralogues of the Endemic Subantarctic Cruciferous Species Pringlea Antiscorbutica and Analysis of their differential Expression during Development and Response to Environmental Stress. Gene 2004;342:199–209.

Igarashi K, Kashiwagi K. Polyamines: Mysterious Modulators of Cellular Functions. Biochem Biophys Res Commun 2000;271:559–64.

Illingworth C, Mayer MJ, Elliott K, Hanfrey C, Walton NJ, Michael AJ. The Diverse Bacterial Origins of the Arabidopsis Polyamine Biosynthetic Pathway. FEBS Lett 2003;549:26–30.

Imai R, Ali A, Pramanik HR, Nakaminami K, Sentoku N, Kato H. A Distinctive Class of Spermidine Synthase is involved in Chilling Response in rice. J Plant Physiol 2004;161:883–6.

Iqbal M, Ashraf M. Changes in Growth, Photosynthetic Capacity, and Ionic Relations in Spring Wheat (Triticum aestivum L.) due to Pre-sowing Seed Treatment with Polyamines. Plant Growth Regul 2005;46:19–30.

Iwata Y, Koizumi N. An Arabidopsis Transcription Factor, AtbZIP60, Regulates the Endoplasmic Reticulum Stress Response in a Manner Unique to Plants. Proc Natl Acad Sci USA 2005;102:5280–5.

Janowitz T, Kneifel H, Piotrowski M. Identification and Characterization of Plant Agmatine Iminohydrolase, the last missing link in Polyamine Biosynthesis of Plants. FEBS Lett 2003;544:258–61.

Jones JDG, Dangl JL. The Plant Immune System. Nature 2006;444:323–9. Kakehi J, Kuwashiro Y, Niitsu M, Takahashi T. Thermospermine is Required for Stem Elongation in Arabidopsis Thaliana. Plant Cell Physiol 2008;49:1342–9.

Kakkar RK, Sawhney VK. Polyamine Research in Plants. A Changing Perspective. Physiol Plant 2002;116:281–92.

Kasinathan V, Wingler A. Effect of Reduced Arginine Decarboxylase Activity on Salt Tolerance and on Polyamine Formation during Salt Stress in Arabidopsis Thaliana. Plant Physiol 2004;121:101–7.

Kasukabe Y, He L, Nada K, Misawa S, Ihara I, Tachibana S. Overexpression of Spermidine Synthase Enhances Tolerance to Multiple Environmental Stresses and up-regulates the Expression of various Stress-regulated Genes in Transgenic Arabidopsis Thaliana. Plant Cell Physiol 2004;45:712–22.

Kasukabe Y, He L, Watakabe Y, Otani M, Shimada T, Tachibana S. Improvement of Environmental Stress Tolerance of Sweet Potato by Introduction of Genes for Spermidine Synthase. Plant Biotechnol 2006;23:75–83.

Kaur-Sawhney R, Tiburcio AF, Altabella T, Galston A. Polyamines in Plants: An Overview. J. Cell Mol Biol 2003;2:1-12.

Khurana N, Saxena RK, Gupta R, Rajam MV. Polyamines as Modulators of Microcycle Conidiation in Aspergillus Flavus. Microbiology 1996;142:517–23.

Kim SA, Kwak JM, Jae SK, Wang MH, Nam HG. Overexpression of the AtGluR2 Gene Encoding an Arabidopsis Homolog of Mammalian Glutamate Receptors Impairs Calcium nutilization and Sensitivity to Ionic Stress in Transgenic Plants. Plant Cell Physiol 2001;42:74–84.

Knott JM, Römer P, Sumper M. Putative Spermine Synthases from Thalassiosira Pseudonana and Arabidopsis Thaliana Synthesize Thermospermine Rather than Spermine. FEBS Lett 2007;581:3081–6.

Kumar A, Altabella T, Taylor M, Tiburcio AF. Recent Advances in Polyamine Research. Trends Plant Sci 1997;2:124–30.

Kumria R, Rajam MV. Ornithine Decarboxylase Transgene in Tobacco Affects Polyamine Metabolism, in Vitro Morphogenesis and Response to Salt Stress. J Plant Physiol 2002;159:983–90.

Kusano T, Yamaguchi K, Berberich T, Takahashi Y. Advances in Polyamine Research in 2007. J Plant Res 2007a;120:345–50.

Kusano T, Yamaguchi K, Berberich T, Takahashi Y. The Polyamine Spermine Rescues Arabidopsis from Salinity and drought Stresses. Plant Signal Behav 2007b;2:250–1.

Kusano T, Berberich T, Tateda C, Takahashi Y. Polyamines: Essential Factors for Growth and Survival. Planta 2008;228:367–81.

Kuthanová A, Gemperlová L, Zelenková S, Eder J, Macháčková I, Opatrný Z, Cvikrová M. Cytological changes and Alterations in Polyamine Contents induced by Cadmium in Tobacco BY-2 cells. Plant Physiol Biochem 2004;42:149–56.

Kuznetsov Vl, Shevyakova NI. Proline under Stress: Biological Role, Metabolism and Regulation. Russ J Plant Physiol 1999;46:274–87.

Kuznetsov Vl, Shevyakova NI. Polyamines and Stress Tolerance of Plants. Plant Stress 2007;1:50–71.

Kuznetsov Vl, Shevyakova NI. Polyamines and Plant Adaptation to Saline Environments. In: Remawat KG, Editor. Desert Plants. Springer-Verlag Berlin-Heidelberg; 2010. p. 261–98.

Kytoviita MM, Sarjala T. Effects of Defoliation and Symbiosis on Polyamine Levels in Pine and Birch. Mycorrhiza 1997;7:107–11.

Larher FR, Aziz A, Gibon Y, Trotel-Aziz P, Sulpice R, Bouchereau A. An Assessment of the Physiological Properties of the so-called Compatible Solutes using in Vitro Experiments with Leaf Discs. Plant Physiol Biochem 2003;41:657–66.

Lepri O, Bassie L, Safwat G, Thu-Hang P, Trung-Nghia P, Hölttä E, Christou P, Capell T.

Over-expression of Human Ornithine Decarboxylase cDNA in Transgenic Rice Plants Alters the Polyamine Pool in a Tissue-Specific Manner. Mol Genet Genomics 2001;266:303–12.

Levine A, Pennell RI, Alvarez ME, Palmer R, Lamb C. Calcium-mediated Apoptosis in a Plant Hypersensitive Disease Resistance Response. Curr Biol 1996;6:427–37.

Lindsay GS, Wallace HM. Changes in Polyamine Catabolism in HL-60 human promyelogenous leukaemic Cells in Response to Etoposide induced Apoptosis. Biochem J 1998;337:83–7.

Liu K, Fu H, Bei Q, Luan S. Inward Potassium Channel in Guard cells as a Target for Polyamine Regulation of Stomatal Movements. Plant Physiol 2000;124:1315–26.

Phyto-chemicals and Ethanobotany **Pages 138-154**
Edited by: Pawan Kumar 'Bharti'
ISBN: 978-93-86841-93-3
Edition: 2019
Published by: Discovery Publishing House Pvt. Ltd., New Delhi (India)

6

Stem Gall of Coriander and Its Management

[1]R.S. Mishra

Coriander (*Coriandrum sativum* L.) is one of the important spices crop grown throughout the world and belonging to family *Apiaceae* (*Umbelliferae*). It is native of Mediterranean region. In India, it is cultivated in Rajasthan, Gujarat, Madhya Pradesh, Tamil Nadu, Utter Pradesh and Bihar. Rajasthan is major growing state and contributes about 40 per cent of coriander production in India. Production of coriander in India is about 314 metric tonnes from the area of 447 thousand hectare with productivity 0.7 metric tonnes per hectares (Anonymous 2014-15). All parts of this herb are in use as flavoring agent and/or as traditional remedies for the treatment of different disorders in the folk medicine systems of different civilizations (Sahib *et al.*, 2012). Coriander (*Coriandrum sativum*) is also widely cultivated in U.P. for green leaf as well as seed, but area, production and productivity is not as per expectation because crop production is influenced by numerous agronomical, ecological and edaphic factors like fertility of soil, cultural practices, pH of soil and infestation by pests and diseases(Dabbas *et al.* 2009). Incidences of insect/pest and diseases have been considered as a major factor in low crop production along with fertility status of soil. The crop affects badly due to number of diseases incited by fungi, bacteria, and viruses. Among of them, fungal pathogens (*Protomyces, Erysiphe, Fusarium, Rhizoctonia* etc.) have been reported to infect the coriander crop drastically.

History and Distribution

Stem gall of coriander is one of the well-known disease of coriander causing heavy damage especially when associated with wilt (Nikam *et al.*, 1959). Stem gall and powdery mildew were reported earlier as minor diseases of less significance in Europe and India by Butler (1918) but now both the diseases considered as the diseases of major significance causing severe yield losses (Gupta, 1954; Mundukar, 1959, Gupta, 1973; Awasthi *et al.*, 1978; Srivastava *et al.*, 1971; Keshwal *et al.*, 1979). Gupta (1954) estimated fruit yield loss is about 15 per cent when 23 per cent plants are infected. Singh *et al.* (1984) noticed

[1] College of Agriculture, Azamgarh, N. D. University of Agril. & Technology, Kumarganj, -224229, Faizabad, UP, India.

the disease was quite prevalent with a total intensity of 7.5-24.4 per cent with 9.0-20.8 per cent expected yield loss. Stem gall disease cause severe loss in yield and quality of seeds (Lakra, 1993). Stem gall disease incited by fungus *Protomyces macrosporus* Unger, a member of sub-division- Ascomycotina, class- Hemiascomycetes order- *Taphrinales* and family- *Protomycetaceae*. The fungus attacks on foliage, stem, flowers and fruits, causing hypertrophy and deformity. Pathogen has been persisted from year to year in the form of chlamydospores in seeds, soil or both (Pavgi and Mukhopadhyay, 1969 a, b), which germinates and initiates fresh infection in the following season. Symptoms were visible by infecting the viable chlamydospores in to 3-6 weeks old seedling (Srivastava, 1955 b). Lakra (1990) studied and reported maximum disease infection 67 per cent with 5 g inoculation of inoculums per plot. The amount of inoculum had no effect on incubation period.

Date of sowing

The date of sowing differs in different agro climatic region as well as states depending on the requirement of crop growth periods. The date of sowing plays on important role in development of disease which ultimately determines the seed yield. The sowing date of coriander is described in between 15 Oct. to 15 Nov. The incidence of stem gall disease is more or less correlated with the time of sowing irrespective of environmental conditions (Mishra and Pandey, 2015)

Tripathi (2003) conducted the experiments during 1999-2001 and reported suitable time of coriander sowing is from 16 October to 16 November. He has found minimum yield loss due to stem gall disease during this sowing period in east zone (Lucknow). Severity of stem gall disease was significantly affected by sowing date. A positive and significant correlation coefficient was recorded between disease intensity and per cent seed yield loss. Early sowing (16 September) and late sowing (10 Dec.) exhibited high disease and low seed yield.

Identification and Characterization of Pathogen

The genus *Protomyces* is an obligate parasite on plants within the *Apiaceae* family. The fungus produces white-green galls on stem, leaves, inflorescence and fruits. The galls on leaves are restricted to petiole, midrib, veins and veinlet's (Reddy and Kramer, 1975). In these gall ascogenous cells are present. The ascogenous cell is formed intercellurily in the intercellular mycelium commonly concentrated along the vascular bundles of the host plant (Buren, 1915, Gjaerum, 1964). The cells of surrounding host tissues shows hypertrophy, hyperplasia and malformation. The hypertrophied seed galls are brittle, rough surfaced, straw yellow and 3-8 times larger than the normal seeds. The seed galls are containing numerous chlamydospores of the pathogen (Pavgi and Mukhopadhyay, 1969) Mycelium of the fungus is found in galled tissue only. The size of the ascogenous cells varies between 42-77 μm in diameter with smooth wall 3-6 μm thick in *Aegopodium podagraria* host plant. Research of molecular studies confirmed Protomycetales are very closely related to Taphrinales with the used of inferences from 18 S rDNA sequence divergence (Nishida *et al.* 1995). Gupta (1962) have found chlamydospores in the floral parts which affected the fruits size and shape. Rao (1972) made extensive studies on morphology and developmental anatomy of the stem galls and malformation of other parts of coriander caused by *Protomyces macrosporus*. The gall formed on stem and other parts of plant due to increased size and number of cortical and phloem cells which showed hypertrophy and hyperplasia. Gupta and Sinha (1964) have described the variation in morphological characters and pathogenicity of the fungus. They have collected samples from various north Indian localities and made comparison of chlamydospores with diameter, thickness of episporium, diameter of germinated branches and septate hyphae in the intercellular spaces of nonvascular tissues. Initiates and development of chlamydospores from hyphae were studied by Gupta and Sinha (1963 a).

Bacigalova, *et al.* (2005) were studied the new species of *Protomyces cirsii-oleracei* Buhr from living leaves of *Cirsiumoleraceum* (L.). This species is formed galls are limpid, white green to yellow, often 2–20 mm long. The septate mycelium of the pathogen is very thin, invades the leaf tissue intercellularly, and concentrates along with vascular tissue. Mature ascogenous cells are 36.5μm long and 35μm wide, it is three-layered, light to yellowish-brown with4.7μm thick. Bacigálová, (2008) has introduced the *Protomyces buerenianus* Buhr, a mycobiota of Slovakia. The fungus was found on the living leaves and stems of neophytic host plant *Galinsogaparvi flora* Cav. (*Asteraceae*). Mycelium is 2–5 μm thick and mature ascogenous cells are 70 μm long and 60 μm wide. The ascogenous cell walls are three-layered, light to yellowish-brown with 5–9μm thick. Bacigálová, (2004) has characterized to the *Protomyces as* bio- trophic, gall forming usually on leaves, stems and fruits. The galls are usually restricted on petiole, veins and veinlets of leaves.

Survival and Spread of Pathogen

The stem gall disease of coriander appears in the form of small tumour like swelling on all herbaceous part of plant starting from stem to seeds. The fungus is restricted in neighboring tissues, resulting the formation of tumour like gall. The infection becomes systemic in host stem before and during the pre-flowering period leading to hypertrophy and hyperplasia in fruit.

Pavgi and Mukhopadhya (1969) reported the *Protomyces macrosporus* Unger inciting the stem gall disease of coriander (*Coriandrum sativum* L.) perpetuated through the resting chlamydospores released in the soil after the monsoon rains from the crop debris and fruit galls of un-cleaned seed lot of coriander planted in the field. The pathogen also survives in the soil through heat-resistant desiccated endo and blastospores, most provably through the chlamydospores, hibernating in an intensively cultivated field. Purple leaf spot of agasta (*Protomycopsis* thirmulacharrii), Angular leaf spot of black and green gram (*Protomycopsis physeoli*) are formed primary inoculums from debris of the previous season soil, that are perpetuated from one season to another season by heat resistant chlamydospores (Haware and Pavgi 1971). The chlamydospores in pericarp are carried to soil along with seed as fresh inoculums (Pavgi and Mukhopadhyay, 1972) and germinate after monsoon rain from crop debris and fruit galls (Pavgi and Mukhopadhyay, 1969). The chlamydospores can survive in soil for a long time and can germinate even after 8 years (Gupta, 1973). Stem gall of coriander disease appear regularly every year at different stage of plant growth. The thick walled chlamydospores resist in higher temperature and desiccate during summer months (May-June). It is survive over prolonged periods in the absence of host crop. A natural rest period of 4-6 months (dormancy) as per requisite to chlamydospore germination was indicated by earlier worker (Bueren, 1915; Butler, 1922; Gauman and Dodge, 1928). This dormancy could not be broken by use of chemicals (Srivastava, 1955-b). Mukhopadhyay and Pavgi (1964) indicated that chlamydospores immersion in water up to one week has been helped to break the thick exospores and fasten germination to as much as 90 per cent. Galls on the stem and fruit exposed to weathering conditions in the field become desiccated during summer, while the chlamydospores embedded in the host tissues remain protected from adverse effects directly. Monsoon rains in July-August initiate rotting of the plant debris gradually releasing the chlamydospores in the soil by disintegration of the host tissues from September onward (Pavgi and Mukhopadhyay 1969). He also studied the period and depth of the soil where the maximum number of chlamydospores were present in per gram of soil. The number of chlamydospores/g soil showed an increase through December and decline in later month. The spore count was nearly similar with slight variation in all the depth i.e. surface, 1 inch and 2 inch. Lakra (2001) noticed the distribution patterns of chlamydospores of *Protomyces macrosporus* in the infected parts of coriander and its relationship with the expression of symptoms. The degree of gall formation was positively correlated with the number of chlamydospores present in the tissue which formed hypertrophied galls in plant parts under field condition. The highest number of chlamydospores was observed in the hypertrophied collar region of stem and lowest in the healthy looking seed and stem of highly infected plants. Mix (1925) had seen annual addition of fresh chlamydospores and blastospores into the soil through intensive cultivation of the susceptible host crop and recurrence of the disease in the same field which lead to soil transmission of this pathogen.

Adejumo *et al.* (2000) described the secondary inoculum (blastospores) causing an increase amount of incidence and severity of leaf smut disease of cow pea caused by *Protomycopsis phaseoli*. Pavgi and Mukhopadhyay, (1972) reported the infection and development of disease stem gall of coriander caused by *Protomyces macrosporus* Unger pathogenic on *Coriandrum sativum* L. becomes systemic in the host stem much before or during the pre-flowering period, inducing organogenic changes in the flowers and fruits due to hypertrophy and hyperplasy. Partial fruit development due to part infection occurs variously and the chlamydospores in the pericarp are carried to the soil with the seed as a fresh inoculums. Pavgi and Mukhopadhyay (1969) tested the viability of coriander seed infected by stem gall disease with triphenyltetrazolium chloride and germination under pot condition. Seed viability was highest healthy seed (95-98%) and none of completely hypertrophied seed was found viable. Mishra and Kumar (2016) reported the viability of coriander seed infected by stem gall disease which tested with triphenyltetrazolium chloride Seed viability (94.60%) and seed germination (90.00%) was maximum in healthy seed, while none of hypertrophied seeds were found viable. Seed germination was more or less in similar pattern.

Germination of Chlamydospores

Soil suspension from different places were separately centrifuged at 1400 r.p.m. supernatant liquid decanted off and the chlamydospores collected in the sediment were treated in acidulate water and induced to germinate on inverted slide mounts in condensed moisture. The recovered chlamydospores indicated 66-89% germinability (Thirumalachar and Pavgi 1950). Numerous isolation modes by Pavgi and Mukhopadhyay (1969) from infected soil sample collected from two different locations resembled salmon red and creamy white type in colony characters and morphology of culture cells. Pathogenicity tests were positive and typical galls appeared in about two weeks later on the inoculated plants. Control plants remain healthy. Tubaki (1957) made extensive studied on nucleus status of chlamydospores. He stated that the nuclei in *Protomyces macrosporus* were neither nucleolus nor chromatin could be differentiated in heidenhain's hemotoxylin stain. Mathur (1962) studied the relation of pH of soil and stem gall disease of coriander. He indicated that highest chlamydospores was germinated at pH 7.4. The minimum infection occurs at pH 4.6, and maximum infection at pH 7.8-8.4. Any further increase or decrease in the pH level tended to increase the inhibition. Haware and Pavgi, (1976) were observed the sequence of the events in germination of chlamydospore (*Protomycopsis patelii* pavgi and thirumulachar) parasitic on mung beens (*Phaseolis mungo* L. and *Phaseolus radiates* L.). Haware and Pavgi, (1976)studied the spore germination of *Protomycopsis thirumalacharii* Pavgi caused purple leaf spot disease of mung beans *(Phaseolus mungo* L. and *Phaseolus radiates* L.) and 'Agasta'*(Sesbania grandflora* Pers.) respectively in Varanasi and the surrounding areas of Uttar Pradesh . The infection is mostly confined in leaflets and chlamydospores developed in the mesophyllar interspaces obscuring the host tissues.

Pavgi and Mukhopadhyay, (1973) I nvestigated the genus *Protomyces macrosporus* Unger, especially the nuclear divisions in the germinating chlamydospores, copulation of spores and developmental cytology within the host tissues. Lakra (2001) find out the distribution patterns of chlamydospores in the infected parts of coriander (*Coriandrum sativum*) and its relationship with the expression of symptoms. The degree of gall formation was positively correlated with the number of chlamydospores of the pathogen which formed hypertrophied tissues in plants under field conditions. The highest number of chlamydospores was observed in the hypertrophied collar region of stem and lowest in the healthy-looking seeds and stems. Adejumo *et al.* (2001) studied the chlamydospores germination in potato dextrose agar with leaf tissues dipped in acidified water (1% H_2SO4) a microscopic slide. The chlamydospores was germinating slowly at 24–28°C temperature with snow white colour that produced globose vesicles.

Disease Severity and Yield

Severe losses from stem gall disease have been reported by many workers (Prasad, 1983; Singh *et al.*, 1984 and Lakra, 1993). At Gwalior, disease intensity was 23% with 15 per cent average yield loss/plant was reported by Gupta (1954). Naqvi (1986) reported that severity of stem gall disease was significantly correlated with yield. Toncer (1998) reported that when the seeds were sown during 15 Nov to 15 March at 15 days interval. The seed yield and essential oil content (0.34%) were highest in seeds sown on 15 November. Gupta (1976) studied the impact of nitrogen phosphorus and manganese on the severity of the disease. The severity of the disease decreased with the application of nitrogen while manganese reverses the effect. Phosphorus at low level reduces the infection but at high level increases it. Yield of infected seeds, total seed yield/ha and per cent yield loss were positively correlated with disease intensity while yield of healthy seeds were negatively correlated in the study conducted for evaluation of coriander cultivars for resistance of stem gall disease (Tripathi, 2001).

Management

In order to get higher yield and quality products, management of disease is essential. It comprises a number of practices to be adopted right from seed sowing to harvest. Numbers of attempts have been made to effectively control the stem gall disease in coriander. Chlamydospores are thick walled and survive in the unfavorable environment over prolonged period in the absence of host. The disease is seed as well as soil borne Mishra and Pandey (2015). Therefore seed and soil management are reviewed.

Chemical Management

Chlamydospores are thick walled and survive in the unfavorable environment over prolonged period in the absence of host. The disease is seed as well as soil borne. Therefore seed and soil treatment have been recommended by several workers. Gupta and Sinha (1963-b) observed control of stem gall disease by spraying sulpha drugs and some common antibiotics. Three soil application of streptomycin and penicillin each at 400 ppm concentration showed a decrease of disease intensity. Combined soil and seed treatment with Thiram gave better results. TCNA (Tetrachloro nitro anisole) @ 0.5 kg/100kg of seeds also gave better results. Mathur and Narula (1963) indicated the effect of certain fungicides, antibiotics and synthetic phytohormones on the germination of chlamydospores of *Protomyces macrosporus*. They found effective for inhibiting the chlamydospores germination by Blitox-50, Dithane Z-78, Aretan, Agllol, Achromycin, Chloromycetin and NAA. Synthetic phytohormone also inhibited 50 per cent germination of chlamydospores with the concentration of 10 ppm spray fluid. Thirumalachar *et al.* (1969) reported the Aureofungin inhibited the growth of *Protomyces macrosporus* @ 2.5μg/ml. Nene *et al.* (1966)

have reported very effective control of stem gall by combined seed and soil treatment with thiram. The dosage for seed treatment is 0.25 kg/100 kg seed and soil treatment @ 8 kg/acre. Seed treatment alone also reduces the disease incidence significantly. Four foliar sprays of thiram (0.2%), captafol (0.2%) or carboxin (0.1%) were found more effective than seed treatment or combined seed and soil treatment in controlling stem gall disease and increasing seed yield of coriander Bhardwaj, and Shrestha (1985). Lakra (2000) examined the effect of seed treatment with Bavistin (Carbendazim), Captan, Thiram and Vitavax (Carboxin) @ 2 and 4 g a.i. /kg seed before sowing and resulted thiram and carbendazim @ 2.0 g/kg seed were more effective in comparison to rest of the chemical. He also sprayed the Carbendazim (0.2%), Carboxin (0.1%), Copper oxychloride (0.3%), mancozeb (0.25%) and Streptomycin (500 ppm)on the infected coriander crop. The disease was effectively controlled with thiram and Carbendazim (0.2%). Tripathi *et al.* (2001) observed highest stem gall disease incidence (38%) with the application of 50 kg phosphorus/ha while the lowest disease incidence with 25 kg/ha. Whereas the highest average seed yield was obtained with application @70:50:25 kg NPK/ha. Tripathi and Bartaria. (2002) also studied the effect of thiram, Captan, Bavistin, Vitavax (Carboxin) and Mancozeb with seed treatment alone and in combination with foliar spray for the control of stem gall disease and resulted all the treatments lowered the disease intensity and gave higher seed yields over control. However seed treatments had gave better resulted than seed treatments combined with foliar spray of fungicides. Kumar *et al.* (2014) reported the effect of seed treatment and foliar spray of bio agents *Trichoderma viride, Pseudomonas fluorescens* and fungicides like Carbendazim, Ridomil, Blitox-50, Hexaconazole and Propiconazole on the incidence of stem gall disease of coriander. The trial was conducted in a Randomized Block Design with three replications and eight treatments including check. Hexaconazole as seed treatment (0.2%) and foliar spray(0.2%) at 40,60 and 75 DAS is found more effective treatment for management of stem gall disease of coriander than seed treatment with bio agent *Trichoderma viride* (0.4%) with foliar spray at 40,60 and 75 days after sowing. Whereas, maximum seed yield was recorded in seed treatment with hexaconazole and propiconazole. The highest cost benefit ratio 1:4.36 was observed in the seed treatment with IISR *Trichoderma* liquid formulation @ 0.4% + foliar spray at 40, 60 and

75DAS. Mishra *et al* (2013) observed that four fungicides namely carbendazim (0.20%), hexaconazole (0.20%), propiconazole (0.20%) and blitox-50 (0.20%) with seed treatment and foliar spray at 40, 60, and 75 DAS were found effective for minimizing the stem gall disease. Among the fungicides 51.0% disease reduction was observed in hexaconazole followed by propiconazole (48.35%), blitox-50 (38.36%) and carbendazim (33.97%).

Organic Management

The increasing population pressure and demand of field resources are introducing chemical fertilizer, pesticides and insecticides in to the soil, but they are disturbing the soil physio-chemical properties including soil texture, porosity and water holding capacity and also disturbed the soil microbial population (Raj *et al.* 2014). Besides this, use of chemical fertilizers and pesticides in agriculture fields lead to environmental degradation. Hence as an alternative to chemicals are used for incensing production and productivity of crop. Panchgavya is also being sought to improve crop establishment and health (Shakuntala *et al.* 2012). It is an organic formulation, which in Sanskrit means the blend of five products obtained from cow i.e. milk, ghee, curd, dung and urine. All these products are individually called as "Gavy" and collectively named as Panchgavya. Panchagavya has got reference in the scripts of Vedas and Vrikshayurveda (Natarajan, 2002). In India use of Panchagavya in organic forming is gaining popularity in recent years especially in state like Tamil Nadu and Kerala (Shailaja *et al.* 2014). It is also called cowpathy treatment based on products obtained from cows used in ayurvedic medicine and of religious significance for Hindu (Srimathi *et al.* 2013). Panchgavya is an organic product recommended for crop improvement in organic agriculture (Sangeetha and Thevanathan, 2010). It is used as a foliar spray, soil application along with irrigation, as well as seed treatment (Natarajan, 2002). Panchgavya has played a significant role in providing resistance to pests and diseases, resulting in an increased over all yields (Tharmaraj *et al.* 2011). Panchgavya possess the properties of fertilizers and bio pesticides and have been resulted in positive effect on growth and yield of crops as reported by Somasundaram *et al,* (2007). Effective microorganisms in panchgavya are a mixed culture of naturally occurring beneficial microbes mostly lactic acid bacteria (*Lactobacillus*), yeast (*Saccharomyces*), actinomycetes (*Streptomyces*), photosynthetic bacteria (*Rhodopsuedomonas*) and certain fungi (*Aspergillus, Penicillium* etc.) (Xu, 2001., Swaminathan *et al.* 2007). Chemolethotrops and autotrophic nitrifiers (Ammonifers and nitrifiers) are present in panchgavya, which colonize on the leaves and increased the ammonia uptake and enhance the total N supply (Papen *et al.* 2002). The P^H of panchgavya was lowered to 4.5 at 30 days of fermentation and this might due to *Lactobacillus* bacteria in panchgavya, which produced more organic acid during fermentation (Mathivanan *et al.* 2006).

Prabhu (2009) prepared panchgavya by using the ingredients viz. cow dung (5kg),cow urine (3liter), cow milk (2 liter), cow curd (2 liter), cow ghee (1 liter), sugarcane juice (3 liter), tender coconut water (3 liter) and ripened banana (12 NO_3). All the above substrates were added to a wide mouthed mud pot and kept open under shade. The content was stirred twice a day for about 20 minutes both in morning and evening to facilitate aerobic microbial activity. The beneficial microorganisms of panchgavya and their establishment in the soil hove improved the sustainability of agriculture as the microorganisms present in the rhizospheric environment i.e. around the roots, which influence the plant growth and crop yield was might due to presence of growth accelerating enzyme in panchgavya which favored rapid cell division and multiplication (Vasumathi 2001, and Sanjutha *et al.* 2008). Naik and Sreenivasa (2009) opined that panchgavya contains bacteria producing plant growth promoting substances. The microbes viz. *Rhizobium, Azotobactor, Azospirillum, Trichoderma* and *Pseudomonas* present in panchagavya act as liquid bio fertilizers and bio pesticides (Ali 2011). Sometimes seed germination and seedling quality have reduced with increasing concentration of organic fortification which might be due to optimal dose of the organic product which is normally specific crops to crop (Henig-Severa *et al.* 2000). Panchgavya enhance the growth and vigour of crops, including resistance to pest and diseases with increasing the keeping quality of vegetables and fruits (Natarajan 2002). Mishra *et al.* (2015) reported that the maximum reduction of mycelium growth was found in cow urine based botanical formulation 50.83 to 56.05% followed by acetone based botanical formulation 49.92 to 54.31%, distilled water based botanical formulation 44.51 to 52.35%. The effectiveness of cow urine based onion extract was 51.58% at 20% concentration after 72 h incubation. Sugha (2005) evaluated the antifungal potentiality of panchagavya against *R. solani, S. rolfsii, F. solani, S. sclerotiorum* and *Phytophthora colocasiae,* which resulted complete suppression of mycelial growth of *R. solani* and other pathogens, the growth inhibition ranged was between 88.1-92.3%. The antifungal activity of panchagavya against major soil borne pathogens *viz. F. solani* f. sp. *pisi, F. oxysporum* f. sp. *pisi, R. solani, S. solfsii* and *S. Sclerotiorum* were studied and found 90 per cent inhibition of *F. oxysporum* f. sp. *Pisi* and *F. solani* f. sp. *Pisi* and 100 per cent inhibition of *S. rolfsii, S. sclerotiorum* and *R. solani.* Dogra (2006).

Basak and Lee (2005) conducted the experiment to study the efficacy of cow urine and dung *in vitro* for controlling wilt caused by *F. oxysporum* f. sp. *Cucumerinum* of cucumber and *F. solani* f. sp. *cucurbitae.* Cow dung solution showed 80-84 per cent and cow urine showed 100 per cent inhibition of wilt pathogens. Out of twelve organic inputs tested, eight inputs *viz.* biosol, matkakhad, agnihotra ash + cow urine, panchgavya, vermicompost, cow pat pit compost, NADEP compost and biodynamic compost showed 60.2-100 per cent mycelial growth inhibition of *S. sclerotiorum* without autoclaving (Shalika 2009). Sreenivasa and Naik (2011) observed 92.1 and 57.3 per cent mycelial growth inhibition of *Fusarium* sp. at 15 and 20 per cent concentrations of cow urine *in vitro.*Plotnikova (1977) observed the presence of mycolytic bacteria in cow manure. The extract of cow dung compost has showed the presence of bacterial isolates, which inhibited the mycelial growth of *Fusarium oxysporum* f.sp. *cucumerinum* and *Helminthosporium sigmoideum* (Kai *et al.* 1990). Czaczyk *et al.* (2000) isolated four strains of *Bacillus* from cow dung compost. All the strains possessed strong inhibition properties 56.2-71.0 per cent against the mycelial growth of *R. solani, Bipolaris sorokiniaria, S. sclerotiorum, Trichothecium roseum, F. solani* and *F. oxysporum*. Chung *et al.* (2000) isolated *Paenibacillus koreensis* from compost that have antifungal activity against *Fusarium oxysporum, Colletotrichum lagenarium, Sclerotinia sclerotiorum, Botrytis cinerea* and *Rhizoctonia solani. Aspergillus niger, Trichoderma harzianum, Bacillus cereus* and *Bacillus subtilis* were found major microbes in cow dung compost. When microbes *Bacillus subtilis* and *B. cereus* were cultured with the seedling blight inducing pathogens such as *Sclerotium rolfsii, F. oxysporum, Pythium aphanidermatum, H. maydis* and *R. solani,* the mycelial growth of all tested pathogenic fungi were inhibited to the tune of 40.0-57.8 and 35.5-53.3 per cent, respectively (Muhammad and Amusa 2003). Charest *et al.* (2005) observed the presence of two bacteria *Pseudomonas aeruginosa* and *Rhizobium radiobacter* in cow dung manure. Both bacterial isolates were evaluated against *Pythium ultimum* and was resulted 2-3 per cent mycelia growth inhibition by *R. radiobacter*. Khaing *et al.* (2008) reported the presence of ten species of beneficial microbes such as *Serratia marcescens, Bacillus megatarium, Azotobacter chroococcum, Pseudomonas medocina* and *Flavobacterium* spp. In vermiwash. Species of *Bacillus, Serratia, Pseudomonas* and Actinomycetes were obtained from panchgavya and evaluated for their antifungal potentiality against soil borne pathogens *viz. S. rolfsii, F. oxysporum, F. solani* and *R. solani*. The maximum inhibition was possessed by *Serratia* (99.0%) followed by *Bacillus* (72.7-99.0%) and Actinomycetes (48.6-99.0%) against all the test pathogens (Ashlesha and Sugha 2008).

Actinomycetes present in cow dung compost possessed antimicrobial activity against fifty three pathogens (Pinto *et al.* 2010). Sinha *et al.* (2010) documented the presence of nitrogen fixing bacteria, phosphate solubilizing bacteria, Actinomycetes and mycorrhizal fungi in vermicompost and vermiwash, which showed antifungal activity against soil borne pathogens. Sreenivasa and Naik (2011) exhibited the presence of beneficial microorganisms in panchgavya and beejamrutha, which has been reported to improve the seed germination, seedling length and vigour in wheat and soybean. There are numerous reports on the effectiveness of cow milk, cow urine and cow dung in the management of viral diseases of ornamental and other plants (Joseph and Sankarganesh 2011).Nakasone *et al.* (1999) advocated the use of cow dung paint for the control of smoky blight canker of apple and obtained 86.7 per cent healing of wounds. Panchgavya-3 (MPG-3) was superior to carbendazim in reducing the plant disease and increasing the vigour of plant and yield. Xu (2001) reported 65 per cent disease reduction incited by *Rhizoctonia solani* in Turfgrass with the application of cow manure and chicken manure. Raja and Kurucheve (1999) studied the fungi toxicity of animal dung and urine against *Fusarium oxysporum* f. sp. *lycopersici*, the causal agent of tomato wilt. The highest seed germination of jamun (96.6%) was found when it was treated with cow dung and urine for 24 h. The increased shoot length was found with cow urine treated seeds (Mohan 2008). Yadav and Lourduraj (2006) reported the effect of panchgavya spray on the yield attributes, grain yield and economics. It is significantly increased the productive tillers per hill, panicle length and filled grains per panicle. Sharma and Deshpande (2006) soaked pigeon pea seeds in 10 per cent cow urine, vermiwash, neem leaf extract, biogas slurry, cow dung slurry, homa farming ash and cow dung slurry (10%) + homa farming ash (10%) for 6 h. All the treatments significantly enhanced seed germination, shoot length, root length and vigour index. Fruit yield of guava was found maximum (38.8 kg/tree) in homa atmosphere followed by 29.2 kg with homa + Rishi Krishi and homa + panchgavya (Mohan 2008). Amendment of cow dung compost in soil minimized more than 50 per cent growth of *Fusarium, Sclerotinia* and *Phytophthora* and 26 per cent growth reduction was observed in *Rhizoctonia solani* (Rakesh *et al.* 2013).

REFERENCES

Adejumo T.O, Ikotun Tand Florini D.A (2000)False Smut of Cowpea is Caused by *Protomycopsisphaseoli* (Ramak and Subraman.) in *Nigeria.* Abstracts of Paper and Poster presented at the *Second World* cowpea *Research Conference,* Accra, Ghana, 3-9 September, 2005.

Adejumo T.O, Ikotun T and Florini D.A (2001) Identification and Survival of the Causal Organism of Leaf Smut Disease of Cowpea in Nigeria. *Mycopathologia,*150(2):85-90.

Anonymous (2014) Annual report of National Horticulture Board New Delhi, Pp.16-17.

Ashlesha and Sugha S.K (2008) *In vitro* Antifungal bio Efficacy of Microbes Present in Panchgavya against Major Soil Borne Pathogens.*Plant Disease Research,*23(1):68-74.

Awasthi P.B, Mishra U.S and Pande B.N (1978) A New Record of *Protomycesmacrosporus* Unger On *FoeniculumvulgareL. Curr. Sci.,*47:832-824.

Bacigalova K (2004) Contribution to the Knowledge of the *Protomycetaceae*in Slovakia.*ThaisziaJ. Bot.,* 14:1-22.

BacigalovaKamila, PiatekMarcin and WolkowyckiMarek (2005) *Protomyces cirsii-oleracei* (Fungi, Protomycetales) A New Species for Poland. *Polish Botanical Journal,* 50(1): 77–82.

Bacigalova K (2008) *Protomyces Buerenianus* (*Protomycetaceae*) a New Species for Slovakia. *Biologia,*63/1: 40-43.

Basak A.Band Lee M.W (2005) Efficacy of Cow Dung in Controlling Root Rot and *Fusarium*wilt of Cucumber. *Indian Journal of Plant Pathology,* 23(1&2): 81-84.

Bhardwaj L. N and Shrestha S. M(1985) Efficacy of Fungicide Application in the Control of Stem Gall of Coriander. *Agriculture Ecosystems and Environment,* 13:319-323.

Buren G (1915) Die Schweizerischen*Protomycetaceen*mitbesonderer.

BerucksichtigungihrerEntwicklungsgeschichte and Biologie.*Beitr.Kryptogamenfl.Schweiz,* 5(1):1-95.

Butler E. J (1918) Fungi and Disease in Plants. *Thacker spink & co., Calcutta,* pp. 547.

Charest M.H, Beauchamp C.J and Antoun H(2005) Effects of the Humic Substances of Deinking Paper Sludge on the Antagonism between two Compost Bacteria and *Pythiumultimum. FEMS Microbiology Ecology* 52(3):219-227.

Chung Y.R, Kim C.H, Hwang I and Chun J(2000)*Paenibacilluskoreensis* sp. *nov.*, a New Species that Produces an Iturin like Antifungal Compound. *International Journal of Systematic and Evolutionary Microbiology*, 50(3): 1495-1500.

Czaczyk K,Trojanowska K and Stachowiak B(2000) Antifungal Activity of *Bacillus* sp. isolated from Compost. *Folia Microbiology*,45(3):552.

Dabbas M.R, Singh D.P. and Prakash H.G (2009) Management of Stemgall of Coriander through IDM Practice. *International Journal of Plant Protection*, 2(2):55-257.

Dogra S. (2006)Anti-fungal Potential of Panchgavya against some Soil Borne Pathogens. M.Sc. Thesis, Department of Plant Pathology, CSK Himachal Pradesh KrishiVishvavidyalaya, Palampur, India.p 76.

Gauman E.A and Dodge C.W (1928) Comparative Morphology of Fungi. *Mc Grow Hill Book Co. Inc.*: pp-701.

Gjaerum H. (1964) *Protomycetes, Protomycopsis* and *Taphridiumin* Norway. *NyttMagasin for Botanik*, 12:19–28.

Gupta J. S (1954) Disease Appraisal of Stem Gall of *Coriandrum sativum* L. *Indian phytopath*, 7(1):53-60.

Gupta J. S (1958) Laboratory Assay of Certain Fungicides, Antibiotics and Sulpha Drugs on the Germination of *Protomyces Macrosporus* Unger. *Agra Unive. Jour. Res.* (Sci.), 7:105-112.

Gupta J. S (1962) Pathological Anatomy of the Floral Parts and Fruits of Coriander Affected with *Protomyces Macrosporus* Unger *Agra Univ. Jour. Res.*, 11:307-311.

Gupta J. S and Sinha S (1963a) Biometrical Grouping in *Protomyces macrosporus* Unger Causing Stem Gall of Coriander.*Proc. Ind. Acad. Sci.*, 33(4):507-510.

Gupta J. S and Sinha S (1963b) Some Therapeutic Control Trials on the Stem Gall Disease of Coriander. Bull. *Indian Phytopath.* Soc., 1:75-78.

Gupta J. S and Sinha S (1964) Variation in Pathogenicity of *Protomyces Macrosporus* Unger. *Proc. Natn. Acad. Sci.*, 34(3):241-244.

Gupta R. N (1973) Longevity of Chlamydospores of Coriander Gall Fungus. *Indian phytopath.*,26(3):581-582.

Gupta R. N (1976) Impact of Nitrogen, Phosphorus and Manganese on the Stem Gall of Coriander. *ActaBotanica Indica*, 40(1):30-35.

Haware M.P, and Pavgi M.S (1971) Perpetuation of *Protomycopsis* Species Causing Purple Leaf' Spot of Legumes in India.*Ann. Phytopath. Soc. Japan*, 37:242-248.

Haware M.P and Pavgi M.S (1976) Chlamydospore Germination in *Protomycopsis*species. Faculty of Agriculture, Banaras Hindu University, India.*Mycopathologia*,59(2):105-111.

Haware M. P and Pavgi M. S (1976) Host Range of Two *Protomycopsis* Species from India. Faculty of Agriculture, Banaras Hindu University, India, 272-274.

Henig-Severa N, Eshelb A, and Neemana G (2000) Regulation of the Germination of Aleppo pine (*Pinushalepensis*) by nitrate, Ammonium and Gibberellin, and its role in post-fire forest regeneration. *Physiologiaplantarum*.108:390-397.

Joseph B and Sankarganesh P (2011) Antifungal Efficacy of Panchagavya.*International Journal of Pharm Tech Research*, 3:585-588.

Khai H, Ueda T and Sakaguchi M. (1990)Antimicrobial activity of bark-compost extracts. *Soil Biology and Biochemistry*,22(7):983-986.

Khaing N.S, Khai A.A, Aye K.S and Khaing O.Z (2008) Maintenance of Beneficial microbes in vermiwash carrier system and its application in crop.*GMSARN International*,14(3):12-16.

Kumar Gagan, Yadav S.K, Patel J.S, Sarkar A, and Awasthi L.P (2014) Management of Stem Gall Disease in Coriander Using *Pseudomonas* and *Trichoderma* (Bio agents) and Fungicides. *Journal of Pure and Applied Microbiology,* 8:(6) :201-205.

Lakra B.S (1993) Effect of Depth and Amount of Inoculum and Time of Inoculation of Chlamydospores of *Protomyces Macrosporus* in Infectivity and Severity of Coriander. *Plant Disease Research,* 5(1):118.

Lakra B.S (1999) Assessment of Losses Due to Stemgall in Coriander. *Plant Disease Research,* 14(1):85-87.

Lakra B.S (2001) Estimation of Chlamydospores of *Protomyces macrosporus* in different Infected Plant Parts of Coriander. *Plant Disease Research,* 16(1): 94-95.

Mathivanan R, Edwin, S.C., Viswanathan K. and Chandrasekaran D (2006) Chemical Microbial Composition and Antibacterial Activity of Modified Panchagavya. *International Journal of Cow Science,* 2(2): (Retrieved 12.02.10 from *Indian Journals.com*).

Mathur S.B (1962) Soil P^H in Relation to Stem Gall Disease of Coriander Caused by *Protomyces Macrosporus* Unger. *Indian Phytopatho.,*15:75-76.

Mathur S.B. and Narula P.N (1963) Effect of Certain Fungicides, Antibiotics and Synthetic Phytohormonesthe Germination of Chlamydospores of *Protomyces Macrosporus* Unger Causing Stem Gall of Coriander. *Proc. Ind. Acad. Sci. Sec.,* 33(4):615-617.

Mishra R.S and Pandey V.P. (2015) Screening of *Coriandrum Sativum* Accessions for Stem Gall Disease Tolerance and Seed Yield. J. *Plant Disease Science,* 10 (2):256-259.

Mishra R.S and Pandey V.P (2015) Evaluation of Varieties of Coriander (*Coriandrum sativam* L.) for Resistance to Stem Gall Disease and Seed Yield. *Curent Advances in Agricultural Sciences,* 7(2):151-153.

Mishra R.S and S. Kumar (2016) Viability of Coriander Seeds from *Protomyces Macrosporus* Infected Plants to Spread of Stem Gall of Coriander. CAAS:26(02):16-20.

Mix A.J (1925) *Ibid.*15:214-222.

Mohan B (2008) Evaluation of Organic Growth Promoters on Yield of Fruits Crops in *India. J. Organ. Syst.,* 3(1):23-36.

Mukhopadhyay A.N and Pavgi M.S (1964) Chlamydospore Germination of Artificial Culture of *Protomyces Macrosporus* Unger. *Experimentia,* 20(11):619.

Muhammad S and Amusa N.A(2003) *In vitro* Inhibition of Growth of Some Seedling Blight Inducing Pathogens by Compost Inhibiting Microbes. *African Journal of Biotechnology,* 2(6):161-164.

MundkurB. B (1959) Fungi and Plant Diseases.*Nacmillan& Co. Ltd., London,* pp. 246.

Nakasone A. K, Bettiole W, and Souze R.M.D (1999) The Effect of Water Extracts of Organic Matter on Plant Pathogens. *Summa Phytopathologica,* 25:330-35.

Naik.N, and Sreenivasa M.N (2009) Influence of Bacteria Isolated from Panchagavya on Seed Germination and Seed Vigour in Wheat. *Karnataka J. Agric. Sci.,* 22(1):231-232.

Natarajan K (2002) Panchagavya : A Manual, Other India Press, Mapusa, Goa, India, pp. 33.

Naqvi S. A. M. H. (1986) Varietal Screening of Coriander Against Stem Gall in Relation to Disease Intensityand Crop loss.*Ind. Jour. Of Myco.& plant patho.,*16(3): 270-276.

Nene Y. L, Siddiqui I.A and Kharbanda P. D (1966) Control of Stem Gall of Coriander by Fungicide. *Mycopath. Mycol. Appl*., 29(1-2):142-144.

Nikam B.C, Kulkami, S.N. and Pawar P.K (1959) Coriander its diseases. *Indian Forming,* Nov.12-13.

Nishida H, Ando K, Ando Y, Hirata A and Sugiyama J. (1995) Mixiaosmundae: Transfer from the Ascomycota to the Basidiomycota based on Evidence from Molecules and Morphology. *Can. J. Bot.*, 73:660-666.

Papen H, Gabler A, Zumbusch E and Rennenberg H (2002) Chemo litho autotrophic Nitrifiers in the Phyllosphere of a Spruce Ecosystem Receiving high Nitrogen Input. *Curr. Microbiol.*, 44:56-60.

Pavgi M. S. and Mukhopadhyay A. N (1969-a) Transmission of *Protomyces macrosporus* Unger, the Incitant of Stem Gall of Coriander. *Ann. Phyto.Patho. Soc. Japan*, 35(4):265-270.

Pavgi M.S. and Mukhopadhyay A. N (1969-b) Viability of Seed in Coriander Infected by *Protomyces Macrosporus* Unger. *Ann.Phyto.Patho. Soc. Japan*, 35(4):271-274.

Pavgi M.S And Mukhopadhyay A.N (1970) Cytology of Chlamydospore Germination in *Protomyces Macrosporus* Unger. Faculty of Agriculture, Banaras University, India. *Cytologia*, 35:359-367.

Pavgi M.S and Mukhopadhyay A.N (1972) Development of Coriander Fruit Infected by *Protomyces Macrosporus* Unger, 37:619-627.

Pinto S.S, Mann M.B, Campos F.S, Franco A.C., Germani J.C and Van Der SST (2010) Preliminary Characterization of Some *Streptomyces* Species Isolated from a Composting Process and their Antimicrobial Potential. *World Journal of Microbiology and Biotechnology*, 26(10): 1847-1856.

Plotnikova L.Z. (1977) Dung Infusion as a means for Controlling Powdery Mildew of Rose. *Zashchita Rastenii*, 2:28.

Prabhu M.J (2009) Panchagavya: Low Cost Organic Input for both Crops and Animals. In: Farmer's Notebook, *The Hindu Online Edition*, 4th June 2009.

Prasad B.K (1983) Free Sugar and Amino Acid Contents of Coriander Infected with Stem Gall Disease. *Indian Phytopath.*, 36(1):150-151.

Raj Abhishek, Kumar Manoj, Toppo Pratap Jhariya, (2014) Cow Dung for Ecofriendly and Sustainable Productive farming. *Environmental Science*, 3:2277-8179.

Raja J and Kurucheve V (1999) Fungicidal Activity of Buffalo (*Babulusbubalis*) Urine: A New Record. *Madras Agricultural Journal* 86(10/12):614-616.

Rakesh K.N, Dileep N, Syed Junaid, Prashith Kekuda T.R, Vinayaka K.S and Noor Nawaz A.S (2013) Inhibitory Effect of Cow Urine Extracts of Selected Plants against Pathogens Causing Rhizome Rot of Ginger. *Science, Technology and Arts Research Journal*, 2(2): 92-96

Rao C. P (1972) Anatomical Studies on Abnormal Growth Caused by *Protomyces Macrosporus* on *Coriandrum Sativum* L. *Indian Phytopath.*, 25(4):483-496.

Reddy M. S and Kramer C. L (1975) A Taxonomic Revision of the Protomycetales. *Mycotaxon*, 3:1–50.

Sahib N.G., Anwar F, Gilani A.H, Hamid A.A, Saari A and Alkharfy K.M (2012) Coriander (*Coriandrum sativum L.*): A Potential Source of High-value Components for Functional Foods and Nutraceuticals–*A Review. J. Phytother. Res.*, 27(9):1002/ptr.4897.

Sanjutha S, Subramanian S, Rani I. and Maheswari (2008) Integrated Nutrient Management in *Andrographispaniculata. Research Journal of Agriculture and Biological Sciences*, 4(2):141-145.

Sangeetha V, Thevanathan R (2010a) Effect of TMV Strains in a Local Lesion Host. Journal of Panchagavya on Nitrate Assimilation by Experimental Ecobiol., 31:28-131.plants, *The Journal of American Science*, 6: 80-86.

Singh S. P, Gupta J. S and Sharma A. K (1984) Disease Appraisal and Crop Loss Estimates in Coriander Attacked by *Protomyces macrosporus* Unger in Uttar Pradesh. *Geobios,* 11(6):276-278.

Singh H.B., Singh A, Tripathi A, Rai S.K., Katiyar R.S., Johri J.K., and Singh S.P. (2003) Evaluation of Indian Coriander Accessions for Resistance against Stem Gall Disease. *Genetic Resources and Crop Evolution,* 50:339-343.

Sinha R.K, Valani D, Chauhan K and Agarwal S. (2010) Embarking on a Second Green Revolution for Sustainable Agriculture by Vermin Culture Biotechnology using Earthworms: Reviving the Dreams of Sir Charles Darwin. *Journal of Agricultural Biotechnology and Sustainable Development,* 2:113-128.

Shakuntala N.M., Vasudevan S.N., Patil S.B, Doddagoudar S.R, Macha RCMSI Vijay and Kumar A.G. (2012) Organic Bio Priming on Seed Vigour inducing Enzyme in Paddy - An Alternative to Inorganics. *Ecoscan,* 1:251-257.

ShailajaB, MishraIpsita,Gampala Srihima, SinghVikramJeet and Swathi K (2014) Panchagavya- an Eco-friendly Insecticide and Organic Growth Promoter of plants. *International Journal of Advanced Research,* 2:(11) 22-26.

Sreenivasa M.N and Naik N (2011) Impact of Bacteria Isolated from Organic Liquid manures on Seed Germination and Seedling Vigour Index of Wheat and Soybean. *Organic Farming Newsletter,*7:3-5.

Srimathi P, Mariappan N., Sundaramoorthy L and Paramathma M (2013)

Efficacy of Panchagavya on Seed Invigoration of Biofuel Crops. *Academic Journals.*8(41): 2031-2037.

Srivastava H.C (1955-b) Studies on Tumour Disease of *Coriandrum Sativum* L. Caused by *Protomyces Macrosporus* Unger. *Proc. 42nd Ind. Sci. Cong.,* Part III: 218.

Srivastava U, Rai R.A. and Agrawal J.M. (1971b) Powdery Mildew of Coriander and Its Control. *Indian Phytopath.,* 24(3):437-440.

Somasundaram, E. and Amanullah M.M (2007) Panchagavya on Growth and Productivity of Crops: *A Review.Green Farming,* 1:22-26.

Sugha S.K (2005) Antifungal Potential of Panchgavya.*Plant Disease Research* 20:156-158.

Swaminathan C, Swaminathan V and Vijay Lakshmi K (2007) Panchgavya Boon to Organic Farming.*International Book Distributing Co. Lucknow,* P. 332.

Tharmaraj K, Ganesh P, Suresh Kumar R, Anandan A and Kolanjinathan K (2011)"A Critical Review on Panchagavya—a Boon Plant Growth," *International Journal of Pharmaceutical and Biological Archive,* 2(6):1611–1614.

Tripathi A.K (2001) Evaluation of Coriander Cultivars for Resistant against Stem Gall Disease and Yield Potncial. *Crop Research Hisar,* 22(3):485-488.

Tripathi A.K. and Bartaria A.M (2002) Chemical Control of Stem Gall Disease (*Protomyces Macrosporus)* of Coriander and its Economics. *Plant Disease Research,* 17(1):119-120.

Tripathi A.K (2003) Effect of Sowing Dates and Weather Parameters on Stem Gall Disease of Coriander. *Indian Phytopath.,*56(2):191-193.

Thirumalachar M.J., Pavgi M.S., and Singh R.A (1969) In Vitro Activity of 3 Antifungal Antibiotics against *Protomyces Macrosporus* Unger, *Taphrinamaculans*and *Corticumsasakii. Hindustan Anti.Biot. Bull.,* 11(3):189-190.

Toncer O,Tansi S and Kizil S (1998) The Effect of different Sowing Time on Essential Oil of Coriander in GAP region. *Anadolu.,* 8(2):101-105.

Tubki K (1957) Biological and Cultural Studies of three Species of *Protomyces.mycologia,* 49:44-54.

Vasumathi R (2001) Influence of Organic Manures, Bio Fertilizers and Plant Density on Growth, Yield and Alkaloid Content of Bhumyamalaki (*Phyllanthusamarus*Schum. And Thonn.) M.Sc., (Hort.) Thesis TNAU, Coimbatore-3. India.

Xu H.L (2001) Effects of a Microbial Inoculant and Organic Fertilizers on the Growth, Photosynthesis and Yield of Sweet corn. *J. Crop Prod.,* 3:183-214.

Yadav B.K and Lourdraj C.A. (2006) Effect of Organic Manures and Panchagavya Spray on Yield Attributes and Economics of Rice (*Oryza sativa*). *Crop Res.,* 31: 1-5.

Phyto-chemicals and Ethanobotany **Pages 155-168**
Edited by: **Pawan Kumar 'Bharti'**
ISBN: 978-93-86841-93-3
Edition: **2019**
Published by: **Discovery Publishing House Pvt. Ltd., New Delhi (India)**

7

Traditional and Classical Medicinal Uses, Pharmacological Activities and Identification of Rare and Endangered Astavarga Plants (Group of Eight Medicinal Herbs)

[1]Anupam Srivastava, Acharya Balkrishna, Rajesh Kumar Mishra, Bhasker Joshi*

ABSTRACT

Astavarga is nature's most extravagant group of flowering plants found in Himalayan region. As the name Astavarga indicates it contains eight medicinal plants belonging to family Asparagaceae, Liliaceae, Orchidaceae and Zingiberaceae. According to Ayurveda this group of medicinal plants are Rasayana (Rejuvenator) in nature and commonly known as Kakoli, Kshirakakoli, Meda, Mahameda, Jivak, Risbhaka, Riddhi and Vridddhi in Sanskrit. These plants are main constituent of various Ayurvedic preparations like Chyawanprasha Rasayan, Ashtavarga Churna, Brimhani Gutika and Vajikara Ghrita, etc. Correct identification of Astavarga plants described in various Nighantus and Samhitas with their corresponding taxonomical description from various floras is given here. These eight rare species are now endangered due to overexploitation, excessive anthropogenic activities and drastic environmental changes in Himalayan region. Conservation and biological propagation of these plants in natural habitat is urgently required for future generations.

Key words: Astavarga, Ayurveda, Conservation, Medicinal herbs.

Introduction

Ayurveda is the eternal science of life. It is associated with the noble, excellent and great tradition of our ancient Vedas and is a part of our prosperous and glorious history. Starting from Brahma, various Rishi's and Maharsi's (Sages) in the tradition of Daksha, Asvini Kumars, Indra, Atreya, Punarvasu,

[1] MD Scholar, Dravyaguna Deptt. Patanjali Bhartiya Ayurvigyan Avum Anusandhan Sansthan, Haridwar, Uttarakhand, India

* Patanjali Herbal Research Department, Patanjali Research Foundation Trust, Haridwar, Uttarakhand, India

Dhanvantri, Bharadwaja, Nimi, Kasyapa and other humanists have enriched and protected the prosperous tradition of *Ayurveda*. It continues to flow from ancient times. The Samhitas of *Ayurveda* are conveyors of this eternal tradition. Lord Dhanvantri described that *Ayurveda* is the science of life (beneficial, non-beneficial, happy and unhappy factors of life). The main purpose of *Ayurveda* is to protect the health of a healthy person and to mitigate the disorders of a patient.

In ancient India, great inventions were made by *Dhanvantri, Asvini Kumars, Susruta* and *Charaka*. Among these, the discovery of *Jivaniya* (Vitality promoter), *Vayasthapana* (Age-sustainer), *Swasthya Vardhaka* (Health promoting), *Rogapratirodhaka ksamata vardhaka* (Immuno modulator), *Shukrajanan* (Spermatogenic) plants of *Astavarga* was a great discovery. In those days, knowledge was transmitted verbally from one generation to another. It was difficult to document this and resulted in depreciation of some valuable knowledge. This is the reason for the present confusion and mystery regarding the identification of valuable medicinal plants.

In due course of time lack of traditional knowledge, laxity in teaching practices, lack of knowledge regarding natural habitat and correct identification of medicinal plants; unavailability of any evident and newly written textual material for centuries, were the major reasons due to which the actual identification of medicinal plants became uncertain and illusory.

This is true that due to the instability in nature and environmental changes, many plants have become rare and endangered. These eight medicinal plants which usually grow in smaller pockets in Himalayas are endangered due to overexploitation and modern developmental activities. Conservation and biological propagation of these plants in natural habitat is urgently required for future generations.

Study Area

Considering the availability of these plants, the study is conducted in different areas of Uttarakhand specially Mussoorie and Dhanaulti. Mussoorie, popularly known as the Queen of Hills, this charming hill station, situated at an altitude of 2003 m above sea-level, in the Garhwal Hills. Dhanaulti is a hill station situated 24 km from the popular hill station of Mussoorie and 31 km from Chamba. It is situated at an altitude of 2286 m and is known for beautiful alpine forests of Deodar, Rhododendron and Oak.

Materials and Methods

Extensive literary research is conducted using different available literature on the drug, such as classical text of *Ayurveda* and other compendium available. Data was also collected from various books, journals, periodicals and some unpublished books (Nighantus). The review of literature was conducted with an interactive strategy of combining the knowledge of *Ayurveda* and modern science. *Astavarga* plants were collected from different areas in Uttarakhand and herbarium was prepared and preserved for further studies.

Members of Astavarga Plants

S.No.	Sanskrit Name	Botanical Name	Family	Common name
1.	Kakoli	*Roscoea purpurea* Sm.	Zingiberaceae	Roscoe's lily, Roscoe's purple lily, Purple Roscoea, Cinnamon Stick, Hardy Ginger
2.	Kshirakakoli	*Lilium polyphyllum* D. Don	Liliaceae	White Himalayan Lily, White lily, Many leaved lily
3.	Jivak	*Crepidium acuminatum* (D. Don) Szlach.	Orchidaceae	The Gradually tapering Malaxis
4.	Rishbhak	*Malaxis muscifera* (Lindl.) Kuntze	Orchidaceae	Adder Mouth Orchid, The fly bearing Malaxis, Snake Mouth Orchid
5.	Meda	*Polygonatum verticillatum* (L.) All.	Asparagaceae	Whorled Solomon's Seal, Whorled leaf Solomon's Seal
6.	Mahameda	*Polygonatum cirrhifolium* (Wall.) Royle	Asparagaceae	King's Solomon's Seal, Tendril leaf Solomon's Seal, Coiling leaf Solomon's Seal. Coiling leaf Polygonatum
7.	Riddhi	*Habenaria intermedia* D. Don	Orchidaceae	Intermediate Habenaria, White Wild Orchid, The in-between Habenaria, Reindeer Orchid.
8.	Vriddhi	*Platanthera edgeworthii* (Hook. f. ex Collett) R.K. Gupta	Orchidaceae	Edgeworth's Habenaria

The First Authentic Identification of *Astavarga* Plants

This is the first authentic and fact based identification of the *Astavarga* Plants based on deep study of Classical *Ayurved*ic literature, comparison with modern botanical description, constant exploration and discussion with different scientists and *Ayurved*ic experts by Patanjali Research Institute. Correct identification of *Astavarga* plants described in various Nighantus and Samhitas with their corresponding taxonomical description from various floras is compared and presented below.

S.No.	Botanical Name	Sanskrit Name	Main classical names & botanical name description for identification
1.	*Roscoea purpurea* Sm.	Kakoli	Anthers bifurcated at the tip. Stem is slightly purple in colour (*Krishnavarni*).
2.	*Lilium polyphyllum* D. Don	Kshirakakoli	Flowers are white in colour, dotted with purple colour within (*Vakuli, Kabari*).
3.	*Crepidium acuminatum* (D. Don) Szlach.	Jivak	Tip of lip edge is straight - linear. Raceme is penicillate (Brush-like) (*Kuracakakara*).
4.	*Malaxis muscifera* (Lindl.) Kuntze	Rishbhak	Leaves 2, centrally bifurcated or 3 lipped. Pseudo-bulb resembles with the shape of bull's horn (*Vrisabhshringvata*).
5.	*Polygonatum verticillatum* (L.) All.	Meda	Leaves are arranged in whorls, four to eight in number, acute, pointed tips (Arrow-like) (*Salyaparni*).
6.	*Polygonatum cirrhifolium* (Wall.) Royle	Mahameda	Leaves are arranged in whorls, 3-6 in number, tip of leaf is tendril like, ascending, grows with support of nearby shrubs (*Vriksharuha*).
7.	*Habenaria intermedia* D. Don	Riddhi	Flowers are white in colour, lobes of petals fimbriated and long in size (spoke-like) (*Rathangi*).
8.	*Platanthera edgeworthii* (Hook. f. ex Collett) R.K. Gupta	Vriddhi	Since it flowers in shravan season (rainy season) (July - August), named (*Shravanapushpi*), Spur is truncated above, petals and ligules are yellow in colour.

Taxonomic features of *Astavarga* plants

1. Roscoea purpurea Sm., Exot. Bot. 2: 97, t. 108. 1805-1808; Baker in Hook. f., Fl. Brit. Ind. 6: 207. 1890; Naithani, B. D., Flora Chamoli 2: 639. 1985.

Perennial, herb 35-50 cm tall. Rhizome slightly blackish in colour. Root fibres thick, fleshy, fascicled, slightly light brown in colour. Stem purple coloured, leafy, elongate, erect and robust. Leaves 5-6, lanceolate, 15 cm × 1.2-2.5 cm, at flowering time sheath broad, imbricate, leaf-sheath green or purplish-red with spots. Flowers few in a sessile spike. Bracts oblong, hidden in the sheaths of the upper leaves. Calyx green, 3.8 cm long, slit deeply down one side as the flower expands. Corolla tube not longer than the calyx, dilated up wards, limb purple rarely pale lilac or white, upper segments about 2.5 cm long, obovate-cuneate while lower lanceolate, decurved, lip broad deeply bifid. Staminode oblanceolate, half as long as the upper segment. Fertile stamen as long as the staminode. Anthers bifurcated at the tip. Anthers tails 0.4 cm long. Capsule cylindrical, 2.5-3.8 cm long. Seeds ovoid, minute, arillate.

Fl. & Fr.: June- September.

Distribution: Uttarakhand-Mussoorie, Dhanolti, Uttarkashi, Chamoli-Valley of flowers, Nainital, Almora, Ranikhet.

Patanjali Research Foundation-601.

2. Lilium polyphyllum: D. Don, Ill. Bot. Himal. Mts. 388. 1840; Hook. f., Fl. Brit. Ind. 6: 351.1892; Naithani, B. D., Flora Chamoli 2: 652. 1985.

Perennial, bulbous herb. Stem 60-120 cm erect, slender. Leaves alternate, lower whorled, lanceolate to linear-lanceolate, 5-13 x 0.5-1.5 cm, acute, margin hairy. Raceme 4-10 flowered. Bracts whorled. Flowers pendulous, fragrant. Pedicel 4-10 cm long, slightly drooping. Tepals dull yellow or greenish outside, white within with purple streaks, 3-4 cm long, oblanceolate. Stamens exserted. Anthers 1.3 cm long. Style very declinate. Fruit capsule.

Fl. & Fr.: August-November.

Distribution: Himachal Pradesh-Narkanda forests, Chail (Solan district), Jammu & Kashmir- Gulmarg, Liddar valley. Uttarakhand- Dhanolti, Gangotri, Kedarnath.

Patanjali Research Foundation-608

3. Crepidium acuminatum: (D. Don) Szlach., Fragm. Florist. Geobot. 3: 123. 1995. *Malaxis acuminata* D. Don, Prodr. Fl. Nepal. 29. 1825; Naithani, B. D., Flora Chamoli 2: 628. 1985. *Microstylis wallichii* Lindl., Gen. Sp. Orchid. Pl. 20. 1830; Hook. f., Fl. Brit. Ind. 5: 686.1890.

Terrestrial, sometimes epiphytic herb. Stem cylindrical, 1.5-7 × 0.4-0.6 cm, fleshy with several nodes, mostly enclosed in sheath. Leaves 3-4, obliquely ovate, ovate-oblong or sub-elliptical, 4-12 × 2.5-6 cm, base contracted into a sheath-like, amplexicaul 2-4 cm long petiole, apex acuminate. Raceme is penicillate, Peduncle 10-30 cm long, wingless. Rachis erect, 3-16 cm long, 10- or more flowered. Floral bracts lanceolate, 3-6 mm long. Flowers purplish red, 1.5 cm in diameter. Dorsal sepal narrowly oblong or broadly linear, 8-9 × 2 mm, margin revolute, apex obtuse. Lateral sepals oblong, 6-7 × 3-3.5 mm, margin revolute, apex obtuse. Petals narrowly linear, 8-9 × 0.8 mm, margin revolute. Lip superior, ovate-oblong or obovate-oblong in outline, 10-11 × 6-7 mm, shallowly bilobed. Auricles narrowly ovate. Column 1-1.5 mm long, stout. Capsule obovoid-oblong, 1.8 × 1 cm. Fruiting pedicel 7 mm long.

Fl. & Fr.: May-July.

Distribution: Himachal Pradesh-Shimla, Chamba, Chail, Narkanda. Uttarakhand-Dehradun, Mussoorie, Tehri, Pauri, Pithoragarh, Nainital, Ramagarh, Almora, Ranikhet.

Patanjali Research Foundation-604

4. Malaxis muscifera: (Lindl.) Kuntze, Revis. Gen. Pl. 2: 673. 1891; Naithani, B. D., Flora Chamoli 2: 628-629. 1985. *Dienia muscifera* Lindl., Gen. Sp. Orchid.

Pl. 22. 1830. *Microstylis muscifera* (Lindl.) Ridl., J. Linn. Soc., Bot. 24: 333. 1888; Hook. f., Fl. Brit. Ind. 5: 689.1890.

Terrestrial, herb up to 40 cm tall. Pseudobulb small, ovoid. Stem flexuous. Leaves 2, unequal, 2-10 × 1-4 cm, elliptic to oblong or oblong-lanceolate, obtuse or acute or sub-acuminate. Sheathing petiole 2-6 cm long. Inflorescence 2.5-25 cm long. Flowers yellowish-green. Bracts slightly shorter than pedicelled ovary. Sepals subequal, 2-2.3 mm long, oblong-lanceolate. Dorsal sepal directed downwards, laterals upwards. Petals linear, spreading. Labellum fleshy, broadly ovate, 2 mm long, basal portion excavated, obscurely angled on either side of base, apex acuminate. Column very short, anthers sessile on its top. Pollinia ovoid and free. Pedicelled ovary up to 3 mm long, pedicel twisted. Fruit capsule, 6-8 mm long, broadly ovoid-oblong, ribbed and of light yellow colour.

Fl. & Fr.: August-November.

Distribution: Himachal Pradesh-Shimla, Chamba. Jammu & Kashmir-Gulmarg, Leh. Uttarakhand- Pithoragarh, Almora, Chakrata, Tehri, Dhanolti, Chamoli.

Patanjali Research Foundation-606

5. Polygonatum verticillatum (L.) All., Fl. Pedem. 1: 131. 1785; Naithani, B. D., Flora Chamoli 2: 656. 1985. *Convallaria verticillata* L., Sp. Pl. 1: 315. 1753; Hook. f., Fl. Brit. Ind. 6: 321.1892.

Terrestrial, herb. Rhizome usually shortly branched, usually tuberous terete, very rarely moniliform, 0.7-1.5 cm thick. Stem erect, 20-80 cm long, glabrous. Leaves in whorls of 3, occasionally alternate near base of stem, sometimes opposite near apex of stem, subsessile, oblong-lanceolate to linear, 6-10 × 0.5-3 cm, apex acute to acuminate. Inflorescences 1 or 2-4-flowered. Flowers pendulous. Peduncle 1-2 cm long. Bracts small or absent. Pedicel 3-10 mm long. Perianth pale purple or white or pale yellow, but probably only when dry, cylindric, 0.8-1.2 cm long. Tepals 6, connate into a tube, 2-3 mm long. Stamens 6 with staminodes, epipetalous. Filaments 0.5-2 mm long, papillose. Ovary 3 mm long. Style 2.5-3 mm long. Berries red, 6-9 mm in diameter, 6-12-seeded.

Fl. & Fr.: May-October.

Distribution: Himachal Pradesh-Shimla, Narkanda. Jammu & Kashmir-Trikuta Hills, Udhampur, Doda. Uttarakhand- Kedarnath, Gangotri, Madmaheshwar.

Patanjali Research Foundation-602

6. Polygonatum cirrhifolium (Wall.) Royle, Ill. Bot. Himal. Mts. 1: 380. 1839; Naithani, B. D., Flora Chamoli 2: 655. 1985. *Convallaria cirrhifolia* Wall., Asiat. Res. 13: 380-382, pl. 5. 1820; Hook. f., Fl. Brit. Ind. 6: 322.1892.

Terrestrial, herb. Rhizome moniliform or tuberous, terete, 1-2 cm thick. Stem erect or scandent, 30-90 cm long, glabrous. Leaves in whorls of 3-6, rarely also a few alternate in proximal part of stem, sessile, narrowly linear to linear-lanceolate, very rarely oblong-lanceolate, margin entire, 4-12 cm × 2-15 mm long and wide, tip usually cirrhose at anthesis. Inflorescences usually 2-flowered. Flowers pendulous. Peduncle 0.3-1 cm long. Bracts 1-2 mm, scarious, veinless or bract absent. Pedicel 3-8 mm. Perianth white, greenish or pale purple, sub-cylindric, slightly constricted in middle, 8-11 mm long. Tepals 2 mm long. Ovary 2.5 mm long. Style 2 mm. Berries red or purple-red, 8-9 mm in diameter, 4-9-seeded.

Fl. & Fr.: May-October.

Distribution: Himachal Pradesh-Shimla, Narkanda. Uttarakhand-Mussoorie, Chakrata, Gaurikund.

Patanjali Research Foundation-603

7. Habenaria intermedia D. Don, Prodr. Fl. Nepal. 24. 1825; Hook. f., Fl. Brit. Ind. 6: 138.1890; Naithani, B. D., Flora Chamoli 2: 622. 1985.

Terrestrial herb, 20-30 cm tall, turning black when dried. Tubers ellipsoid, 1.5-3 × 1-2 cm, fleshy. Stem erect, terete, stout. Leaves 3-5, laxly arranged. Leaf blade ovate-lanceolate, 3.5-8 × 2-4 cm, base amplexicaul, apex acute. Raceme 1-4-flowered, 5-15 cm long. Flowers large, green and white. Floral bracts ovate, 4-5 cm long, nearly as long as ovary, apex acuminate. Ovary twisted, terete, including pedicel 3.8-4.5 cm long. Flowers white or greenish. Sepals ciliate, green. Dorsal sepal erect, ovate-oblong, concave, 2.2 × 1.2 cm, 7-veined, apex acute. Lateral sepals reflexed, obliquely falcate-lanceolate, 3 × 0.6 cm, 7-veined, apex acute. Petals white, forming a hood with dorsal sepal, erect, white, obliquely subovate-falcate, 2.2 × 0.8 cm, margin ciliate, unlobed, apex acute. Lip pale or yellowish-green, 2.8-3 cm long, base spurred, deeply 3-lobed above base, lobes ciliate. Lateral lobes linear, outer margin with 10 filiform lobules. Mid-lobe linear, 1.8-2.0 cm long, slightly shorter than lateral lobes, apex acute. Spur pendulous, cylindric, 7-8.5 cm long, much longer than ovary, slightly dilated near end, apex obtuse. Connective 2 mm wide. Pollinia ovoid. Caudicles linear. Viscidia orbicular, small. Rostellum with elongate arms. Stigmas clavate.

Fl. & Fr.: May-October.

Distribution: Himachal Pradesh-Koti (Shimla) Summer Hill Indian Shimla (Fagu), Dalhousie (Chamba). Jammu & Kashmir-Poonch, Pirpanjal Range. Uttarakhand-Dehradun-Mussoorie Company bagh, Bhatta Fall, Kampty fall, Tehri, Chamoli, Valley of flowers, Gaurikund, Utarrkashi, Bhagirathi Valley.

Patanjali Research Foundation-605

8. Platanthera edgeworthii (Hook. f. ex Collett) R.K. Gupta, Fl. Nainital. 349. 1968. *Habenaria edgeworthii* Hook. f. ex Collett, Flora Simlensis 504, f. 166. 1907; Naithani, B. D., Flora Chamoli 2: 622. 1985.

Terrestrial, leafy herbs with unidivided, oblong tubers and fleshy root fibres. Stem with the raceme 30-45 cm long, leafy from about 5 cm upwards, internodes ensheathed by leaf bases. Leaves erect, 4-9 × 0.8 – 1.2 cm, lanceolate, setaceously acuminate, acute, indistinctly 5-7 veined, bases sheathing. Flowers 1.5 cm broad when spread out, in elongated terminal racemes. Peduncles as long as the racemes with about two leafy, sterile, acuminate bracts. Floral bracts leafy, 2.4 × 1.1 cm, broadly lanceolate-ovate, acuminate, acute, initially 3-5-veined but soon branching to give a 9-veined appearance. Dorsal sepal 6 × 4 mm, oblong-ovate, obtuse, 3-veined, lateral veins branching. Lateral sepals 7 × 4 mm, broadly and obliquely ovate, obtuse, 3-veined, the lateral veins branching giving a 5-7-veined appearance. Petals 7 × 2 mm, yellowish-green, bilobed, lobes variable in length and breadth. Upper lobe lanceolate, about half as long as the lower linear lobe, incurved, 2-veined. Lip 5 × 2 mm, purple, inserted at the base of the column, broadly 3-lobed, fleshy, lobes variable in length, obtuse. Spur 1.7 cm long, narrowly clavate, mouth provided with a ligule. Column 3.4 × 3 mm with a small, triangular rostellum and two viscid, sausage-shaped stigmas. Anthers lateral, adnate to the column, 2-loculed. Pollinia 2, granular, golf club-shaped, stalked, 1.3-1.6 × 0.6 mm, each with a long slender caudicle 2.2-2.4 mm long, attached to a minute gland. Staminodes short and fleshy, arising from the sides of the column and protruding above as granular masses. Ovary with pedicel 2 cm long.

Fl. & Fr.: May-October.

Distribution: Himachal Pradesh-Summer Hills, Shimla, Chamba, Narkanda. Uttarakhand- Mussoorie, Dhanolti, Uttarkashi, Valley of flowers, Gobindghat, Nainital, Almora, Almora, Ranikhet.

Patanjali Research Foundation-607.

Status of *Astavarga* Plants (Red Data Book of Indian Plants)

S.No.	Name	Status
1	*Roscoea purpurea* Sm.	Common
2	*Lilium polyphyllum* D. Don	Endangered
3	*Crepidium acuminatum* (D. Don) Szlach.	Rare
4	*Malaxis muscifera* (Lindl.) Kuntze	Rare, Threatened
5	*Polygonatum verticillatum* (L.) All.	Threatened
6	*Polygonatum cirrhifolium* (Wall.) Royle	Rare
7	*Habenaria intermedia* D. Don	Common
8	*Platanthera edgeworthii* (Hook. f. ex Collett) R.K. Gupta	Rare

Substitutes of *Astavarga* Plants

S.No.	Name	Substitute
1.	*Roscoea purpurea* Sm.	Aswagandha [*Withania somnifera* (L.) Dunal] and Kali Musali (*Curculigo orchioides* Gaertn.)
2.	*Lilium polyphyllum* D. Don	Aswagandha [*Withania somnifera* (L.) Dunal], Safed Musali (*Chlorophytum arundinaceum* Baker), *Fritillaria cirrhosa* D. Don and *Nomocharis oxypetala* (D. Don) E.H.Wilson
3.	*Crepidium acuminatum* (D. Don) Szlach.	Vidarikand [*Pueraria tuberosa* (Willd.) DC.], Safed behmen (*Centaurea behen* L.) and Guduchi [*Tinospora cordifolia* (Willd.) Miers], *Dienia cylindrostachya* Lindl. and *Crepidium mackinnonii* (Duthie) Szlach.
4.	*Malaxis muscifera* (Lindl.) Kuntze	Vidarikand [*Pueraria tuberosa* (Willd.) DC.] and Lal behmen [*Centaurium centaurioides* (Roxb.) S.R.Rao & Hemadri]
5.	*Polygonatum verticillatum* (L.) All.	Satavari (*Asparagus racemosus* Willd.), Salam Mishri [*Graphorchis campestris* (Wall.) Kuntze]
6.	*Polygonatum cirrhifolium* (Wall.) Royle	Satavari (*Asparagus racemosus* Willd.), Nagbala [*Sida cordata* (Burm.f.) Borss.Waalk.], Shakakul Mishri [*Polygonatum multiflorum* (L.) All.] and Prasarani (*Paederia foetida* L.).
7.	*Habenaria intermedia* D. Don	Varahikand (*Tacca integrifolia* Ker Gawl.), *Bala* (*Sida cordifolia* L.) and *Chiriya Musali* (*Asparagus filicinus* Buch.-Ham. ex D. Don)
8.	*Platanthera edgeworthii* (Hook. f. ex Collett) R.K. Gupta	*Varahikand* (*Tacca integrifolia* Ker Gawl.), Salam Panja [*Dactylorhiza hatagirea* (D. Don) Soo] and Mahabala (*Sida acuta* Burm.f.) and *Habenaria griffithii* Hook. f.

Medicinal Uses of *Astavarga* Plants

S. No.	Name	Medicinal Uses
1	*Roscoea purpurea* Sm.	Rhizome-anti-rheumatic, febrifuge, galactagogue, haemostatic, eye tonic, expectorant, sexual stimulant, diuretic, tonic, sweet, bitter and cooling properties.Reported to be useful in haematemesis, excessive thirst and rheumatic pain.The ethanolic extract of its rhizomes exhibit immunostimulant potential in mice.
2	*Lilium polyphyllum* D. Don	The bulbs are sweet, bitter, refrigerant, galactagogue, expectorant, aphrodisiac, diuretic, antipyretic and tonic shows soothing, astringent and anti-inflammatory properties.Useful in agalactia, cough, bronchitis, vitiated conditions of pitta, semen related weakness, strangury, burning sensation, polydipsia, hypertension, intermittent fever, haematemesis, rheumatalgia and general debility.
3	*Crepidium acuminatum* (D. Don) Szlach.	The pseudobulbs are sweet, refrigerant, aphrodisiac, ferbrifuge and tonic. Useful in haematemesis, fever, semen related weakness, burning sensation, dipsia, emaciation, tuberculosis and general debility.

4.	*Malaxis muscifera* (Lindl.) Kuntze	Pseudobulb: Sweet, aphrodisiac, haemostatic, antidiarrhoeal, styptic, antidysentric, febrifuge, cooling and tonic.It is useful in sterility, vitiated conditions of pitta and vata, semen related weakness, internal and external haemorrhages, dysentry, fever, emaciation, burning sensation and general debility.
5.	*Polygonatum verticillatum* (L.) All.	It is diuretic, used as a pain reliever, for pyrexia, for burning sensation, phthisis and for treating general debility.Rhizome-Aphrodisiac, emollient, appetizer, tonic and galactagogue.The extract of its aerial parts showed leishmanicidal activity against *Leishmania major* which causes Kala azar.The crude methanolic extract of its rhizome exhibit antinociceptive activity in rats.
6.	*Polygonatum cirrhifolium* (Wall.) Royle	Rhizome-Cooling, mild laxative, galactagogue, aphrodisiac, depurative, wound healer, febrifuge, expectorant and tonic. Compounds extracted from its rhizome exhibit fungicidal activities.
7.	*Habenaria intermedia* D. Don	Tuber-Sweet, cooling, emollient, brain tonic, aphrodisiac, depurative, appetizer, antihelmintic, rasayana (rejuvenator) and tonic.It is useful in burning sensation, thirst, fever, cough, asthma, muscular pain, sprains, arthritis, sciatica, insanity, leprosy, skin diseases, anorexia, worms, emaciation, gout and general debility.
8.	*Platanthera edgeworthii* (Hook. f. ex Collett) R.K. Gupta	Tuber-Cooling, emollient, brain tonic, blood purifier, appetizer, aphrodisiac, rasayana (rejuvenator) antihelmintic and tonic.Tuber is useful in treating burning sensation, excessive thirst, fever, cough, asthma, insanity, leprosy, skin diseases, anorexia, worms, emaciation, gout and general debility.

Pharmacological Activities

(*a*) Pseudobulb of Jivak is useful in sterility, vitiated conditions of Pitta and Vata, internal and external hemorrhages, dysentery, fever, emaciation, burning sensation and general debility.

(*b*) ***Jivaniya* (Vitality promoter)**–*Astavarga* plants are vitality promoter, maintain the balance between three doshas of Vata, Pitta and Kapha. They increase the energy, body strength, glow and other properties of the body.

(*c*) ***Brmhaniya* (Body mass promoter)**–These medicinal plants are body mass promoter. The *Astavarga* plants especially *Kakoli* and *Kshirkakoli* fall in this category.

(*d*) ***Ayusya* (Longevity)**–These medicinal plants mitigate the disorder of the body and specifically alleviate Tridosaja disorder in the body to increase the longevity and slow down the process of aging.

(*e*) **Antioxidant activity**–Extract of pseudobulb of *Crepidium acuminatum* (D. Don) Szlach. shows antioxidant activity.

(*f*) **Antifungal and Antibacterial activity**–Extract of *Crepidium acuminatum* (D. Don) Szlach. Shows antifungal and antibacterial activity.

(*g*) **Anti-inflammatory activity**-The ethanolic extract of *Crepidium acuminatum* (D. Don) Szlach. pseudobulb exhibit analgesic and anti-inflammatory activity in experimental animals.

Classical Medicinal Uses

(*a*) *Mahamayurghrita* processed with *Jivaka* and other herbs is useful in *dhatugata vikara*, , svarabhransa (Aphesia), asthma, cough, facial paralysis, vaginal diseases, blood disorders and semen related problems.

(*b*) Intake of powder prepared from *Astavarga* plants mixed with proper quantity of honey and crystal sugar, is useful in cough and cardiac diseases.

(*c*) *Vacaditaila* processed with Jivaka and other herbs used as *anuvasanavasti* (type of medicated enema); is beneficial for gulma (type of abdominal disorders), distention, vata associated disorders and urinary incontinence.

(*d*) *Jivaniyaghrita* processed with Jivaka is useful for the whole body vitiated with gout and Vata associated disorders

(*e*) *Citrakaditaila* processed with *Jivaka* and other herbs is useful in Vata associated disorders, sciatica, kyphosis, gout and urinary disorders.

(*f*) *Mahapadmataila* processed with *Jivaka* and other herbs is useful in gout and fever.

(*g*) *Jivaniyaghrita* processed with *Jivaka* and other herbs, used properly, can be effective in treating gout and other chronic Vata associated disorders.

(*h*) *Asthapanavasti* (type of medicated enema prepared with oil and decoction of medicinal plants) processed with *Jivaka* and other medicinal herbs is useful in treating gulma, metrorrhagia, anaemia, malaria,

(*i*) Intake of *Ghrita* processed with *Devadaru*, *Kakoli*, *Jivaka* and other medicinal herbs given in proper dose is useful in child emaciation.

(*j*) *Himavanaagada* (preparation useful in poisoning) prepared with the powder of *Pancavalkala* (group of five bark), *Jivaka* and other herbs, mixed with honey to make a paste and external application of this paste on snake bite reduces the toxicity. It also alleviates other symptoms like edema (swelling), erysipelas, boils, fever and burning sensation.

Traditional Medicinal Uses

(*a*) Decoction prepared from Jivaka pseudobulb is useful in general deblity.

(*b*) Intake of powder prepared from Jivaka pseudobulb is useful in seminal weakness.

(*c*) Intake of Jivaka pseudobulb powder promotes lactation.

Conservation of *Astavarga* Plants

The *Astavarga* plants have been listed as rare and endangered, however, based on its low density and frequency in natural pockets in Himachal Pradesh, Jammu & Kashmir and Uttarakhand, now it should be categorized as critically endangered for the region. The habitat of these species in the Himalayas should be urgently identified and conservation measures like biodiversity parks or reserve protected areas must be proposed by concerned authorities for *Astavarga* plants. Mostly underground parts of the plants like, bulbs, pseudobulbs, rhizome and tubers of these species are used in traditional and classical medicine, therefore indiscriminate harvesting of whole plant with underground parts by local people and trade of these species need to be controlled by state governments and forest department strictly. These plants are main constituent of various *Ayurvedic* preparations like *Chyawanprasha Rasayan* and *Ashtavarga Churna*. To meet the demand of pharmaceutical industry *in-situ* and *ex-situ* conservation of these endangered medicinal plants is an important option which will dilute the harvesting pressure on these plants in nature and help conservation activity in the region.

Roscoea purpurea Sm.

Lilium polyphyllum D. Don

Crepidium acuminatum (D. Don) Szlach.

Malaxis muscifera (Lindl.) Kuntze

Polygonatum verticillatum (L.) All.

Polygonatum cirrhifolium (Wall.) Royle

Habenaria intermedia D. Don

Platanthera edgeworthii (Hook. f. ex Collett) R.K. Gupta

Acknowledgements

The authors are grateful to Param Pujya Swami Ramdev Ji of Patanjali Yogpeeth, Haridwar for providing all the necessary facilities for research and documentation work.

REFERENCES

Balkrishna, A. (2012). *Secrets of Astavarga Plants (for vitality and anti-aging)*, Divya Prakashan, Patanjali Yogpeeth, Uttarakhand, Haridwar.

Balkrishna, A., Mishra, R. K., Srivastava, A., Patel, S. P., Vashistha, R. K., Singh, A., Jadon, V. & Saxena, P. (2012). *Astavarga* plants—Threatened Medicinal Herbs of the North-West Himalaya. *Int. J. Med. Arom. Plants*, 2(4): 661-676.

Chauhan, R.S., Nautiyal, M.C., Prasad, P. & Purohit, H. (2008). Ecological Features of an Endangered Medicinal Orchid, *Malaxis Muscifera* (Lindl.) Kuntze, in the Western Himalaya. *MIOS Journal*, 9(6): 8-12.

Chubey, D.R. (1986). *Abhinava Nighantu* Chaukhamba Sanskrit Series, Varansai.

Collet, H. (1980). *Flora Simlensis, A Hand Book of the Flowering Plants of Shimla and Neighbourhood*, Bishen Singh Mahendra Pal Singh, Dehradun.

Dev, A. (1960). *Ayurveda ka Brihat Itihas*, U.P. Govt. Rajrshi Purshotam Das Tandon, Hindi Bhavan Lucknow.

Deva, S. & Naithani, H. B. (1986). *The Orchid flora of North West Himalaya*, Print and Media Associates, New Delhi, India.

Dey, A.C. (1982). *Indian Medicinal Plants used in Ayurvedic Preparations*, Bishan Singh Mahender Pal Singh, Dehradun.

Duthie, J.F. (1906). The Orchids of North-Western Himalaya, *Ann. Roy. Bot. Gard. Calcutta*, 9: 81-211.

Dwivedi, V. (1977). *Bhav Prakash Nighantu*, Motilal Banarsi Das, Delhi.

E-Flora of China. (n.d.). Retrieved from http://www.efloras.org/flora_page.aspx?flora_id=2

E-Flora of Pakistan. (n.d.). Retrieved from http://www.efloras.org/browse.aspx?flora_id=5

Gupta, A.D. (2002). *Asthangha Samgraha*, (Vol. II). Krishana Das Academy Varanasi.

Hooker, J.D. (1997-1999). *Flora of British India*. Bishen Singh Mahendra Pal Singh, Dehradun, (Vol. V-VI) (reprints).

Kamat, S. D. (2002). *Studies on Medicinal Plants and Drugs in Dhanvantari-Nighantu*, Chaukhamba Sanskrit Pratishthan, Delhi (First Published).

Khan, H., Saeed, M., Gilani, A., Khan, M., Dar, A., Khan, I. (2010). The Antinociceptive Activity of *Polygonatum Verticillatum* Rhizomes in Pain Models. *Journal of Ethnopharmacology*, 127(2): 521-527.

Lattoo, S.K., Dhar, A. K. & Jasrotia, A. (2001). Epicotyle Seed Dormancy and Phenology of Germination in *Polygonatum Cirrhifolium* Royle. *Current Science*, 81(11): 1414-1417.

Lattoo, S.K., Khan, S. & Dhar, A.K. (2005). A New Chromosome Number in *Polygonatum Cirrhifolium* Royle: An Endangered Liliaceous Medicinal Herb. *Current Science*, 89(7): 1080-1081.

Mathur, D.R. (2003). *Yogtarangini*. Chaukhamba Vidhyabhawan: Varanasi.

Naithani, B.D. (1985). *Flora of Chamoli*. Howrah, Botanical Survey of India.

Nautiyal, A.R., Nautiyal, M.C. & Purohit, A.N. (1997). *Harvesting Herbs-2000: Medicinal and Aromatic Plants- An Action Plan for Uttarakhand*. Proceeding of a Seminar on Harvesting Herbs-2000. Bishen Singh Mahendra Pal Singh, Dehra Dun, pp. 196.

Polanin, O., Stainton, Adam. 1984. *Flowers of Himalaya*, Oxford University Press, Delhi.

Ramprasad, P. (1998). *Madanpal Nighantu*, Khemraj Shri Krishanadass, Mumbai.

Sharma, A.R. (2001). *Susruta Samhita*, Chaukhamba Surbharti Prakashan, Varansi.

Sharma, P.V. (1993). *Dravya Guna Vijnana*, Chaukhamba Bharti Academy, Varanasi.

Sharma, P.V. (2003). *Dravyaguna Vijnana*, Chaukhamba Bharti Academy, Varanasi.

Singh, A. P. (2006). *Astavarga*- Rare Medicinal Plants. *Ethnobotanical Leaflets*, 10: 104-108.

Uniyal, M. (1975). *Astavarga Sandigdha Vanaushadhi*, Dhanwantri Patrika, Shri Jwala *Ayurved* Bhavan, Aligarh.

E-Flora of Pakistan. (n.d.). Retrieved from http://www.efloras.org/flora_page.aspx?flora_id=5

Flowers of India. (n.d.). Retrieved from http://www.flowersofindia.net/

Nayar, M.P. & Sastry, A.R.K. (1987). Red data book of Indian plants.

Phyto-chemicals and Ethanobotany **Pages 169-177**
Edited by: Pawan Kumar 'Bharti'
ISBN: 978-93-86841-93-3
Edition: 2019
Published by: Discovery Publishing House Pvt. Ltd., New Delhi (India)

8

Medicinal Properties of *Murrayakoenigii* and *Calendula Officinalis*

[1]Dr. Ashok K. Rathoure

Introduction

Medicinal plant products are the natural products which have been very useful for human to cure various ailments and as an alternative medicine for conventional therapy. However, bacteria in natural environments are mainly exist in biofilm formation and are more susceptible to cause severe infections than the planktonic counterparts. Nature always stands as a golden mark to exemplify the outstanding phenomena of symbiosis. Natural products from plant, animal and minerals have been the basis of the treatment of human disease. Today estimate that about 80% of people in developing countries still relays on traditional medicine based largely on species of plants and animals for their primary health care. Herbal medicines are currently in demand and their popularity is increasing day by day. About 500 plants with medicinal use are mentioned in ancient literature and around 800 plants have been used in indigenous systems of medicine. India is a vast repository of medicinal plants that are used in traditional medical treatments. Himalaya as the best habitat of medicinal plants. Since then the science of medicinal plants has progressively evolved to the present state. Himalayan is one of the major repositories of medicinal plants. The Indian Himalayan Region includes parts of Trans North West Himalaya, Jammu & Kashmir, Himachal Pradesh, West Himalayas, Kumaun, Garhwal, Central Himalaya, Sikkim, Darjeeling district of west Bengal, East Himalaya, Arunchal Pradesh. The various indigenous systems such as Siddha, Ayurveda, Unani and Allopathy use several plant species to treat different ailments.

Herbal medicines as the major remedying traditional system of medicine have been used in continue today because of its biomedical benefits as well as place in cultural beliefs in many parts of world and have made a great contribution towards maintaining human health. In India around 20,000 medicinal plant species have been recorded recently but more than 500

[1] Independent Researcher, India.

traditional communities use about 800 plant species for curing different diseases. The use of herbal is medicine becoming popular due to toxicity and side effects of allopathic medicines. This led to sudden increase in the number of herbal drug manufactures. Currently 80% of the world population depends on plant-derived medicine for the first line of primary health care for human alleviation because it has no side effects. Plants are important sources of medicines and presently about 25% of pharmaceutical prescriptions in the United States contain at least one plant-derived ingredient. In the last century, roughly 121 pharmaceutical products were formulated based on the traditional knowledge obtained from various sources.

Murrayakoenigii (Curry leaf, Sweet Neem leaves)

Kingdom	:	Plantae
Division	:	*Magnoliophyta*
Class	:	*Magnoliopsida*
Order	:	*Sapindales*
Family	:	*Rutaceae*
Genus	:	*Murraya*
Species	:	*koenigii*

Murrayakoenigii is a member of the large Rutaceae family and represented by about 150 genera and 1600 species. *M. koenigii* is one of the most widely used plants whose leaves are added to curries to improve flavour. It is usually cultivated for its aromatic smell which is used as natural flavorings in curries and sauces as reported by Sastri in 1952. The intensive pungent, aromatic leaves are best when fresh, but adequately retain their potency for some time after picking. This plant is originated from Tarai of Uttar Pradesh, India and distributed throughout India and Andaman Islands. This plant is an unarmed, semi deciduous, aromatic, shrub or small tree of about 3-5 meter high with strong woody stem. The branches are covered with dark grey bark. The woody stem has a closely crowded, shady crown. The leaves are pinnate, with 11-21 leaflets, each leaflet 2-4 cm long and 1-2 cm broad, have slightly pungent, bitter and feebly acidulous taste. The flowers are **white corymbose cymes** 1 cm long and the small fruits berries occur in close clusters. It turned from green to red and ultimately black on ripening (Biswas et al., 2012; Mitraet al., 2012; Deviet al., 2012).

Various parts of this plant have many medicinal uses and values as raw material for traditional medicine and popular in India. It have been reported that the leaves and the roots can cure piles and heat removal of the body, inflammation and itching, while the powdered leaf is used to aid healing of fresh cuts. As an external application, barks and roots are used to relieve skin eruptions and the bites by poisonous animals. Drury (1978) reported that the green leaves could be eaten in raw for the treatment of dysentery. Curry leaf odors every house yard of South India. Generally, this plant has also been used in the industry, where fresh leaves are steam distilled under reduced pressure to yield volatile oils which can be used as a fixative for a heavy type of soap perfume. The anti-oxidant and anti-diabetic properties of plant were reported. Saritha in 2009 reported the presence of iron in Curry leaves which is good for healthy hair. The antimicrobial activity and anti-inflammatory activity of curry leaves was also reported by many investigators.Marigold flowers (carotenoids, saponosides, sterols, flavonoids, mucilages, essential oil, tannins, Mn^{2+} ions) are used both internally and locally for their healing action in burns, wounds and various inflammatory skin disorders. Experimental models and randomized clinical trials have shown that topical preparations (especially ointments) with Calendulaeflos extracts stimulate the wound-healing process in numerous skin problems (Lievre et al., 1992;Lavagna et al., 2001; Pommier et al., 2004). The medicinal value of leaves and oil of *Murrayakoenigii*listed below:

Name	Parts used	Types of plant extracts	Medicinal uses of plant	Pathogens used for biofilm	Activities	References
Murrayakoenigii	Leaves, essential oil	Ethanol, aqueous	Tonic, chronic wound, stomachic, inflammation, itching, vomiting, cure piles	*Pseudomonas aeruginosa*	Antibiofilm, antiulcer, antidiarrhoea, antidiabetics activities, cholesterol reducing property, phagocytic activity, and more useful medicinal properties	Handral et al., 2012; Ganesh and Vital, 2015

Calendula officinalis (Ganda, Golsbloom, Marigold)

Kingdom	:	Plantae
Division	:	*Magnoliophyta*
Class	:	*Magnoliopsida*
Order	:	Asrerales
Family	:	Calenduleae
Genus	:	Calendula
Species	:	officinalis

Calendula officinalis was cultivated by the Egyptians, Greeks, Hindus and Arabs, has been used medicinally since the 12thcentury. Its name comes from the Latin word, *calends*, the first day of every month, because of its long flowering period. *Calendula*pot; marigold is a genus of about 12–20 species of annual or perennial herbaceous plants. Marigolds are hardy plants that typically bloom in bright yellows, reds, and oranges throughout the summer and well into the fall. Marigold is cultivated throughout India. It flowers from July to September. It is a short-lived aromatic perennial plant, growing to 80 cm tall, with sparsely branched lax or erect stems. The leaves are oblong-lanceolate, 5–17 cm long, hairy on both sides, and with margins entire or occasionally waved or weakly toothed. The inflorescences are yellow, comprising a thick capitulum or flower head 4–7 cm diameter surrounded by two rows of hairy bracts; in the wild plant they have a single ring of ray florets surrounding the central disc florets. The disc florets are tubular and hermaphrodite, and generally of a more intense orange-yellow colour than the female, tridentate, peripheral ray florets.

Calendula was taken internally to treat fevers, promote menstruation and treat cancer. Most importantly, the flowers were made into extracts, tinctures, balms and salves and applied directly to the skin to help heal wounds and to soothe inflamed and damaged skin. In India, herbal compounds including calendula are used topically to treat hemorrhoids. Calendula is used in Italian folk medicine as an antipyretic and anti-inflammatory. Tea made from calendula are used as eye washes, gargles or compresses to treat conjunctivitis, pharyngitis, aphthous stomatitis and gingivo stomatitis, diaper rashes and other inflammatory conditions of the skin and mucus membranes. The medicinal properties of flowers of *Calendula officinalis*is listed below:

Name	Parts used	Types of plant extracts	Medicinal uses of plant	Pathogens used for biofilm	Activities	References
Calendula officinalis	Flowers	Water	Measles, smallpox, jaundice, costiveness, ointment for wound, ulcer, frostbite, skin damage, scars, and blood purification	*Salmonella, Shigelladysenteriae, Shigellaflexneri, Shigellasonnei*and *Escherichia coli*	Antibacterial, antibiofilm, antiedematous, antiseptic action, antioxidant, antispasmodic activities	Muley et al., 2009; Ghaima et al., 2013

Phytochemicals in Plants

Phytochemicals, which are non-nutritive plant chemicals, constitute a heterogeneous group of substances. In general, the plant chemicals that protect plant cells from environmental hazards such as pollution, stress, drought, UV exposure and pathogenic attack are called as Phytochemicals. Recently, it is clearly known that they have roles in the protection of human health, when their dietary intake is significant. These compounds are known as secondary plant metabolites and have biological properties such as antioxidant activity, antimicrobial effect, modulation of detoxification enzymes, stimulation of the immune system, decrease of platelet aggregation and modulation of hormone metabolism and anticancer property. There are more than thousand known and many unknown Phytochemicals. It is well-known that plants produce these chemicals to protect themselves, but recent researches demonstrate that many Phytochemicals can also protect human against diseases. Because of this property, many researchers have been performed to reveal the beneficial health effects of Phytochemicals. Phytochemicals are not essential nutrients and are not required by the human body for sustaining life, but have important properties to prevent or to fight. Nowadays there is an urgent need for discover of new antimicrobial compounds with chemicals structure as effective drug against microbial infections.

Classification of Phytochemicals

Alkaloids: Alkaloids are naturally occurring chemical compounds containing basicnitrogen atoms. The name derives from the word alkaline and was used to describe any nitrogen-containing base. Alkaloids are produced by a large variety of organisms, including bacteria, fungi, plants, and animals and are part of the group of natural products (also called secondary metabolites). Many alkaloids can be purified from crude extracts by acid-base extraction. Many alkaloids are toxic to other organisms. Some alkaloids have a bitter taste.

The majority of drugs currently in common use are derived from alkaloids, for example paclitaxel from the plant *Taxusbrevifolia*. Alkaloids, which are nitrogen containing compounds, created via diverse biosynthetic pathways; continue to provide an extensive range of therapeutic compounds. There is much interest in the identification of new alkaloids either as drugs or as pivotal intermediates in the synthesis of new drugs. The use of alkaloids as drugs started in the early 1950s, when camptothecin isolated from the stem of the Chinese ornamental *tree. Camptotheca acuminate* was shown to be an effective anticancer agent. Many alkaloids derived from plants have anticancer properties. The anticancer drug Taxol has been reported to exhibit side effects including numbness, nausea and migraine. This is not uncommon, and as a consequence, there is a continuing search for new anticancer compounds that are active and selective with minimal side effects. They often have pharmacological effects and are used as medications and recreational drugs. Examples are the local anesthetic and stimulantcocaine, the stimulant caffeine, nicotine, the analgesicmorphine, or the antimalarial drugquinine.

Terpenoids: The terpenoids, sometimes called isopreniods, are a large diverse class of naturally occurring organic chemicals. They are derived from five carbon isoprene units assembled and modified in thousands of ways. Some terpenoids have unusual seven-carbon ring structures. Plant terpenoids are used widely for their aromatic qualities; they play a major role in traditional herbal therapies and are under investigation for antibacterial, antineo plastic and other pharmaceutical functions. Terpenoids contribute to the scent eucalyptus, the flavors of cinnamon, cloves, and ginger and the color of yellow flowers. Monoterpenoids are well known of their antimicrobial activity. Several terpenoids showed antifungal activity against microsporum cookie and Trichophytonmentagrophyes and fusaruim.

Another type of biological active terpenoids is saponins that are agroup of triterpenoids which have been isolated from different plant e.g. rapanea, dolichos, camellia, and primula. Saponins show a wide range of biological activities including antibacterial activity. They often have pharmacological effects and are used as medications and recreational drugs. Examples are the local anesthetic and stimulantcocaine, the stimulant caffeine, nicotine, the analgesic morphine, or the anti-malarialdrugquinine. Saponins are considered to be an exception among antifungal compounds in that their antifungal activity is usually correlated with the sugar moiety glycosylated to the 3-hydroxyl group of the terpenoids and thus a polar part of the molecule, whereas most other antifungal constituents tend to be strongly lipophilic and inactive in glycoside form.

Tannins: Tannins are polyphenols that are obtained from various parts of different plants belonging to multiple species. Deriving it name from the technical word tanning that meant converting animal hides to leather through chemical processes; tannin is basically used for this function. It is found in abundance in the tree bark, wood, fruit, fruitpod, leaves, and roots and also in plant gall. Tannins are found as shapeless yellowish or light brown masses like powder, flakes or sponge. Interestingly, tannins are found almost in all plants and in all climates all over the world. Although algae, fungi and mosses do not contain much tannin the percentage of tannins present in the plants, however, varies. While they are present in significant proportions in some plants, many others have too little of them. Tannins are usually found in large quantities in the bark of trees where they act as a barrier for micro-organisms like bacteria and fungi and protect the tree. The astringent effect of tannins is beneficial in the treatment of diarrhea. Antiseptic effect on skin and mucous membranes has been studied with antimicrobial activity. Presence of phenolic group is responsible for this effect.

Tannins are a basic ingredient in the chemical staining of wood, tannic acid is used in the conservation of ferrous (iron based) metal objects to passivity and inhibit corrosion. Tannic acid reacts with the corrosion products to form a more stable compound, thus preventing further corrosion from taking place. After treatment the tannic acid residue is generally left on the object so that if moisture reaches the surface the tannic acid will be rehydrated and prevent or slow any corrosion. Tannic acid treatment for conservation is very effective and widely used but it does have a significant visual effect on the object, turning the corrosion products black and any exposed metal dark blue. It should also be used with care on objects with copper alloy components as the tannic acid can have a slight etching effect on these metals. In tanning industry, for converting animal hide into leather. Tannins are also used in dyeing, photography, ripening beer and wine as well as an astringent in medicines.

Aromatic compounds: Aromatic compounds are compounds that are similar to benzene in structure and chemical behavior. Benzene, C6H6, is a cyclic compound commonly written as a hexagon with alternating double and single bonds. A large proportion of aromatic substances that are extracted from plants often show antifungal activity. These include simple and alkylated phenols, phenolic acids, phenylpropanoids, coumarins, flavonoids, isoflavonoids, stillbenoids, quinones and xanthones.

Flavonoids: Flavonoids bioflavonoids derive from the Latin word *flavus* meaning yellow, also collectively known as Vitamin P and citrinare a class of plant secondary metabolites or yellow pigments having a structure similar to that of flavones. Flavonoids are the most important plant pigments for flower coloration producing yellow or red blue pigmentation in petals designed to attract pollinator animals. Flavonoids are polyphenolic compounds that are ubiquitous in nature and are categorized, according to chemical structure, into flavonols, flavones, flavanones, isoflavones, catechins, anthocyanidins and chalcones. Over 4,000 flavonoids have been identified, many of which occur in fruits, vegetables and beverages like tea, coffee, beer, wine and fruit drinks. The flavonoids have aroused considerable interest recently because of their potential beneficial effects on human health; they have been reported to have antiviral, antiallergic, anti-inflammatory, antitumor and antioxidant activities.

Need of New Antimicrobials

The discovery of antimicrobial agents marked a new era in the history of medicine. In past 60 years, hundreds of tons of antimicrobial agents have been released on bacterial populations, which have responded to deluge with a progeny, which is no longer susceptible but flourishes. Antimicrobial drug resistance is a global concern today as the resistant microorganisms have emerged and spread throughout the world because of their genetic plasticity. During the past 2 decades, new infectious diseases have appeared and old ones previously thought to be controlled have reemerged and continue to pose threat in this century. Antimicrobial resistance have been reported in for the most predominant pathogenic microorganisms like *Staphylococcus aureus, Staphylococcus epidermidis, Escherchia coli, Pseudomonas aeruginosa, Salmonella typhimurium, Klebsiellapneumoniae, Candida albicans, Cryptococcus neoformans.* The emerging number of incidences of resistance of microbes towards synthetic drugs and antibiotics of microbial origin has turned the attention of scientists, towards traditional medicines especially herbal drugs or drugs of plant origin.

The use of traditional medicines and medicinal plants in most developing countries as therapeutic agents for the maintenance of good health has been widely observed. Modern pharmacopoeia still contains at least 25% drugs derived from plants and many others, which are synthetic analogues, built on prototype compounds isolated from plants. Interest in medicinal plants as are-emerging health aid has been fuelled by the rising costs of prescription drugs in the maintenance of personal health and wellbeing and the bio-prospecting of new plant-derived drugs. The medicinal properties of plants could be based on the antioxidant, antimicrobial antipyretic effects of the Phytochemicals in them. According to World Health Organization, medicinal plants would be the best source to obtain a variety of drugs. Therefore, such plants should be investigated to better understand their properties, safety and efficacy.

Conclusion

Large group of traditional medicinal plants is used for different medicinal properties, which have a greater potential to cure various diseases. Furthermore, various extracts from different medicinal plant parts such as leaves, flowers, essential oils, root, and barks were also found to possess the anti-biofilm activity.Marigold flowers are used both internally and locally for their healing action in burns, wounds and various inflammatory skin disorders. The emerging number of incidences of resistance of microbes towards synthetic drugs and antibiotics of microbial origin has turned the attention of scientists, towards traditional medicines especially herbal drugs or drugs of plant origin. There should be public awareness about the medicinal plant and their uses, so that the public can take benefits of natural resources.

REFERENCES

Ghaima KK, Rasheed AF, Ahmed EF. Antibiofilm, Antibacterial and Antioxidant Activities of Water Extracts of *Calendula officinalis*flowers. Int J Biol Pharm Res 2013;4(7): 465-70.

Muley BP, Khadabadi SS, Banarase NB. Phytochemical Constituents and Pharmacological Activities of *Calendula Officinalis* (Asteraceae): A review. Trop J Pharm Res 2009; 8(5): 455-65.

Handral H.K., Pandith A, Shruthi SD. A Review on *Murrayakoenigii*: Multipotential Medicinal Plant. Asian J Pharm Clin Res 2012; 5(4): 5-14.

Ganesh PS, Vital RR. *In vitro* Antibiofilm Activity of *Murrayakoenigii*essential Oil Extracted using Supercritical Fluid CO2 Method Against *Pseudomonas aeruginosa* PAO1. Nat Prod Res 2015; 29(24): 2295-8.

Biswas A.K.; Chatli M.K.; Sahoo. Antioxidant Potential of Curry (Murrayakoenigii L.) and Mint (Menthaspicata) Leaf Extracts and their Effect on Colour and Oxidative Stability of Raw Ground Pork meat during Refrigeration Storage. J. Food Chemistry 2012; 133(2): 467-472

MitraElina; Ghosh Arnab K; Ghosh Debosree. Protective Effect of Aqueous Curry Leaf (Murrayakoenigii) Extract against Cadmium-induced Oxidative Stress in Rat Heart. Food andChemical Toxicology. 2012;50(5): 1340-53

Devi K.R.; Jael P.M.; Kusumlatha C. Protective Role of Murrayakoenigii Leaf Extract on Adriamycin Induced Micronuclei in Mice Bone Marrow Erythrocytes. International Journal of Pharm Tech Research. 2012; 4(1): 156-161

Lievre M, Marichy J, Baux S, Foyatier JL, Perrot J, Boissel JP, Controlled Study of three Ointments for the Local Management of 2nd and 3rd degree Burns, Clin Trials Metaanal, 1992; 28(1): 9–12.

Lavagna SM, Secci D, Chimenti P, Bonsignore L, Ottaviani A, Bizzarri B, Efficacy of Hypericum and Calendula oils in the Epithelial Reconstruction of Surgical Wounds in Childbirth with Caesarean Section, Farmaco, 2001;56(5–7):451–453.

Pommier P, Gomez F, Sunyach MP, D'Hombres A, Carrie C, Montbarbon X, Phase III Randomized Trial of Calendula Officinalis Compared with Trolamine for the Prevention of Acute Dermatitis during Irradiation for Breast Cancer, J Clin Oncol, 2004; 22(8): 1447–1153

Phyto-chemicals and Ethanobotany **Pages 178-194**
Edited by: Pawan Kumar 'Bharti'
ISBN: 978-93-86841-93-3
Edition: 2019
Published by: Discovery Publishing House Pvt. Ltd., New Delhi (India)

9

Nutraceutical Properties of *Capparis spinosa* as a Mediterranean Medicinal Plant

[1]Amal A. Mohamed, [2]Hossam S. El-Beltagi, [3]Sami I. Ali

ABSTRACT

Medicinal plants, the oldest source of pharmacologically active compounds continue to cater the therapeutic need of majority of population in the developing world and played a dominant role in the introduction of new therapeutic agents. Based on the knowledge of plants gathered from various ancient medical writings, and civilizations, field observation and consultation with folk medicine men, research on medicinal plants have been undertaken all over the world for development of new herbal drugs. In addition, environmental factors like alterations in climatic variables and abiotic stress are known sources for oxidative stress. The ability of plant cells to fight against these factors is important for maintenance of their health growth .Capparis spinosa L. (Caper) is a perennial spiny bush that bears rounded, fleshy leaves and big white to pinkish-white flowers. It is native to the Mediterranean region and growing wild on walls or in rocky coastal areas throughout India. It contains a number of bioactive compounds, mostly polyphenols. Even though it has been used in traditional Indian system of medicines for various human diseases, the summation of its medicinal properties is lacking. Hence, the present review focused to provide collective information regarding the medicinal value of C. spinosa.

Keywords: Capparis spinosa L., medicinal properties, nutritional value, phytochemicals

1. Introduction

Plants are able of producing a great amount of relatively small organic chemicals that are defined as secondary metabolites that eliciting pharmacological or toxicological effects. Pharmaceutical preparations from medicinal plants

[1] Plant Biochemistry Dept., National Research Centre, 33 El Bohouth St., Dokki, Giza, Egypt. P.O. 12622, ID: 60014618.

[2] Chemistry Dept., University College - Umm Al-Qura University, Saudi Arabia.

[3] Cairo University, Faculty of Agriculture, Biochemistry Department, PO. Box 12613, Gamma St, Giza, Cairo, Egypt.

created a new expanding market as herbal components of health foods and preventive medicine under nutraceuticals.

In recent years, there has been a great deal of attention toward the field of free radical chemistry. Reactive oxygen species (ROS) are produced by living organisms as a result of normal cellular metabolism. Free radicals and antioxidants have become commonly used terms in modern discussions of disease mechanisms (Ebadi, 2001).

ROS include the superoxide anion (O_2^-), hydrogen peroxide (H_2O_2), and hydroxyl radicals (OH^-), all of which have inherent chemical properties that confer reactivity to different biological targets (Fig. 9.1.). ROS are often associated with the principle of oxidative stress, which suggests that ROS induce pathology by damaging lipids, proteins, and DNA (Tafani *et al.*, 2016). By the other words, oxidative stress can induce radical mediated damage to cellular biomembranes resulting in lipid peroxidation, that lead to the generation of a variety of oxidized products including reactive electrophiles, such as epoxides and aldehydes, which are capable of modifying DNA, proteins, and other macromolecules. ROS leads to persistent changes in signal transduction and gene expression that, could lead to cell death. A balance between ROS generation and scavenging ultimately determines the oxidative load. The delicate balance between ROS generation and ROS scavenging is disturbed by the different types of stress factors like salinity, drought, extreme temperatures, heavy metals, pollution, high irradiance, pathogen infection, etc. (Fig. 9.1).

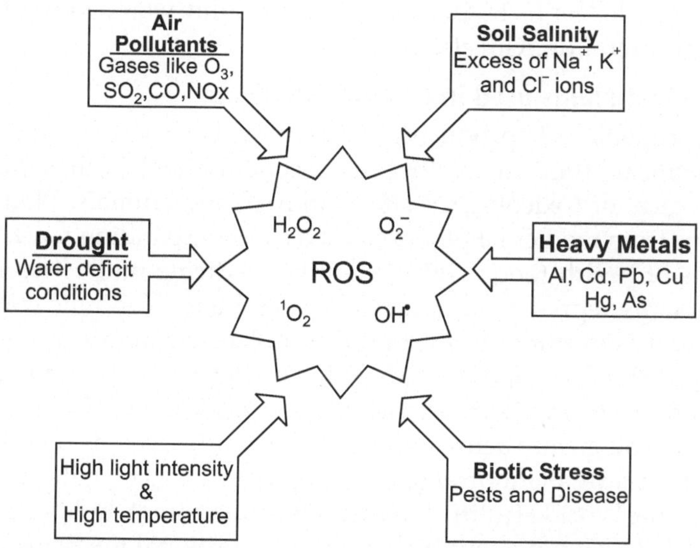

Fig. 9.1: Various causes responsible for the generation of ROS. Photo credit: Kaushik Das and Aryadeep Roychoudhury

To reduce the damaging effects of ROS, aerobic organisms evolved both non-enzymatic and enzymatic antioxidant defences. Non-enzymatic defences include compounds of intrinsic antioxidant properties, such as vitamins C and E, glutathione, and ß-carotene. Purely enzymatic defences, such as superoxide dismutases (SOD), and catalases (CAT), protect by directly scavenging superoxide radicals and hydrogen peroxide, converting them to less reactive species. SODs catalyze the dismutation of $O_2^{\cdot-}$ to H_2O_2, and CAT and peroxidases reduce H_2O_2 to $2H_2O$. The similarity between the SOD and CAT reactions is that each is an oxidation-reduction in which the substrate, $O_2^{\cdot-}$ for SOD and H_2O_2 for CAT, is both reductant and oxidised, whereas different registrants are required for the peroxidases, depending upon their specificities (Fig. 9.2). Under some conditions CAT can act as an efficient peroxidase. SODs deal with the first product of the univalent reduction of O_2, converting it to H_2O_2, which must then be destroyed by CAT and/or peroxidases (Day *et al.*, 2012).

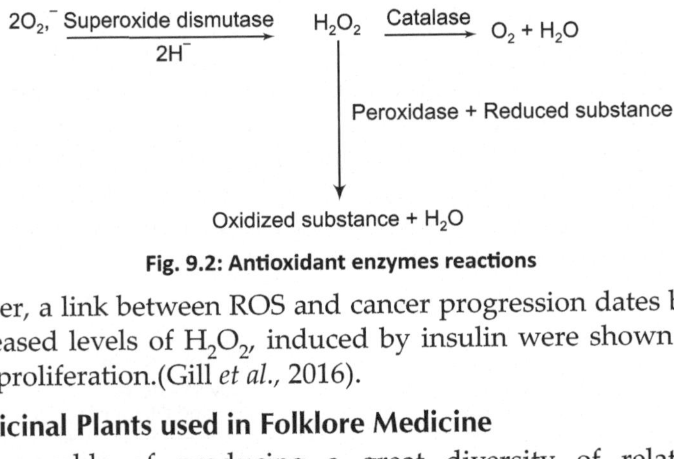

Fig. 9.2: Antioxidant enzymes reactions

However, a link between ROS and cancer progression dates back to 1981 when increased levels of H_2O_2, induced by insulin were shown to promote tumor cell proliferation.(Gill *et al.*, 2016).

Ethno-medicinal Plants used in Folklore Medicine

Plants are capable of producing a great diversity of relatively small organic chemicals that are defined as secondary metabolites that eliciting pharmacological or toxicological effects in man and animals. Pharmaceutical preparations from medicinal plants created a new expanding market as herbal components of health foods and preventive medicine under "nutraceuticals. Medicinal plants represent an important health and economic component of biodiversity. It is essential to make the complete inventory of the medicinal component of the flora of any country for conservation and sustainable use. Natural products from plants are rich sources of chemical diversity and most of the pharmacologically active principles currently used as drugs, including anticancer agents are plant products or directly inspired by natural substances. According to the World Health Organization, approximately 80% of the world's population in developing countries relies on traditional medicines, which are mostly derived from plants, for their primary health care (Chivian, 2002). Epidemiological studies have shown that many of the phytochemicals from medicinal plants possess anti-inflammatory, antiatherosclerotic, antitumor, antimutagenic, anticarcinogenic, antibacterial, or antiviral activities (Ozkan *et al.*, 2016). Moreover, several formulations such as herbal teas, extracts, decoctions, infusions, tinctures, etc. are the methods mostly used for the preparation of the folk Medicines, Several medicinal plants and their extracts works as a scavenger of reactive oxidative species (ROS) by donating hydrogen atoms to peroxy radicals, superoxide anions, and singlet oxygen and hydroxyl radicals; it also functions as a terminator and chelator of metal ions that are capable of oxidizing lipid peroxidation. Furthermore, there is an increasing preference for natural antioxidant rather than synthetic molecules because of the safety of the natural sources.

Capparis Spinosa

Capparis spinosa, a wild plant of the family *Capparidaceae,* is said to be native to the Mediterranean basin and found in many parts (Fig. 9.3.). Fruits of *C. Spinoza,* also known as caper berries, is ellipsoid, ovoid to pear-shaped (Fig. 9.4.). In Mediterranean countries, pickled bud is a commercial commodity According to Sher and Alyemeni (2010), many parts of caper are still being used as drugs and traditional healers in Saudi Arabia describe oral administration of dried fruits of *C. spinosa* with water to treat hypertension and diabetic complications. Hot-water extract of *C. spinosa* prevents lead acetate-induced lipid oxidation in rats (Al-Soqeer, 2011). The strong flavor of capers is usually due to the very pungent methyl isothiocyanate that is released after an enzymatic reaction with a mustard oil glycoside named glucocapparin (methyl glucosinolate)

Fig. 9.3: Morphology of (a) *Capparis spinosa* plant and (b) caperberries

Fig. 9.4: *Capparis spinosa* Fruits

This plant is established to have highly diverse economic and medicinal value in different systems of medicines like in Iranian, Unani, Chinese, Ayurvedic and Greco-Arabi System of medicines. *C. spinosa* is well known with its common name 'Capers' in different countries.

Phytochemical Compounds in C. *Spinosa*

Dfferent secondary metabolites have been found in caper plant, nevertheless a wide range of phytochemical compounds such as flavonoids, alkaloids, and glycosides, in addition to lipids and vitamins, which are responsible for its health-promoting effects have been reported in this plant (Zhao*et al.*, 2013). Although numerous of these substances have existed in low concentrations and significant changes in their content occurred through processing. In addition, there is insignificant scientific evidence regarding any side effects (Valid *et al.*, 2017). It is well known that, roots, the flower buds, and fruits, of the C. *spinosa* have been used in folk medicine and considered as precious sources of glucosinolates (glucocapparin (N.), glucobrassicin, glucoiberin andsinigrin), alkaloids including spermidine alkaloid (A.), isocodonocarpine (B.), capparisinine (C.), capparidisine (D.), capparine, and capparinine as well as codonocarpine (E.), capparisine (F.), cadabacine-26-*O*-ß-D-glucoside (G.), capparipine-26-*O*-ß-D-glucoside, N-acetylated spermidine alkaloids, 15-N-acetylcapparisine (H.), 14-N-acetyl isocodonocarpine (I.), unsaponifiable matter sterols (ß-sitosterol (J.)), aliphatic, triterpenic alcohols, carotenoids (ß-carotene (O.)), tocopherols, andguanosine (K.), capparine A (L.),capparine B (M),Flazin (P.) and 5-hydroxymethylfuraldehyde (Q.) (Fig. 9.5.) (Zhou *et al.*, 2010; Rathee *et al.*, 2011; Gull et al., 2015). Butylisothiocyanate and isopropyl-isothiocyanate (R.) are the major components of the root oils and fruit of *C. spinosa* (Nabavi *et al.*, 2016).

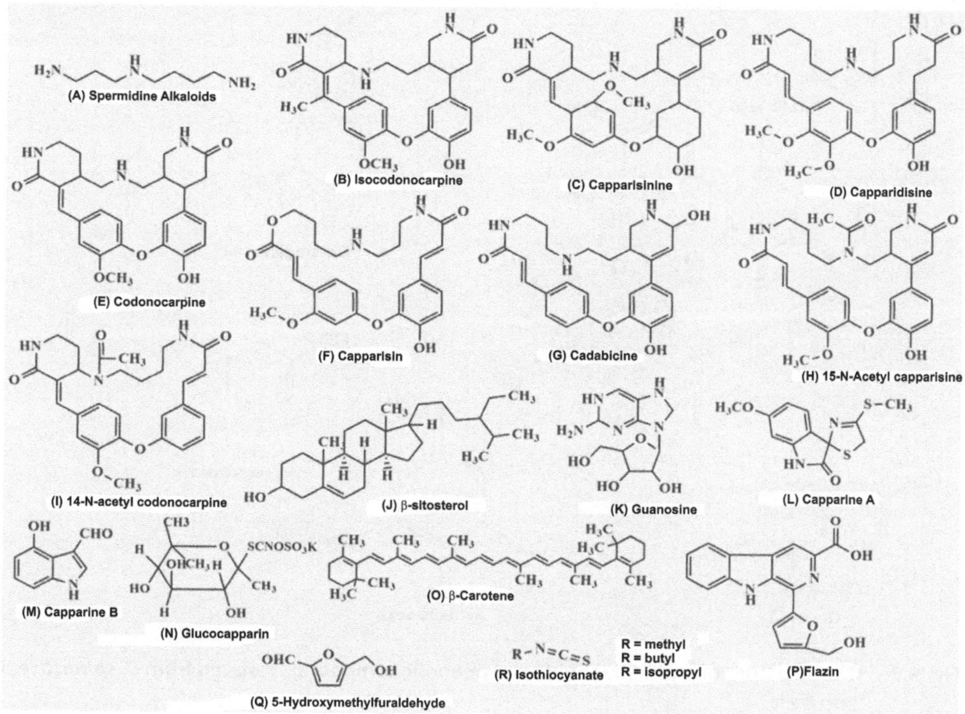

Fig. 9.5: Some of bioactive compounds structures of *Caper spinosa* plant (Rathee *et al.*, 2011)

Several phenolic compounds and flavonoids including chlorogenic acid,catechin, coumarin, ferulic acid, caffeic acid, kaempferol, quercetin, luteolin, resveratrol, rutin, syringic acid, and vanillic acid have been identified in leaves and fruit of C. spinosa (Fig. 9.6.) (Vahid*et al.*, 2017). All of these compounds are known to supply health-improving benefits due to their different biological activities such as antioxidant, antimutagenic, anti-inflammatory and anticancerogenic (Tlili *et al.*, 2017).

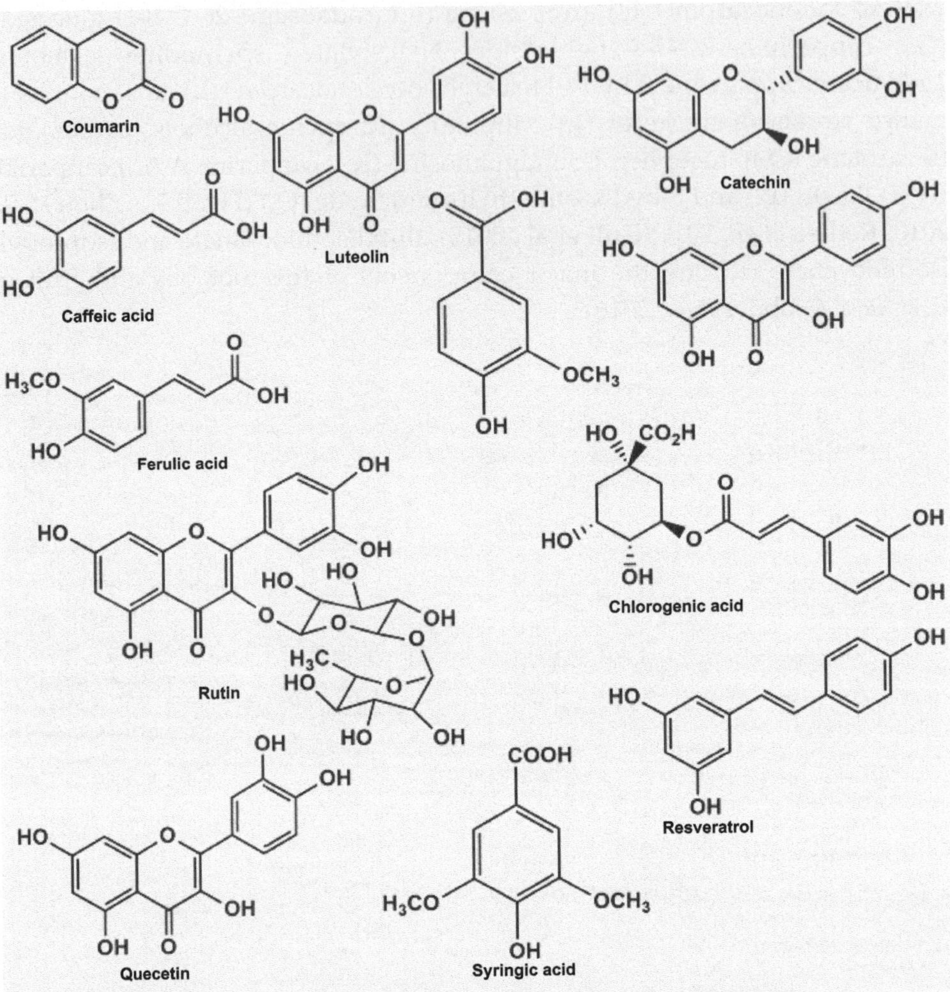

Fig. 9.6: The structure of main flavonoids and phenolic compounds isolated from *C. spinosa* leaf and fruit

Additionally, the caper is think to be rich in volatile organic compounds such as essential oils and the common components of *C. spinosa* identified by (SPME-GC- MS) were benzyl alcohol, benzoic acid, octanoic acid, carvacrol, α-terpinolene, 4-fluoro benzaldehyde and zingerone (Fig. 9.7) (Aliyazicioglu *et al.*, 2015).

In addition, GC–MS analysis revealed the identification of 26 components in essential oil from aerial part ofC. *spinosa*amounting for (95.46%) of the oil. The sulfated compounds were present in a relatively high percentage (40.3%), which are responsible for the aroma of *C. spinosa* volatile oil (Bakr and El Bishbishy 2016). Isopropyl isothiocyanate (28.92%), methyl isothiocyanate

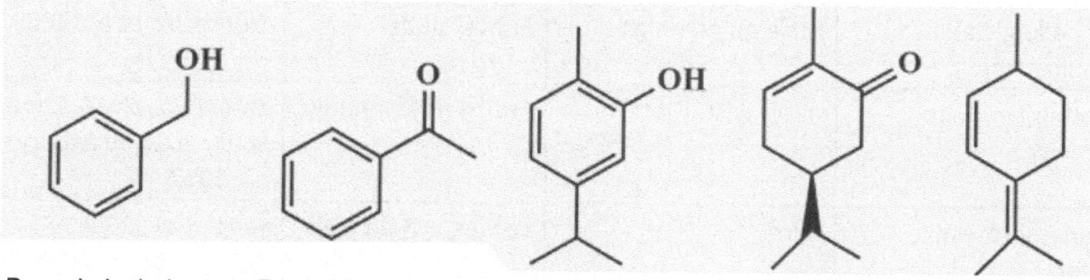

Fig. 9.7: Essential oils main components of *Capparis spinosa* L.

(25.60%), butyl isothiocyanate (16.65%), 3-*p*-menthene (3.08%), 2-butenyl isothiocyanate (2.24%) and 3-methylthio-1-hexanol (2.03%) were the major constituents (Muhaidat *et al.,* 2013).Furthermore, leaves of *C. spinosa* is one of the important sources of Quercetin, which is considered as the main hepatoprotective factor, it is one of the most strong antioxidants owing to its highest capacity to scavenge free radicals (Kalantari *et al.,*2017). These observations make this plant a potential source of bioactive compounds that can be used as herbal medicaments in Saudia Arabia and the reports on the toxicity of the plant further show that the plant is non-toxic to humans.

Pharmacological Properties

Due to its diverse economic, ecological, and medicinal attributes, *C. spinosa* ranks among the most important species of the genus Capparis have been reviewed. It exerted many pharmacological effects, including antioxidant, cytotoxic, anti-diabetic, anti-inflammatory, antimicrobial effect and many others. Table (1) generally referred to the pharmacological effects of the plant.

Table 9.1: Summary of the Major Pharmacological Effects of *C. spinosa*

Pharmacological activity	Animal model	Part of the plant	References
Antioxidant	Albino rats	Fresh buds and aerial parts	Bonina *et al.,*2002, Yang*et al.,* 2008, Sultan and Çelik 2009, Alsabri *et al.,* 2012
Antimicrobial	Gram-positive and negative bacteria	Whole plant and roots	Muhaidat *et al.,* 2013, Shayeb 2012
Antifungal activity	Valsamali fungi	Seeds	Yang *et al.,* 2008, Lam and Ng 2009
Antiviral and immunomodulatory	Herpes simplex virus (Type HSV-2)	Flower buds	Arena*et al.,* 2008
Antidiabetic and hypolipidemic	Type 2 diabetic patients and C57BL/6J mice	Fruits, Specimens	Lemhadri *et al.,* 2007, Yang *et al.,* 2008, Mishra *et al.,* 2012, Mohammadi*et al.,* 2012

Antiallergic and antihistaminic	Male guinea-pigs	Flower buds	Trombetta *et al.*, 2005
Anti-inflammatory activity	mice, wistar rats	Fruits, flower buds	Zhou*et al.*, 2010, Zhou et al., 2011, El Azhary *et al.*, 2017
Hepatoprotective effect	mice	Leaves, whole plant	Yang *et al.*, 2008, Kalantari*et al.*, 2018, Aghel *et al.*, 2012
Antiobesity	C57BL/6J mice	Specimens	Lemhadri *et al.*, 2007
Genotoxic and antimutagenic effects	In vitro	Flower buds	Zhou et al., 2011
Diuretic effect	Wistar rats	Fruits	El-Guendouz *et al.*, 2017
Antiproliferative and Anticancer effect	Colon human cancer HT29,human breast cancer MCF-7, T47D, human hepatoma HepG2, In vitro (HEP-2 and HELA cancer cells lines), prostate cancer cell, Ehrlich ascites carcinoma (EAC)-bearing Swiss albino mice	Seeds,Leaf, fruit, whole plant	Lam and Ng 2009, Luecha et al., 2009, Al-Daraji 2010, Venugopal et al., 2011, Al-Asady et al., 2012, Rathee et al., 2012
HIV-1 reverse transcriptase inhibitors	DNA molecule	Seeds	Lam and Ng 2009
Antihypotensive	Rats and Spotaneously hypertensive rats	Specimens	Ali *et al.*, 2007
Anti-Helicobacter pylori	Clinical isolates of Helicobacter pylori	Plant crude extracts	Masadeh *et al.*, 2014

1. Antioxidant Activities

Phenolic compounds are one of the most diverse groups of secondary metabolites found in edible plants. They are found in a broad variety of vegetables, fruits, seeds, nuts. Flavonoids are powerful antioxidants, metal chelators and free radical scavengers; they suppress lipid peroxidation and show different physiological activities including anti-allergic, anti-inflammatory activities.

The antioxidant molecule is a free radical scavenger, it donates an electron to the potentially damaging free radical (Fig. 9.8). A stable electron pair is formed, stabilising the free radical. The antioxidant itself becomes oxidised (loses an electron).Antioxidant activity of various parts of *C. spinosa* was studied (Aliyazicioglu *et al.*,2013). Fresh and pickled flower buds were the

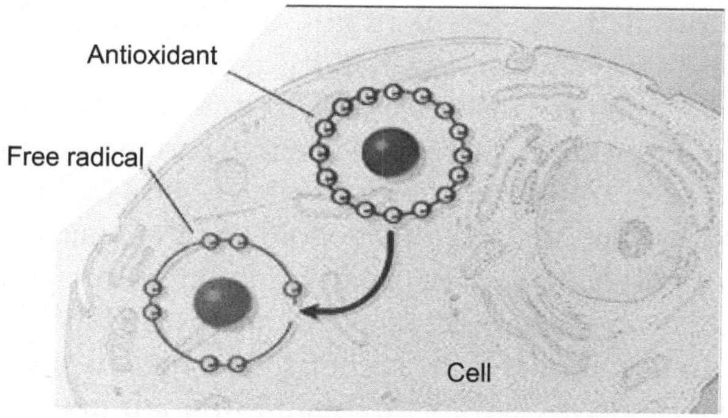

Fig. 9.8: Reactive oxygen species and antioxidants

most studied parts of the plant. According to *Tlili et al.* (2010), phenolic content of fresh buds and leaves from *C. spinosa* exceeded those of many commonly known rich sources of these compounds such as bilberry and raspberry. Recently, growing advantage on phenolic compounds from grapes have concentrated on their biological activities connected to human health benefits, such as antioxidant, anticancer, antimicrobial and cardioprotective properties. Interestingly, *C. spinosa* contains different flavonoid sub-groups. Quercetin, has been identified in the buds of Capparis (Rodrigo et al., 1992), while several derivatives of quercetin glycosides have been isolated from different other parts of Capparis including its fruits (Sharaf et al., 2000). Numerous studies have stated a direct relationship amongst phenolic contents in extracts of medicinal plants and its antioxidant properties (El-Beltagi and Mohames, 2013; Mohamed et al., 2016).

2. Antimicrobial Activity

Medicinal plants have been used to treat different diseases since the beginning of human beings. Wide-ranging observations on the therapeutic effect and effectiveness of several medicinal plants considerably contribute to the discovery of their medicinalactivities, thus they are regularly prescribed, although their full chemical compositions are not well-known. Medicinal utilization of plant products for human ailmenttreatment hassomeadvantages, including inexpensive to produce; they are biodegradable and easily available. Active plant extracts have the ability to kill different pathogenic bacteria without any lethal side effects and environmental risks (Ray *et al.,* 2004). The antimicrobial effect of different phenolic compounds was attributed to deactivation of cellular enzymes, whichcorrelatedto the proportion of diffusion of the substance inside the cell or affected by variations of membrane permeability (Moreno *et al.,* 2006). Increased membrane permeability is a most important factor which affects the mechanism of antimicrobial activity, where active compounds can penetratecellular membranes causingdisturbanceof cellular integrity followed by cell death. Phytochemical analysis of fruits of *C. spinosa* showed the different profile of components. The presence of alkaloid, such as stachydrine, capparispine,cadabicine, capparispine 26-O-β-d-glucoside in addition tocadabicine 26-O-β-d-glucoside hydrochloride was demonstrated in fruit and roots, but the alkaloid content of *C. spinosa* root was higher than that of its fruits and quercetin content was higher in fruits than in roots (Moghaddasian et al., 2012). Flavonoids as the major class of phenolic group, show antimicrobial activity throughinhibition of synthesis of nucleic acids, function of cytoplasm membrane and energy metabolism (Hendra*et al.*, 2011). Fruits aqueous extract with higher total phenolic and total flavonoid content than roots aqueous extract exhibited lower antimicrobial activity.

3. Anticancer Activity

Cancer, was described as, cell proliferation which invades other tissues as well or an uncontrolled growth. The mechanism beyond tissue invading is through direct cell migration or lymphatic system and blood. The hazard agents for cancer consist of an unhealthy diet, environmental factors, infection, radiations, chemicals and smoking (Anand *et al.*, 2008). Hundred various kinds of cancer named by the type of cell or tissue or organ in which they start. Their intensity may be benign (earlier stage) or malignant (end stage, called cancer) (Bakeret *et al.*, 2009). Natural products from biological sources and plants still stay an uncondensed source and unlimited of new nutraceuticals and phytochemicals. Itcontinues to produce the most dramatic effect in the field of cancer (Ahmad *et al.*, 2017). Traditional herbal founded drugs could be hopeful candidates for novel cancer treatments with minimal side effects. They are coming to play a more vital role in the reduction and prevention of cancer (Saad *et al.*, 2008). *Capparis spinosa* is one of the mostprevalent medicinal plants, contained a wide range of phytochemical constituents, used extensively in several parts of the world as a treatment for many human diseases. Many reports confirmed it isable to inhibit many types of cancer cells (Al-Snafi 2015). A new protein is separated from caper, which inhibited proliferation of MCF-7 (breast cancer), HepG2 (hepatoma), and HT29 (colon cancer) cells (Lam and Ng 2009). *Capparis spinosa* essential oil and aqueous infusion appeared marked inhibitory effect on nuclear factor kappa B (NF-KB) activity and on HT-29 cell proliferation(Kulisic *et al.*, 2012). Furthermore, *C. Spinoza* extracts mediated apoptosis through the mitochondrial pathway in SGC-7901 cells (Ji and Yu 2014).The aqueous leaf extracts of caper induced significant inhibitory effect on Hep-2 (human epidermoid larynx carcinoma) and Hela (human cervix uteri epitheloid carcinoma) with low concentration (Al-Daraji 2010).Also, different extracts (aqueous and methanolic) of *C. spinosa* fruit showed Cytotoxic and cytogenetics effects on *in vitro* Hep-2 and HeLa tumor cell lines (AL-Asady *et al.*, 2012). Finally, the extract of *C. spinosa*root bark revealed anticancer effectversus Ehrlich Ascites carcinoma in mice. It considerably reduced the volume of tumor and packed cellsbesides cell count viability (Rathee *et al.*, 2012; Venugopal *et al.*, 2011)

4. Antidiabitics Activity

Diabetes is mainly due to excessive oxidative stress, which cause deterioration of the leading processes which fail throughout diabetes, action of insulin and insulin excretion and an increase in reactive oxygen species that can cause disorder actions. A lot of medicinal plants comprise diverse amounts of antioxidant compounds, primarily tannins, phenolic, flavonoid, vitamins (C and E) that can preserve the performance of β-cells and reducethe levels of glucose in the blood as stated by Pari and Suman (2010).Lots of valuable reports recommended *Capparis spinosa*as a valuable source for bioactive constituents with prospective medicinal and chemotherapeuticvalues. However, little is known about the metabolomics profiles of the different compounds isolated from each part of the selected plant. Different chemical compounds including glycosides,alkaloids,tannins,triterpenoids, carbohydrates,phenolics and flavonoids were identified in the alcoholic extract, whereas flavonoids, steroids,glycosides,saponins and carbohydrates were identified in the aqueous extract of*C. spinosa* (Fu *et al.*, 2007).Many ethnopharmacological studies showed that *C. spinosa* extracts and its components possess powerful antidiabetic activities, particularly antihyperglycemic and hypolipidemic effects (Vahid *et al.*, 2017). It®s reported that, caper treatment appeared a hypoglycemic effect through a decrease of endogenous glucose production and amelioration of insulin sensitivity in diabetic mice (Eddouks *et al.*, 2017). Treatment with hydroalcoholic extract of *C. spinose* significantly increases β cells number, diameter of islets and amount of insulin in diabetic rats (Mohammadi *et al.*, 2012). In addition, several studies showed that, treatment with the fruit and seed of *C. spinosa* decreases the total cholesterol, serum triglyceride, low-density lipoprotein (LDL), liver lipids content and increases high-density lipoprotein (HDL) in diabetic animals, which prove its hypolipidemic effect (Huseini *et al.*, 2013; Kazemian *et al.*, 2015). The suggested mechanisms by which C. spinosa reduces blood glucose may be, it decreases carbohydrate absorption from small intestine, inhibits gluconeogenesis in liver, improves glucose uptake by tissues, and protects beta cells against degradation (Azemi *et al.*, 2016; Jalali *et al.*, 2016; Selfayan and Namjooyan 2016). Along with *C.spinose* properties as an antihyperglycemic and hypolipidemic, justifies its beneficial effects on diabetic complications, including liver damage, nephropathy and cardiovascular disorders (Vahid *et al.* 2017).

Conclusions and Future Prospects

*C. spinosa*has been consumed for a long time. *C. spinosa* health benefits are assumed to arise primarily from their polyphenols and glucosinolate content which are the primary bioactive components that are responsible for different biological properties of C. *spinosa*, including antimicrobial, antioxidant, anti-inflammation, anticancer, cardioprotective and antiaging activities, which are thoroughly accompanying to the prevention of diseases and promotion of health, creating superior potential for C. *spinosa* in the industrial field of nutritional and pharmaceutical agents. Excessive progress has been achieved for the extraction andidentificationof different bioactive components especially polyphenols in C. *spinosa*,besides evaluation of its different biological properties. The structure of polygons underlying its mode of actions in biological system has been studied, and the attained results might help to modify polyphenol structures as well as to design and synthesize new structures of polyphenol possess new biological function.

REFERENCES

Ahmad R, Ahmad N, Naqvi A A, Shehzad A, Al-Ghamdi MS (2017). Role of Traditional Islamic and Arabic Plants in Cancer Therapy. Journal of Traditional and Complementary Medicine 7, 195-204.

Ahmad MK, Khan AA, All SN, Mahmood R (2015). Chemoprotective Effect of Taurine on Potassium Bromate-induced DNA Damage, DNA-protein Cross-linking and Oxidative Stress in Rat Intestine. Plos One,10(3): e0119137.

Al-Asady AAB, Khalil KH and Barwari SSM. (2012). Cytotoxic and Cytogenetics Effects of Aqueous, Methanolic and Secondary Metabolites Extracts of Capparis Spinosaon Tumor Cell Lines in Vitro. Jordan Journal of Biological Sciences, 5(1), 15- 30.

Al-Daraji MNJ. A Study of the Inhibitory Effect of the Capar, Capparis Spinosa L. (2010). Aqueous Crude Leaf Extract on the HEP-2 and HELA Cancer Cell Line. Iraqi Journal of Desert Studies, 2(1), 67-73.

Aghel N, Rashidi I, Mombeini A. (2010). Hepatoprotective Activity of *Capparisspinose* L. Root Bark against CCl4 Induced Hepatic Damage in Mice. Iran J Pharmaceutical Res. 6(4): 285-90.

Ali Z. N., Eddouks M., Michel J.B., Sulpice T., and Hajji L. (2007). Cardiovascular Effect of *Capparis spinosa* Aqueous Extract. Part III: Antihypertensive Effect in Spontaneously Hypertensive Rats. American Journal of Pharmacology and Toxicology 2(3): 111-115.

Aliyazicioglu R., O.E. Eyupoglu, H. Sahin, O. Yildiz, N. Baltas (2013). Phenolic Components, Antioxidant Activity, and Mineral Analysis of *Capparis spinosa* L. Afr. J. Biotechnol., 12 (2013), pp. 6643-6649.

Aliyazicioglu, R., Tosun, G., and Eyupoglu, E. (2015). Characterisation of Volatile Compounds by Spme and gc-fid/ms of Capers (Capparis spinosa L.). Afr. J. Agric. Res. 10, 2213–2217.

Alsabri S, Zetrini A, Ermeli N, Mohamed S, Bensaber S, Hermann A, Gbaj A. (2012). Study of Eight Medicinal Plants for Antioxidant Activities. J Chem Pharm Res. 4: 4028-4031.

Al-Snafi AE (2015). The Chemical Constituents and Pharmacological Effects of Capparis Spinosa -An Overview. Indian Journal of Pharmaceutical Science & Research 5,93-100.

Al-Soqeer A.. (2011). Antioxidant Activity and Biological Evaluation of Hot-water Extract of Artemisia Monosperma and *Capparis spinosa* against lead Contamination Res. J. Bot., 6 pp. 11-20

Anand P, Kunnumakkara AB, Sundaram C, et al. Cancer is a Preventable Disease that requires Major Lifestyle Changes. Pharm Res. 2008; 25:2097-2116.

Arena A, Bisignano G, Pavone B, Tomaino A, Bonina F, Saija A, et al. Antiviral and Immunomodulatory Effect of a Lyophilized Extract of C. *Spinosa* L. buds. Phytother Res. 2008; 22(3): 313-317.

Azemi M.E., Namjoyan F., Shahr-babak M.S. (2016). Investigating the Antioxidant Capacities, Total Phenolic Contents, and a-amylase Inhibitory Activities of Capparis Spinosa L. Methanolic Extracts, International Journal of Pharmaceutical Research & Allied Sciences 5 (2), 363–369.

Becker WM, Kleinsmith LJ, Hardin J, Bertoni GP. The World of the Cell. 7nd ed. San Francisco: Pearson Education, Inc., publishing as Pearson Benjamin Cummings; 2009:757-790.

Bonina F, Puglia C, Ventura D, Aquino R, Tortora S, Sacchi A, Saija A, Tomaino A, Pellegrino ML, de Caprariis P. (2002). In Vitro Antioxidant and in Vivo Photoprotective Effects of a Lyophilized Extract of *Capparis spinosa* L. buds. J Cosmet Sci. 53(6): 321-35.

Day AM, Brown JD, Taylor SR, Rand JD, Morgan BA, Veal EA. (2012). Inactivation of a Peroxiredoxin by Hydrogen Peroxide is Critical for Thioredoxin-mediated Repair of Oxidized Proteins and Cell Survival. Mol Cell. 2012;45:398–408

Eddouks M, Lemhadri A, Hebi M, Ahmed EL H, Zeggwagh NA, Bachir EL B, Lhoussaine H, Burcelin R. Capparis Spinosa L. Aqueous Extract Evokes Antidiabetic Effect in Streptozotocin-induced Diabetic Mice. Avicenna J Phytomed, 2017; 7 (2): 191-198.

El Azhary K., Jouti N.T., El Khachibi M., Moutia M., Tabyaoui I., El Hou A., Achtak H., Nadifi S., Habti N., BadouA. (2017). Anti-inflammatory Potential of *Capparis spinosa* L. *in vivo* in Mice through Inhibition of Cell Infiltration and Cytokine Gene Expression. BMC Complementary and Alternative Medicine (2017) 17:81.

El-Beltagi HS, Mohamed HI (2013). Reactive Oxygen Species, Lipid Peroxidation and Antioxidative Defense Mechanism. Not Bot Hort Agrobo Cluj 41:44–57.

El-Guendouz S., Al-Waili N., Aazza S., Elamine Y., Zizi S., Al-Waili T., Al-Waili A., Lyoussi B. (2017). Antioxidant and Diuretic Activity of co-administration of Capparis Spinosa Honey and Propolis Incomparison to Furosemide. Asian Pacific Journal of Tropical Medicine 10(10), 974–980.

Fu XP, Alsa HA, Abdurahim M, Yill A, Aripova SF and Tashkhodzhaev B. (2007). Chemical Composition of *Capparis spinosa* fruit. *Chemistry of Natural compounds*, 43(2), 181-183.

Gill J. G., Piskounova E., Morrison S. J. (2016). Cancer, Oxidative Stress, and Metastasis. *Cold Spring Harbor Symposia on Quantitative Biology*. 81: 163–175.

Hendra R, Ahmad S, Sukari A, Shukor M.Y, Oskoueian E. (2011). Flavonoid Analyses and Antimicrobial Activity of various parts of *Phaleriama crocarpa* (Scheff.) Boerl fruit. Int J Mol Sci; 12:3422-3431.

Huseini H.F., Hasani-Rnjbar S., Nayebi N., Heshmat R., Sigaroodi F.K., Ahvazi M., Alaei B.A., Kianbakht S. (2013) Capparis Spinosa L. (Caper) Fruit Extract in Treatment of Type 2 Diabetic Patients: a Randomized Double-blind Placebo-controlled Clinical Trial, Complementary Therapies in Medicine 21 (5) 447–452.

Jalali M.T., Mohammadtaghvaei N., Larky D.A. (2016) Investigating the Effects of Capparis Spinosa on Hepatic Gluconeogenesis and Lipid Content in Streptozotocin-induced Diabetic rats, Biomedicine & Pharmacotherapy 84, 1243–1248.

Ji YB, Yu L. (2014). N-butanol Extract of Capparis Spinosa L. Induces Apoptosis Primarily through a Mitochondrial Pathway involving mPTP open, Cytochrome C Release and Caspase Activation. Asian Pac J Cancer Prev. 15:9153-9157.

Kalantari H., Foruozandeh H., Khodayar M. J., Siahpoosh A., Saki N., Kheradmand P. (2018). Antioxidant and Hepatoprotective Effects of Capparis Spinosa L. Fractions and Quercetin on Tert-butyl Hydroperoxide- Induced Acute Liver Damage in Mice. Journal of Traditional and Complementary Medicine 8:120-127.

Kamiloglu, S., Toydemir, G., Boyacioglu, D., Beekwilder, J., Hall, R.D., Capanoglu, E. (2015).A Review on the Effect of Drying on Antioxidant Potential of Fruits and Vegetables. Crit. Rev. Food Sci. Nutr. Pages S110-S129

Kazemian M., Abad M., reza Haeri M., Ebrahimi M., Heidari R. (2015) Anti-diabetic Effect of Capparis Spinosa L. Root Extract in Diabetic Rats, Avicenna Journal of Phytomedicine 5(4), 325-332.

Kulisic-Bilusica T, Schmollerb I, Schnabeleb K, Siracusac L, Rubertoc G. (2012). The Anticarcinogenic Potential of Essential Oil and Aqueous Infusion from Caper (*Capparis spinosa* L.). Food Chem. 132:261-267.

Lam Sze-Kwan, Ng Tzi-Bun. A Protein with Antiproliferative, Antifungal and HIV-1 Reverse Transcriptase Inhibitory Activities from Caper (*Capparis spinosa*) Seeds. Phytomedicine. 2009; 16:444-450.

Lemhadri A, Mohamed E, Thierry S, Remy B (2007). Anti-hyperglycaemic and Anti-obesity Effects of *Capparis Spinosa* and Chamaemelum Nobile Aqueous Extracts in HFD Mice. American J. Pharmacol. Toxicol., 2(3): 106-110, 2007.

Luecha P, Umehara K, Miyase T, Noguchi H. (2009). Antiestrogenic Constituents of the Thai Medicinal Plants *Capparis flavicans* and *Vitexglabrata*. J Nat Prod. 72(11): 1954-1959.

Masadeh M.M., Alkofahi A.S., Alzoubi K.H., Tumah H.N., Bani-Hani K. (2014). Anti-Helicobactor Pylori Activity of Some Jordanian Medicinal Plants. Pharm Biol, 52(5): 566–569.

Mishra PR, Panda PK, Chowdary KA, Panigrahi S. Antidiabetic and Antihyperlipidemic Activity of *Capparis spinosa* L. Extract. Int J Pharm Sci Rev Res. 2012; 14(1): 38-43.

Moghaddasian B, Eradatmand Asli D, Alaghemand A. (2012). Quantitative Analysis of Quercetin in different parts of Capparis Spinosa by HPLC. Ann Biol Res 3(12), 5775-5778.

Mohamed AA., Ali SI., Sameeh MY., Abd El-Razik TM. (2016). Effect of Solvents Extraction on HPLC Profile of Phenolic Compounds, Antioxidant and Anticoagulant Properties of Origanum Vulgare. Research J. Pharm. and Tech 9(11), 2009-2016.

Mohammadi J, Mirzaei A, Delaviz H, Mohammadi B. (2012). Effects of Hydroalcoholic Extract of *Capparis Spinosa* on Histomorphological changes of Pancreas in Diabetic Rats Model. J Birjand Univ Med Sci. 19(3): 235-244.

Muhaidat R., Al-Qudah M.A., Al-Shayeb A., Jacob J.H., Al-Jaber H.I., Hussein E., Al-Tarawneh I.N., Abu Orabi S.T. (2013). Chemical Profile and Antibacterial Activity of Crude Fractions and Essential Oils of *Capparis ovata* Desf. and *Capparis spinosa* L. (Capparaceae). International Journal of Integrative Biology, 14(1): 39-47.

Moreno S., Scheyer T., Romano C., Vojnov A. 2006. Antioxidant and Antimicrobial Activities of Rosemary Extracts linked to their Polyphenol Composition. Free Radic. Res. 40(2):223-231.

Nabavi S.F., Maggi F., Daglia M., Habtemariam S., Rastrelli L., Nabavi S.M., (2016). Pharmacological Effects of *Capparis spinosa* L, Phytotherapy Research 30 (11) 1733–1744.

Okalie N P and Ikewuchi JC. (2004). Cataractogenic Potential of Bromate Mediated Oxidative Stress in Rabbits. Journal Medical Science 4: 158-163.

Ozkan G, Kamiloglu S, Ozdal T, Boyacioglu D, Capanoglu E.(2016). Potential Use of Turkish Medicinal Plants in the Treatment of Various Diseases.Molecules. 2016 Feb 25;21(3):257.

Pari L, and Suman S. (2010). Antihyperglycemic and Antilipidperoxidative Effects of Flavanoid Natringin in Streptozotocin-nicotinamide Induced Diabetic rats. Int. J. Biol. Med. Res. 1, 206-210.

Rathee P, Rathee D, Rathee D, Rathee S. (2012). *In vitro* Anticancer Activity of Stachydrine Isolated from *Capparis decidua* on Prostate Cancer lines. *Nat Prod Res*, 26(18), 1737-1740.

Ray AB, Sarma BK, Singh UP (2004). Medicinal Properties of Plants: Antifungal, Antibacterial and Antiviral Activities. Lucknow, International Book 600 pp.

Rodrigo M, Lazaro M, Alvarruiz A, Giner V. (1992). Composition of Capers (*Capparisspinosa*): Influence of Cultivar, Size and Harvest date. J Food Sci 57: 1152–1154.

Saad B, Azaizeh H, Said O. Arab Herbal Medicines. Bot Med. 2008;16:32.

Selfayan M., Namjooyan F. (2016) Inhibitory Effect of Capparis Spinosa Extract on Pancreatic Alpha-amylase Activity, Zahedan Journal of Research in Medical Sciences 18 (4), e6450.

Sharaf M, El-Ansari M, Saleh N. 2000. Quercetin Triglycoside from Capparis Spinosa. Fitoterapia 71: 46–49.

Shayeb A. Chemical Composition of Essential Oil and Crude Extract Fractions and their Antibacterial Activities of *Capparis spinosa* L. and *Capparis cartilaginea Decne*. from Jordan: MSc thesis, Yarmouk University, Faculty of Science; 2012.

Sher, H., Alyemeni M.N. (2010), Ethnobotanical and Pharmaceutical Evaluation of *Capparis spinosa* L, Validity of Local Folk and Unani System of Medicine J. Med. Plants Res., 4 pp. 1751-1756.

Sultan A.O., Çelik T.A. (2009). Genotoxic and Antimutagenic Effects of *Capparis spinosa* L. on the Allium Cepa L. Root tip Meristem Cells. International Journal of Cytology, Cytosystematics and Cytogenetics62(2): 114-123.

Tafani M., Sansone L., Limana F., Arcangeli T., De Santis E., Polese M., Fini M, Russo MA. (2016). The Interplay of Reactive Oxygen Species, Hypoxia, Inflammation, and Sirtuins in Cancer Initiation and Progression. *Oxidative Medicine and Cellular Longevity*. 2016, Article ID 3907147, http://dx.doi.org/10.1155/2016/3907147

Tlili N, Khaldi A, Triki S, Munne-Bosch S. Phenolic Compounds and Vitamin Antioxidants of Caper (*C. spinosa*). Plant Foods Hum Nutr. 2010; 65(3): 260-265.

Tlili N, Feriani A, Saadoui E, Nasri N, Khaldi A.(2017). Capparis Spinosa Leaves Extract: Source of Bioantioxidants with Nephroprotective and Hepatoprotective Effects. Biomed Pharmacother.; 87:171e179.

Trombetta, D., Occhiuto, F., Perri, D., Puglia, C., Santagati, N. A., Pasquale, A. D., Saija A., Bonina F. (2005). Antiallergic and Antihistaminic Effect of two extracts of *Capparis Spinosa* L. Flowering Buds. Phytother. Res. 19, 29–33.

Ueno H, Oishi K, Sayato Y and Nakamuno K. (2000). Oxidative Cell Damage in Kat- Sod Assay of Oxyhalides as Inorganic Disinfection by-products and their Occurrence by ozonation. Arch. Environ. Contam. Toxicol., 38: 1-6.

Vahid, H., Rakhshandeh, H., Ghorbani, A. (2017). Antidiabetic Properties of Capparis Spinosa L. and its Components. Biomedicine and Pharmacotherapy. (92), 293-302.

Venugopal Y, Ravindranath A, Kalpana G. Antitumor Activity of *Capparissepiaria* on Ehrlich Ascites Carcinoma in Mice. (2011). Int J Biomed Res. 2(4): 264-271.

Yang T, Liu YQ, Wang CH, Wang ZT. Advances on Investigation of Chemical Constituents, Pharmacological Activities and Clinical Applications of *C. spinosa*. Zhongguo Zhong Yao Za Zhi. 2008; 33(21): 2453-8.

Zhou, H., Jian, R., Kang, J., Huang, X., Li, Y., Zhuang, C., Yang, F., Zhang, L., Fan, X., Wu, T., 2010. Anti-inflammatory Effects of Caper (Capparis spinosa L.) Fruit Aqueous Extract and the Isolation of Main Phytochemicals. J. Agric. Food Chem. 58, 12717–12721.

Zhou HF, Xie C, Jian R, Kang J, Li Y, Zhuang CL, et al. Biflavonoids from Caper (Capparis Spinosa L.) Fruits and their Effects in Inhibiting NF-kappa B Activation. J Agric Food Chem. 2011; 59(7): 3060-3065.

Zhao H.-Y., Fan M.-X., Wu X., Wang H.-J., Yang J., Si N., Bian B.-L. (2013). Chemical Profiling of the Chinese Herb Formula Xiao-Cheng-Qi decoction using Liquid Chromatography Coupled with Electrospray Ionization Mass Spectrometry. J. Chromatogr. Sci., 51 (2013), pp. 273-285

INDEX